TOWARDS PROFESSIONAL WISDOM

Towards Professional Wisdom
Practical Deliberation in the People Professions

LIZ BONDI

DAVID CARR

CHRIS CLARK

and

CECELIA CLEGG
University of Edinburgh, UK

ASHGATE

Published by
Ashgate Publishing Limited
Wey Court East
Union Road
Farnham
Surrey GU9 7PT
England

Ashgate Publishing Company
Suite 420
101 Cherry Street
Burlington, VT 05401-4405
USA

www.ashgate.com

British Library Cataloguing in Publication Data
Towards professional wisdom:practical deliberation in the people professions.
   1. Professional ethics–Congresses. 2. Professional employees–Attitudes–Congresses. 3. Decision making–Moral and ethical aspects–Congresses.
   I. Bondi, L. (Liz)
   174–dc22

Library of Congress Cataloging-in-Publication Data
Towards professional wisdom:practical deliberation in the people professions/by Liz Bondi ... [et al.].
      p. cm.
   Includes bibliographical references and index.
   ISBN 978-1-4094-0742-3 (hbk.:alk.paper)—ISBN 978-1-4094-0743-0 (pbk.:alk. paper)—ISBN 978-1-4094-0744-7 (ebook) 1. Practical judgment.2. Professions—Psychological aspects. 3. Human services—Psychological aspects. I. Bondi, L. (Liz)
   BF447.T69 2011
   001—dc22

2011003884

ISBN 9781409407423 (Hbk)
ISBN 9781409407430 (Pbk)
ISBN 9781409407447 (ebk)

Printed and bound in Great Britain by the
MPG Books Group, UK

Contents

List of Tables

Acknowledgements

This volume has its origins in a conference held at the University of Edinburgh in March 2008. We are most grateful to the College of Humanities and Social Science for financial support towards that event, and to Arlene Sievwright for her superb assistance in the organisation and administration of the conference. We also wish to thank all the conference delegates, whose enthusiasm helped to ensure the realisation of this volume.

At later stages in its preparation, Hillarie Higgins and Marlies Kustatscher provided much-appreciated editorial assistance, for which we are most grateful.

We are also very grateful to the following for permission to reproduce material previously published elsewhere: Elsevier for kind permission to reproduce as Chapter 9 of this volume an article originally published in *Emotion, Space and Society*, 1(1) (2008), 14–17, and for permission to reproduce as Table 3.2 material originally published in *Social Science and Medicine*, and Sage Publications for kind permission to reproduce as Chapter 11 text from an article originally published in the *Journal of Social Work*, 9(2) (2009), 222–35.

Notes on Contributors

Liz Bondi is Professor of Social Geography at the University of Edinburgh, where she contributes of professional education in counselling and psychotherapy. She is founding editor of two journals: *Gender, Place and Culture* (first published 1994) and *Emotion, Space and Society* (first published 2008). She has published over 50 papers in refereed journals, and over 25 book chapters. She is co-author of *Subjectivities, Knowledges and Feminist Geographies* (Rowman and Littlefield, 2002) and co-editor of *Education and Society* (Routledge, 1988, with M.H. Matthews), *Emotional Geographies* (Ashgate, 2005, with J. Davidson and M. Smith), *Working the Spaces of Neoliberalism* (Blackwell, 2005) and *Emotion, Place and Culture* (Ashgate, 2009, with M. Smith, J. Davidson and L. Cameron).

Elizabeth Campbell is a Professor in the Department of Curriculum, Teaching and Learning at the Ontario Institute for Studies in Education, University of Toronto. Dr Campbell's scholarship and teaching focus on the areas of professional ethics in education and the moral dimensions of teaching. Among her publications are her book *The Ethical Teacher* (Open University, 2003) and articles in the *Journal of Teacher Education, Teachers and Teaching: Theory and Practice, International Journal of Educational Change, Educational Research and Evaluation: An International Journal on Theory and Practice, Journal of Educational Policy* and *Cambridge Journal of Education*. She is an editor of the journal *Curriculum Inquiry.*

David Carr is Emeritus Professor at the University of Edinburgh, where he was formerly Professor of Philosophy of Education. He is author of *Educating the Virtues* (Routledge, 1991), *Professionalism and Ethics in Teaching* (Routledge, 2000) and *Making Sense of Education* (Routledge, 2003), as well as of nearly 200 philosophical and educational papers and book chapters on ethics, values, professional judgement and other philosophical issues. He is also editor of *Education, Knowledge and Truth* (Routledge, 1998), *Virtue Ethics and Moral Education* (Routledge, 1999, with Jan Steutel), *Spirituality, Philosophy and Education* (Routledge, 2003, with John Haldane) and the *Sage Handbook on*

Philosophy of Education (Sage, 2010, with Richard Bailey, Robin Barrow and Christine McCarthy).

Chris Clark is Emeritus Professor at the University of Edinburgh, where he was formerly Professor of Social Work Ethics. He is author of *Social Work Ethics: Politics, Principles and Practice* (Palgrave Macmillan, 2000) and editor of *Private and Confidential: Handling Personal Information in the Social and Health Services* (The Policy Press, 2008, with Janice McGhee). His recent work addresses the hermeneutics of practical reason and life practice in professional action.

Cecelia Clegg is Senior Lecturer in Practical Theology at the University of Edinburgh. She is co-author of *Moving Beyond Sectarianism: Religion, Conflict, and Reconciliation in Northern Ireland* (Columba Press, 2001), *Skills for Transformation: Working with Groups in an Inter-Church Context* (MNNI, 2001) and *Faith Communities and Local Government in Glasgow* (Scottish Executive Social Research, 2005), as well as papers and book chapters on reconciliation, conflict transformation and social cohesion.

Joseph Dunne is Cregan Professor in Philosophy of Education at Dublin City University, and Head of Human Development at St Patrick's College, Dublin. He is author of *Back to the Rough Ground: Practical Judgment and the Lure of Technique* (University of Notre Dame Press, 1997). He has co-edited *Questioning Ireland: Debates in Political Philosophy and Public Policy* (IPA, 2000, with Attracta Ingram and Frank Litton), *Childhood and its Discontents: The First Seamus Heaney Lectures* (Liffey Press, 2002, with James Liffey) and *Education and Practice: Upholding the Integrity of Teaching and Learning* (Blackwell, 2004, with Padraig Hogan). His *Persons in Practice: Essays in Education and Public Philosophy* is forthcoming from University of Notre Dame Press.

Alison Elliot's work straddles the university, civil society and the Church. Formerly a lecturer in psychology, she is currently an Honorary Fellow at New College, University of Edinburgh, where she is Associate Director of the Centre for Theology and Public Issues. In 2004 she became the first woman to be appointed Moderator of the General Assembly of the Church of Scotland. She has represented her Church on many ecumenical and civic bodies. She is Convener of the Scottish Council for Voluntary Organisations.

Jeannie Kerr is a PhD student in Educational Studies at the University of British Columbia in Vancouver, Canada, under the supervision of Dr Daniel Vokey. She completed her Master of Arts in Educational Administration and Leadership at UBC in 2007. Her current research is an hermeneutical inquiry into intuition and judgement through analysis of texts from Indigenous, Buddhist and Aristotelian traditions. Jeannie is particularly interested in neo-Aristotelian perspectives on *phronesis*. Jeannie was a classroom and special education teacher specialising in inner-city schools for 11 years prior to her PhD programme.

Kristján Kristjánsson is Professor of Philosophy of Education, School of Education, University of Iceland. He is the author of various articles in international journals on issues in philosophy and education, and a number of books, including *Justifying Emotions* (Routledge, 2002), *Aristotle, Emotions and Education* (Ashgate, 2007) and *The Self and Its Emotions* (Cambridge University Press, 2010).

Michael Luntley is Professor of Philosophy at the University of Warwick. His interests include the philosophy of mind, Wittgenstein and the philosophy of education. He is especially interested in the nature of learning, the acquisition of concepts and the role both might have in an understanding the nature of expertise. Recent publications related to these last interests include 'Understanding expertise', *Journal of Applied Philosophy*, 26(4) (2009); 'On Education and Initiation', *Journal of Philosophy of Education*, 43, special supplementary issue: 'Reading Peters Today' (October 2009), and 'What do nurses know?', *Nursing Philosophy*, 12(1) (2011).

Kathleen Marshall is a solicitor and child law consultant. Her early experience was in local government. From 1989 to 1994 she was Director of the Scottish Child Law Centre, and since then her work has focused on children's rights. After ten years as an independent child law consultant, she was appointed Scotland's first Commissioner for Children and Young People, with a remit to promote and safeguard children's rights. Since demitting office in 2009, she has been writing and speaking about children's rights, and is currently working on projects dealing with historic abuse of children in care and youth justice.

Maggie Mellon is a social worker with many years' experience of practice, management and policy in both local government and the voluntary sector. Her previous posts include Director of Children and Family Services with Children 1st, 2005–2009, Head of Public Policy with Action for Children (formerly NCH) and Principal Officer Children and Young People, Lothian Region and City of Edinburgh. Maggie currently works as an independent adviser on policy and practice issues. She is the Chair of the Scottish Child Law Centre, and a member of the board of NHS Health Scotland. Maggie's qualifications include MSc, CQSW and Diploma in Child Protection.

Susie Orbach is a psychoanalyst and writer whose interests have centred on feminism and psychoanalysis, the construction of femininity and gender, globalisation and body image, emotional literacy, and psychoanalysis and the public sphere. She co-founded The Women's Therapy Centre in 1976, and is convener of Anybody,[1] an organisation campaigning for body diversity. Her books include *Fat is a Feminist Issue* (Hamlyn, 1978), *Hunger Strike* (Penguin, 1993), *On Eating* (Penguin, 2002), *What's Really Going on Here* (Karnac, 1995), *Towards Emotional Literacy* (Virago, 1999), *The Impossibility of Sex* (Karnac, 2005) and the recently published *Bodies* (Profile Books, 2009). Susie is Chair of the Relational School in the UK, and has a clinical practice catering for individuals and couples.

John Swinton is Professor of Practical Theology and Pastoral Care at the University of Aberdeen. He is also an honorary Professor at Aberdeen's Centre for Advanced Studies in Nursing. He has worked as a registered nurse specialising in psychiatry and learning disabilities, and as a community mental health chaplain. His areas of research include the relationship between spirituality and health, and the theology and spirituality of disability. In 2004 he founded the Centre for Spirituality, Health and Disability at the University of Aberdeen.[2] His recent writings include *Raging with Compassion: Pastoral Responses to the Problem of Evil* (Eerdmans, 2007) and *Practical Theology and Qualitative Research Methods* (SCM Press, 2006, with Harriet Mowat).

Nick Totton is a therapist and trainer with over 25 years' experience. Originally a Reichian body therapist, his approach has become broad-based and open to the spontaneous and unexpected. He has written or edited 12 books, including *Psychotherapy and Politics* (Sage, 2000), *Body Psychotherapy: An Introduction* (Open University Press, 2003), *Press When Illuminated: New and Selected Poems* (Salt Publishing, 2004) and *Wild Therapy: Undomesticating Inner and Outer Worlds* (PCCS Books, 2011).

Daniel Vokey is Associate Professor in Philosophy of Education with the Department of Educational Studies at the University of British Columbia. His research investigates how teachings from the world's wisdom traditions can help promote just, sustainable and fulfilling ways of life through education. In this work, he draws upon his academic background in religious studies and the philosophy of education, his professional experience facilitating wilderness-based leadership programmes (Outward Bound) and his training in the contemplative pedagogies of Shambhala Buddhism. He serves on the Executive of the Canadian Philosophy of Education Society, and as Chair of the Philosophy of Education Society's Ethics SIG. A recent publication is '"Anything you can do I can do better": Dialectical argument in philosophy of education', *Journal of Philosophy of Education*, 43(3) (2009).

---

1   <www.endangeredspecieswomen.org.uk>.
2   <www.abdn.ac.uk/cshad>.

Sue White is Professor of Social Work (Children and Families) at the University of Birmingham. Her research focuses principally on the analysis of professional decision-making in child welfare, with a particular emphasis on safeguarding. She was a member of the Social Work Task Force, and currently sits on the Social Work Reform Board. She is a member of the reference group informing the Munro Review into reducing bureaucracy in child protection. She is currently Chair of the Association of Professors of Social Work, and Editor-in-Chief of the international journal *Child and Family Social Work.*

Introduction: Towards Professional Wisdom

David Carr, Liz Bondi, Chris Clark and Cecelia Clegg

The editors of this volume are professional colleagues to the extent of having been academic contemporaries in different schools and departments of the University of Edinburgh over the course of many years. They have all also been directly concerned, beyond the groves of academe, with the pre- and in-service education and training of practitioners for various fields of professional work such as (precisely, in the case of these editors) education, social work, counselling and ministry. It is also probably little exaggeration to say that despite working in professional fields with common occupational interests and concerns, the present editors barely knew each other until a few years ago. Moreover, we suspect that this general state of affairs is not unusual in most major universities in Britain and more widely.

The origins of the present volume may be traced back to a meeting between two editors following the discovery that both were working on much the same issues and problems of professional concern, albeit in rather different professional fields. One editor, exercised by the problem of how to understand the nature of professional deliberation and judgement in social work, was alerted – ironically, while on study leave at a university on the other side of the world – to the work of another editor working in his home university on much the same issues in the context of teacher education and training. It was soon apparent from the meeting following this discovery that professional fields such as education and social work, given their common concerns with general social welfare and health, could only stand to benefit from closer dialogue and co-operation between those bent on further understanding the character and effective conduct of such practices. Aside from the scandal of academic apartheid between researchers working on similar issues and problems of professional practice in such relative academic isolation – particularly in contemporary contexts of professional policy-making in which practitioners are increasingly encouraged or required to work in closer collaboration – it is not very hard to see how reflection on the issues and problems in a field such as social work may be a potentially rich source of professional insight to teachers, and vice versa.

Indeed, it soon became clear that that the issues and problems that had brought together two editors of this volume were not just confined to education and social work, but common to a wide range of professional or quasi-professional occupations that have been variously referred to as 'semi-professions', 'vocations', 'caring professions' or (in the preferred terminology of many contributions to this volume) 'people professions'. It was but a short further step from appreciating the common occupational concerns of education and social work to recognising that such other occupations as (for example) counselling, ministry and nursing raised and faced precisely analogous questions and problems. In particular, it was clear that these and other occupations are implicated in issues of human association, welfare and flourishing that engender complex and difficult questions about the nature and status in such contexts of effective professional reflection and deliberation: issues, precisely, about what might be said to constitute *wise* judgement and conduct in such fields.

To clarify such questions, we could start by asking how the professional reflection of teachers, social workers, counsellors, nurses and ministers might generally be distinguished from that of other human professions, trades or services. First, it seems to be widely agreed that the rational powers required for the effective pursuit of such occupations might or should be regarded as forms of 'practical reason', procedural knowledge or 'reflection in action'. That said, the precise logical form of such knowledge, reason or reflection is also a matter of lively debate, and it is to some of these disputes that the chapters in Part One of this volume are addressed. Moreover, one key topic of debate in this connection is whether the knowledge or rational judgement required for the effective conduct of caring or people professions is reducible to the technical 'evidence-based' rationality to which modern professions as medicine seem sometimes to have aspired. There can be little question that the spectacular technical advances of modern medical science – no doubt reinforced by modern social scientific attempts to explain human behaviour in quasi-natural scientific terms – have encouraged general conceptions of professional practice as instruments or vehicles of social engineering. On such 'scientistic' views of professional practice, if the overall goals of human health, welfare and progress may be determined by rational scientific inquiry, and the means to such goals can be established by empirical research and experiment, then the desired goals might in principle be achieved by straightforward implementation of such identified means. There can be little doubt that education was widely so conceived in much influential twentieth-century educational theorising as a technology of pedagogy grounded in a (behavioural) science of learning.

A key difficulty about any such conception of profession, however, is that it is far from clear that either social or natural science is well-placed to determine the goals of human welfare and flourishing. The basic problem is that questions of human welfare and flourishing appear to be located in the space of 'value' rather than (social or natural) fact, and are as such – not least in Western and other liberal and plural democracies – inevitably and invariably contested. While this is not, of course, to deny that values are either rational or objective, that sane and sensible values may need to be constrained by facts or evidence, or that there may be rationally better and/or worse ways of rationally resolving value disputes, it is to concede that the kind of inquiry appropriate to appraising values is primarily moral or ethical rather than scientific. Thus, in so far as 'people professional' deliberation is inevitably implicated in such value disputes, it is arguably also more (or more centrally) *moral* or *ethical* than scientific – and, to be sure, it is now widely recognised that courses of education and training in such fields as education, nursing and social work might or should include a core ethical component.

However, in so far as the nature of ethical or moral reflection, deliberation, judgement and conduct is also philosophically contested, this clearly raises no less complex issues about the precise direction that professional ethics should take, and about the consequent best course of 'people professional' education and training. Indeed, one key issue here – of enormous significance for professional judgement in people or caring professions – concerns the extent to which any morally correct or defensible professional judgement may be expressed in the form of well-defined rules or principles of the kind found in the ethics of deontology and utilitarianism, and which are also the staple fare of much official professional policy and regulation. In this connection, some moral philosophers and theorists of professional ethics have inclined to a perspective known generally as 'ethical particularism' which effectively denies, given the highly situation-specific or context-sensitive character of moral thought and/or judgement, that such thought is at all susceptible to such regulation or codification. However, although particularism usually cites the authority and support of Aristotle (or of ancient and/or modern Aristotelian virtue ethics), and although Aristotle clearly did hold that the virtuous moral response should be a matter of particular context-sensitive judgement, it is no less clear that he also explicitly subscribed to general moral rules and principles, and saw particular moral judgements as nevertheless dependent upon some framework of such principles. In this regard, it probably makes best sense to observe some Aristotelian 'mean' between the more uncompromising moral regulation of deontic ethics and the more radical rejection of moral rules of latter-day particularists. (More modest forms of particularism are defended by some contributors to this volume; but for criticisms of radical particularism, see Luntley, Chapter 2 in this volume, and Kristjánsson [2007] and [2010].) Nevertheless, it is clear enough that such 'people (and other) professional' occupations as teaching, social work and nursing do require practitioners to make highly particular context-sensitive judgements in the course of their work, and that any ethics for such professions would need to include an adequate account of the logical grounds of such judgements.

Furthermore, it should be noted that the kind of virtue-theoretical perspective that is often enlisted in support of (radical or moderate) ethical particularism parts company with the moral rationalism of deontic ethics (the ethics of duty and utility) by insisting that genuine or full moral (virtuous) judgements or responses are by no means exclusively matters of reason or cognition – or at least of reason as cognitively conceived. For past and present virtue ethicists, virtues are dispositions to moral conduct that are no less *affective* than cognitive. Indeed, as one editor of this volume has expressed this elsewhere (Carr, 2009), the virtues of virtue ethics are more or less equivalent to states of emotion, feeling or appetite ordered in accordance with some deliberative ideal of practical wisdom. But if moral (virtuous) responses and judgements are construed in this affectively grounded way, then this would seem to have consequences for those human occupations – such as, precisely, the 'people professions' – in which the emotional dimensions of human association are significantly implicated. Indeed, while some perspectives on professional ethics seem to have supposed that professional relations should always be 'impersonal' or 'disinterested' and seek to eschew the emotional involvements or attachments that might lead to bias or other distorted judgement, it seems rather more intuitive to suppose that good social workers need to be sympathetic to clients, that good nurses need to be caring towards patients, and that good teachers need to be capable of warm and supportive relations with pupils. Virtue ethics can generally (and arguably better than other moral theories) be pressed in support of this more intuitively plausible view of the professional value of properly ordered feeling and emotion. So far, so good. But this also raises difficult questions and issues – some of which are addressed in Part Two of this volume – about how such affective qualities might be developed, fostered and monitored in the education and training of 'people professionals'.

This volume addresses, directly or indirectly, all of these aforementioned questions, issues and problems about the nature of reflection and conduct in people professions. The volume has its origins in a successful and internationally well-attended University of Edinburgh conference, 'Towards Professional Wisdom: Practical Deliberation in the "People Professions"', organised and staged by the editors in March 2008. The main aim of that conference was to encourage interdisciplinary dialogue on issues of common concern to a wide variety of professional fields such as education, social work, counselling, nursing and ministry. The conference set out to focus mainly on issues and problems concerning the character of deliberation and judgement in such 'people professions', specifically with a view to exploring the possibility that such occupations require the development of a special kind of reflection or deliberation (perhaps along the lines of Aristotle's *phronesis*, or practical wisdom). In the event, however, the conference also addressed such related but wide-ranging issues as: the impact of official prescription and regulation on professional judgement; conflicts of professional judgement and public/political accountability; tensions between universal justice and equality and particular client need; the limits of professional concern for the personal problems of clients; the extent to which 'people professional' practice is grounded in theory; alternative models of professional deliberation to 'technical rationality'; the role of emotion and affect in 'people professional' practice; the possibility of non-scientific (narrative) sources of professional wisdom, and the role of the supervisor in the training and practice of people professionals.

In the wake of this meeting and the widespread professional interest that it provoked, the editors decided that there would be much academic and professional value and merit in assembling a collection of invited essays on this wider range of conference themes: that, indeed, there seemed to be a quite regrettable gap in the literature of professional issues for work specifically addressed to such 'people-professional' themes in an appropriately inter-disciplinary and cross-professional way. Contributions were commissioned from a broad constituency of distinguished scholars in the fields of professional ethics and expertise from relevant 'people-professional' backgrounds and a wide range of academic disciplines such as philosophy, theology, politics, sociology and psychology (see also Clark et al., 2009). The second section of this introduction will therefore provide brief summaries of the 15 chapters that comprise the volume.

* * *

Part One of the collection investigates the nature of knowing and deliberation in practice. The professions have an ambivalent relationship with technical and scientific knowledge: while it is universally acknowledged as the prime distinguishing and legitimising characteristic of modern professionals, it is much less clear that the whole of the professional's wisdom and skill in deliberating over difficult cases can be encompassed within the realm of scientifically validated technical expertise.

In Chapter 1, Joseph Dunne contrasts the technical rationality that informs productive activities with the practical wisdom, derived from Aristotelian *phronesis*, essential to effective engagement in human affairs. Members of a community of practice are committed to its characteristic outcomes; to sustain that commitment, they nurture the characteristic capabilities or virtues of the practice. While the capabilities of a practice are both technical and practical, it follows from Dunne's exegesis that the cardinal virtue of people practices must be wise judgement, or *phronesis*. The practically wise professional employs a capacity for engaged understanding and discerning judgement; he or she is able to distinguish unusual situations from everyday concerns and respond appropriately, mediating with generalities while always respecting the particularity of the case.

In Chapter 2, Michael Luntley challenges the widespread supposition – previously exemplified by Dunne in the preceding chapter with the common notion that the potter has 'know-how in his or her hands that is irrecoverable in any explicit propositions' (page 20, this volume) – that the knowledge of expert practitioners is somehow different in kind from the ordinarily recognised knowledge expressible in propositions. Luntley expands the concept of a proposition, arguing that propositional knowledge is no less than such merely because it resists precise articulation or codification. He further maintains that it is not the thought-processes of the expert that represent extraordinary skill and judgement in response to difficult or unusual problems; on the contrary, it is the special procedures and knowledge application attributed to the novice that are extraordinary.

In Chapter 3, Chris Clark further explores the reach and limits of technical rationality by examining 'evidence-based practice', now widely promulgated as the necessary and sole legitimate foundation of good practice in a growing range of human services. Notwithstanding its superficial attraction, evidence-based practice has in actuality been founded on a narrowly positivist conception of scientific evidence. Considering knowing for practice, Clark distinguishes actors' background knowledge, whose content they are normally largely unaware of, from the foreground tools, both conceptual and tangible, that they consciously employ to carry out a task. Evidence-based practice may be a helpful source of foreground tools, but fails entirely to ground the broader process of practical reasoning, or the practical wisdom which distinguishes the deeply experienced professional.

In Chapter 4, Daniel Vokey and Jeannie Kerr carry the discussion of practical reasoning into the arena of moral choices. They question the reliability of moral decision-making, and ask what might serve as evidence of learning by students of the capacity to make better moral choices. Noting that moral decision-making commonly occurs in contexts of complexity that cannot be conclusively addressed by standard inferential reasoning, they argue that we must posit forms of non-inferential cognition, including moral intuition and moral judgement. Vokey and Kerr draw on Haidt's (2001) social intuitionist model of moral judgement that emphasises the priority of felt apprehensions over logical reasoning. They identify discernment – the proper mean between rashness and timidity in moral judgement – as the capacity needed to meet the challenge of complexity.

In the final chapter of Part One, addressing issues of professional deliberation, Elizabeth Campbell probes what is needed to prepare students of education to show appropriate moral example and engage in effective ethical deliberation in their eventual professional practice. In her own research, students appeared barely conversant with normative ethical standards, but did tend to remember rules or prohibitions pertaining to notorious but rare infractions. They were particularly impressed by their negative experiences of the unethical practice of their supervising teachers. Campbell notes that while the development of moral and ethical judgement mostly occurs before entering training, real understanding of professional issues only develops as the fruit of professional experience. All the same, she argues that there is a case for more explicit and focused pre-service teaching of professional ethics.

Part Two takes up questions about the personal and affective dimensions of professional engagement. For some in the people professions, emotional connections with others are a key reward of their work. But is such emotional involvement wise? How can the requirement for professionals to treat their 'clients' impartially be combined with the inevitably personal nature of their interaction with those for whom they care or those whose development they seek to facilitate? How do we equip professionals to manage the emotional nature of their work? What expectations do we hold about how we engage with our own and others' emotional experiences of professional relationships? Part Two addresses such questions, and explores ways in which wise personal and affective engagement might be thought about and developed in professional practice.

In Chapter 6, David Carr explores the relationship between the personal and the interpersonal in 'people professional' relationships from a philosophical and conceptual viewpoint. He argues that some of the philosophical trouble arises from conceptual confusion between the terms 'impartial' and 'impersonal'. But even if impartiality need not be equated with impersonal forms of behaviour, prevailing deontological approaches to professional ethics provide no satisfactory guidance in relation to emotional engagement within professional practice. He therefore turns to two possible alternatives: the ethics of care, and Aristotelian virtue ethics. As he explains, the latter places better emphasis on the moral character required of professionals and the importance of its cultivation in the training, practice and ethical frameworks of people professionals.

In Chapter 7, Kristján Kristjánsson picks up on questions concerning the moral character of professionals, with a particular focus on schoolteachers, noting the recent proliferation of studies of teachers' professional identities and the emotional dimension of teaching. He argues that the literature on both issues has become saddled with what he calls the 'constructivist-cognitive' paradigm, according to which agents, including teachers and other professionals, have multiple identities but no actual selves, and emotions are understood either as non-cognitive thrusts or as exercises of social power. He exposes the weaknesses of this paradigm, and paves the way for an Aristotle-inspired alternative.

Historically, one aspect of identity of particular relevance to the composition and character of professions has been gender. The growth of the people professions has been associated with what is sometimes called the 'feminisation' of professions. In Chapter 8, Liz Bondi explores the natures of these trends, and poses questions about the impact of gender on what we understand by professional wisdom. Using debates about emotion as an example, she shows how ideas about 'feminine' and 'masculine' attributes and orientations continue to have an impact on the value accorded to different aspects of professional wisdom.

Work is where many of us live for many hours a day, yet the emotional importance of work in people's lives is often downplayed. In Chapter 9, Susie Orbach argues for greater emotional literacy at work, focusing on professions in which relationships with others are key. Her account explores questions of the underlying motivations that draw people into these professions, and offers concepts from psychoanalysis to help us think about and manage the emotional dilemmas we face at work. She concludes by using the Jungian concept of the shadow, which posits that there are always forces at work that seek to undo or do the opposite of our conscious intent and the overt intentions of the organisations in which we work.

In Chapter 10, which concludes Part Two, John Swinton argues that imagination is a vital ingredient of professional wisdom, which he considers needs to be combined with the idea of practitioners in the people professions serving as guides and healers for individuals, particularly in times of personal crisis. In this context, he explores the wisdom of L'Arche communities, which offer support for people with learning disabilities based on Jean Vanier's 'The Way of the Heart' (Vanier, 1999). As he shows, this approach is not simply another mode of caring for people, but is a way of being with and learning from people with intellectual disabilities.

As a form of professional wisdom, it requires us to think in new ways about the relevance of friendship.

Part Three addresses often complex issues around the effect of legislation and regulation on professional judgement, and the ways, both positive and negative, in which the demands of the state or of professional bodies have an impact on how professionals deliberate and decide. This part includes contributions from the fields of social work, counselling, ministry and social policy.

In Chapter 11, Sue White notes the disparity between the way clinicians often display uncertainty about technologies and their own diagnoses, and the way social workers and practitioners are much less equivocal in offering opinions about human relationships. She uses ethnographic research conducted in children's departments in England and Wales to illustrate the effect of a raft of government reforms, particularly the electronic assessment instruments which are, she argues, pushing social workers towards precipitous categorisations and action.

In Chapter 12, Kathleen Marshall and Maggie Mellon draw on research by the office of the Scottish Commissioner for Children and Young People to show how state regulation originally intended to protect children has led to paranoia and risk-aversive behaviour in innocent adults. They graphically illustrate by means of three stories how the mechanisation of relationships between adults and children has developed, denying children the creative play that they need for development, and leaving adults searching for 'guidelines' to follow that will exonerate them in the eyes of the media and society at large should things go wrong. We are, they argue, at risk of undermining healthy social relationships between adults and children – relationships that both children and adults need.

The next two chapters address, from very different perspectives, the area of professional judgement in ministry. In Chapter 13, Alison Elliot reflects on the way ministers have to negotiate the boundaries between the voluntary, professional and business sectors, whose attitudes and values are potentially in conflict. She explores how the concept of the psychological contract can bridge some of the differences. Illustrating her argument from research on a faith-based project about homelessness, she demonstrates that reflective ministerial practice can be remarkably robust in navigating the challenges of voluntary action in the present culture of regulation.

In Chapter 14, Cecelia Clegg assesses the lack of accountability in the profession of ministry that has, until the middle of the last decade, managed to avoid professionalisation and regulation. Noting that the practitioner is the main 'tool' in ministry, she argues that pastoral supervision must be a major element in developing wise practice. This is especially true in light of the particular features of pastoral ministry, in terms of the movement of the Spirit and making religious truth claims, which both require accountability and discernment if they are to be lived positively. With the formation of the Association of Pastoral Supervisors and Educators (APSE) in 2008 and the subsequent opening of a route for accrediting pastoral supervisors, there is now a formal structure to underpin and encourage the practice of pastoral supervision – one in which she contends the Churches must invest.

The closing contribution of the collection comes from Nick Totton, who in a provocative essay argues that good therapy cannot also be 'safe'. He contrasts the emphasis on boundaries with creativity and relationship, claiming that therapy should not be domesticated, but wild. He laments the rise of the 'normal' practitioner and the re-medicalisation of therapy driven by the rise in therapist numbers and hunger for status. He favours 'local knowledge' and 'thick description' over the primacy given to expert knowledge, contending that scientific research has shown that 'neither technique nor training significantly affect the benefits reported' (page 239, this volume). Teasing out the current context in terms of a society that wants to control life, especially the unconscious, and to alleviate suffering, he argues that individual psychotherapists and the psychotherapy profession must choose whether or not to stand against this fantasy.

While the editors, as sometime contributors to the literature on these issues, have also seen fit to contribute invited chapters to this volume, they would like to express their especial thanks to the authors of invited contributions in this work. It is largely due to these distinguished colleagues that this volume has been able to present – so we believe – a wide range of quality pioneering essays on the nature of professionalism and professional practice from leaders in the field of contemporary reflection on these issues. In this regard, the editors have every confidence that the volume will be of considerable academic and professional value to a wide professional clientele – including theorists of the professions, policy-makers and practitioners – in such fields as teaching, social work, nursing, ministry, psychotherapy and counselling, as well as other professions.

References

Carr, D. (2009), 'Virtue, mixed emotions and moral ambivalence', *Philosophy*, 84, 31–46.

Clark, C., Bondi, L., Carr, D. and Clegg, C. (2009), Editorial, special issue: 'Towards Professional Wisdom', *Ethics and Social Welfare*, 3(2), 113–14.

Haidt, J. (2001), 'The emotional dog and its rational tail: A social intuitionist approach to moral judgement', *Psychological Review*, 108(4), 814–34.

Kristjánsson, K. (2007), *Aristotle, Emotions, and Education*, Aldershot: Ashgate.

—— (2010), *The Self and Its Emotions*, Cambridge: Cambridge University Press.

Vanier, J. (1999), 'The Way of the Heart', in *Becoming Human*, 2nd edn, New York: Paulist Press.

Part I
Practical Wisdom and Professional Deliberation

1 'Professional Wisdom' in 'Practice'[1]

Joseph Dunne

The claims of any profession or would-be profession, in terms of its authority with clients, the esteem it enjoys in the wider society, the exclusivity of its members' mandate to practise – and, not least, the scale of remuneration it commands – are closely tied to the kind of knowledge it embodies. In this chapter, I will focus on a particular kind of knowledge, much valorised in the wider culture of modernity, that has increasingly been called on to inform expert activity and to ground claims to professional status in many diverse fields. My analysis will show how this kind of knowledge, assembled according to the norms of what may be called 'technical rationality', negates wisdom as a capacity for engaged understanding and discerning judgement. And my main purpose will be to offer an account of wisdom – largely by contrast with technical reason – and to argue that, all pressures to the contrary notwithstanding, it remains indispensable in those domains of activity designated in this book as the 'people professions' – or at least that this is the case if the essential fabric of these domains is to be respected and they are to realise, without distortion, their own proper ends.

Practices and their Internal Goods

I begin by replacing 'profession' with 'practice', a concept I borrow mainly from Alasdair MacIntyre (1984 [1981]) and Aristotle's *Nicomachean Ethics* (Book 6, trans. Thompson, 1976); I do so in the belief, to be substantiated in the subsequent analysis and argument, that anything worth defending in the concept of profession is already included in the concept of practice – and that anything *not* so included is best jettisoned anyhow. By a practice,

---

1   This chapter draws on material from my previous essays Dunne (2004) and Dunne (2005).

I mean a more or less coherent and complex set of activities that has evolved co-operatively and cumulatively over time, and that exists most significantly in the community of those who are its practitioners – so long as they are committed to sustaining and developing its internal goods and its proper standards of excellence. 'Internal goods' here includes the desirable outcomes characteristically aimed at through a practice, for example patients restored to good health, well-educated students, and clients' achievement of greater resourcefulness in dealing with emotional conflict – in the cases, respectively, of medical practice, teaching and psychotherapy. What all these examples show are the characteristic end-results of a practice, the attainment of which is its essential end or *telos* as a practice. And these are the first kind of what I call internal goods of a practice.

Internal goods of a second kind reside in practitioners themselves: capabilities or qualities acquired and exercised by them through their apprenticeship into the practice, their answerability to its standards of excellence, and their submission to the demands of striving to achieve, regularly and reliably, its characteristic ends (in the sense of the first kind of internal good). These qualities are themselves of two kinds: competencies proper to each practice, and virtues of character that transcend any particular practice, though they may receive a unique modulation in the context of some particular practice. The former are technical proficiencies (for example, in making an accurate assessment of a patient's or a student's state of immediate need or readiness); but to exercise these proficiencies in striving to realise the proper ends of the practice, one may need virtues such as patience, temperance, courage, honesty or humility. Together, these qualities focus and direct one's energy and attention, disciplining one's desires, putting one at the disposal, so to speak, of what needs to be accomplished in each situation where the ends of the practice are at stake, and joining one in non-rivalrous partnership with others similarly disposed.

Internal goods are at the constitutive core of a practice, definitive of it as the quite specific practice that it is. But there are also external goods – chiefly, rewards in terms of pay, recognition and status. And also, somewhat external (though necessary if a practice is to survive with more than a fugitive presence in the world) is an institutional framework: a set of structures that mediates between it and wider social, economic and political agencies – in the case of the type of practices to be considered here, for example, securing and managing adequate resources, formulating and invigilating codes of practice, devising regulatory procedures, determining entry requirements or credentialising aspirant practitioners. At their best, these institutional structures serve the achievement of the practice's internal goods. But they can also, and often do, compromise this achievement, leading to greater or lesser distortions and corruptions of practice – distortions and corruptions that can be identified and addressed only in the light of a clear recognition and understanding of the internal goods defined and pursued at what I am calling the practice's constitutive core.

This MacIntyrean (1984 [1981]) conception of practice, sufficiently generic to include a wide variety of specific domains and even kinds of domain – for example, performance arts (dancing, flute-playing), productive professions and crafts (architecture, weaving), theoretical pursuits (physics, history) and games (soccer, chess) – differs from Aristotle's original concept of *praxis*. For the latter was not domain-specific, but rather designated the open set of activities through which one strove to live a worthwhile life in the light of some conception of the overall human good, or of flourishing as the ultimate goal of all one's living; and one did this precisely *not* as an expert in any particular field – and, if in any role, simply as a citizen of the *polis*. Now the practices to which this book is devoted might be said to instantiate *both* of these senses of practice: on the one hand, they are enclaves of specialised competency and concern, while on the other – since their ends lie in significant changes to the human beings whose needs are addressed by their specific forms of interaction – they are unavoidably implicated in basic, and of course always contestable, issues concerning human well-being.

Technical Rationality and the Drive Towards 'Professionalisation'

My concern here is not singly with any one of these latter practice-domains, but rather with all of them as sharing, so I shall claim, an internal feature that is essential to their integrity as practices. Returning us to the theme broached at the outset, this feature has to do with the kind of *knowledge* that they embody, a kind that I shall designate as 'practical'. I shall return presently to analyse the nature of this knowledge, whose kinship with wisdom will, I hope, become manifest. But I turn now to consider that other kind of knowledge which, by its growing dominance, has threatened to eclipse it – while at the same time driving the movement in many areas towards more assertive forms of professionalism.

This latter form of knowledge has been intimately linked to the great esteem placed in modernity on rationality, or rather, a specific mode of rationality that has established an epistemic hegemony, so that only knowledge assembled within its frame is recognised as properly rigorous, and only activity organised according to its dictates is recognised as properly efficacious – claims for the efficacy of the activity being grounded in prior claims for the rigour of the knowledge. This mode is often and understandably related to modern science (though it needs to be recognised that, as practices of inquiry, the sciences do not actually follow it). And it also has deep roots in Western philosophy, being traceable back to the Platonic valorisation of *techne* which provides the etymological basis for its designation as *technical* rationality.

Within the frame of technical rationality, the context-dependence of first-person experience is suppressed in favour of the detachment of third-person procedures. These procedures give a privileged role to a kind of observation and experimentation that is standardised and measurable, to modes of testing that specify precisely what can count as counter-evidence, to findings or outcomes that are clearly formulated and replicable, and to a language-in-use that is maximally freed from possibilities of misinterpretation by its being maximally purged of the need for interpretation itself. Within this frame, a subject can disengage from her or his environing milieu and take an objectifying and instrumental stance towards it. This stance promises enormous mastery: everything in the environment is potentially a means to be controlled in achieving pre-designed ends. And with mastery there is also maximisation: optimal effectiveness in achieving ends and optimal efficiency in achieving them with the least – or most economical – input of means.

It is in control over *matter* that technical rationality has achieved the spectacular success now so evident in our built environment and vast array of technological devices. What concerns me here, however, is the persistent attempt to organise and regulate according to its dictates the kind of *human action* and *interaction* involved in the people-centred practices considered in this book. Its prestige has grown to the point where it is no longer seen as *a* form of rationality, with its own limited sphere of validity, but as coincident with rationality *as such*. Knowledge of any kind that does not accord with it is deemed to be non-rational, and hence to be incapable of delivering progress in an area of practice – or, as is now easily assumed, of underwriting its claims as a profession. Any area of practice that does not rationalise itself according to its standards – that persists in giving a strong function to other modes of knowledge – is under pressure to adopt its procedures and accommodate to its norms. This pressure has long been exerted in practices strongly linked to natural science, such as medicine and dentistry, and in recent decades has also been very evident in practices such as education, law and nursing, or in newer practices (such as psychotherapy or social work) keen to assert their 'professional' status.

To technicise a practice is to make it over in such a way that control over its key operations is maximally assured by a method whose implementation can be monitored systematically. This will involve devising new procedures or extracting from established ones a rational core that can be made transparent and replicable. Typically, this entails disembedding the knowledge implicit in the skilful performance of the characteristic tasks of the practice from the immediacy and idiosyncrasy of the particular situations in which it is deployed, and from the background of experience and character in the practitioners in whom it resides. Through this disembedding, it is supposed that what is essential in the knowledge and skill can be abstracted for encapsulation in explicit, generalisable formulae, procedures or rules – which can in turn be applied to the various situations and circumstances that arise in the practice in order to meet the problems that they present. These problems are assumed to contain nothing significant that has not been anticipated in the analysis which yielded the general formulae, and hence to be soluble by a straightforward application of the formulae without need for any new insight or discernment in the actual situation itself. Control, efficiency and proper 'accountability' seem to be assured because the system is minimally dependent on the discretion or judgement of individual practitioners, with all the hazard and lack of standardisation that this might entail. The ideal to which technical rationality aspires, one might say, is a practitioner-proof mode of practice.

Wisdom in Practice

My articulation of the nature of technical rationality has just brought out its inherent opposition to practitioners' knowledge, or its drive to supplant what might be called an alternative mode of *practical* rationality. How, then, is this alternative mode of rationality to be characterised? It is here that wisdom re-enters the discussion. In the Aristotelian tradition, the answer will rely heavily on the notion of *phronesis* elaborated, somewhat sketchily, in Book 6 of the *Nicomachean Ethics* and usually translated as 'practical wisdom' (or good 'judgement' as the capability to make good judgement-calls reliably). I will outline here a few key, inter-related features of *phronesis*: its role as an action-orientating form of knowledge; its irreducibly experiential nature; its entanglement (beyond mere knowledge) with character; its non-confinement to generalised propositional knowledge; its need to embrace the particulars of relevant action-situations within its grasp of universals, and its ability to engage in the kind of deliberative process that can yield concrete, context-sensitive judgements (see Dunne, 2009).

To have *phronesis* (to be practically wise or a person of good judgement) is to be able to recognise situations, cases or problems as perhaps standard or typical – that is to say, of a type that has been met previously and for which there is an already established and well-rehearsed rule, recipe or formula – or as deviating from the standard and conventional, and in either case, to be capable of dealing with them adequately and appropriately. One respects the particularity of the case – and thus does not rigidly impose on it an ill-fitting application of the general rule. At the same time, one tries to find a way of bringing this particularity into *some* relationship, albeit one yet to be determined, with the body of general knowledge codified in rules and formulae. It is not that one disregards this general knowledge, but rather that it is available to one, like the measuring rule used by builders at Lesbos, which Aristotle (trans. Thompson, 1976) approved because, being made of lead, it was pliable enough to measure the surfaces of irregularly shaped stones (unlike, for example, a wooden rule). One's adeptness as a person of judgement, then, lies neither in the knowledge of the general as such nor in an entirely unprincipled dealing with particulars. Rather, it lies precisely in the mediation between general and particular, in the ability to bring both into illuminating connection with each other. This requires perceptiveness in reading particular situations as much as flexibility in one's way of possessing, being informed by, and 'applying' general knowledge.

Practical wisdom is more than the possession of general knowledge just because it is the ability to actuate this knowledge with relevance, appropriateness, or sensitivity to context. In every fresh actuation there is an element of creative insight through which it makes itself equal to the demands of a new situation. Because of this element of 'excess', beyond what has already been formulated, which it proves itself recurrently capable of generating, judgement is at home with the implicit – a fact closely related to its experiential character. One thinks here of how the past experience of 'experienced' people is at their disposal, informing in intimate detail their way of meeting and interpreting what is *now* appearing within their experience *here*. What comes up here and now, what challenges one in a new situation, may not be comfortably encompassed by one's previous experience, but rather may require that experience be reconstructed; and this reconstruction (a key motif of Dewey's philosophy; see, for example, Dewey, 1997 [1938]) *is* what we mean by significant learning. It may be, of course, that there are many situations in or from which we need to, but do not, learn, so that our experience settles into stale routine; it is sometimes said of teachers, for example, that although they may have been teaching for ten years, they have only one year's experience – their first year in practice, more or less repeated thereafter.

The kind of openness that allows one's experience to be quickened by new learning so that one develops finely discriminating judgement can be characterised as *cognitive*; but it also brings into play some of those virtues of *character* mentioned earlier. There is, for example, patience in sticking with a problem, or in waiting with a person until she or he has found a way to tell a story; or courage in entertaining an unpopular or unwelcome thought, or in trying to deal with rather than avoid a risky situation, or in confronting a person whom one may have good reason to fear (perhaps because of some power the person can wield over one), or temperateness so that one is not too easily swayed by first impression or by impulse or irritation, and can thus keep one's attention on what is salient in dealing with a problematic situation. Receptivity to the problem is called for, rather than keenness to master it with a solution. This receptivity may call for a high level of imaginative and emotional engagement by the self; but it does not gratify the 'fat relentless ego' (Murdoch, 1970, 52). One might therefore be tempted to speak of it as 'impersonal'; but the springs of judgement are deeply recessed in one's mind, character and being, and therefore are expressive of the kind of person – as well as, or rather in and through, the kind of practitioner – that one has become.

The kind of attentive receptivity that I have just invoked may seem to draw us too uncomfortably close to the 'mystical' or to states of mind whose cultivation is sought through 'spiritual' disciplines. However, our ordinary linguistic usage already registers the need for – indeed, the very fact of – receptivity: we speak of a question *arising* or an insight *coming* (as sleep comes or tears come). Language here points us to the fact that what we need is not always under our control in the sense of being at our command; it is a matter, rather, of our not obstructing, but allowing – or being available to – what needs to happen or to emerge. I introduce these intimations of ordinary language because their very ordinariness may seem more reassuringly legitimate than any recourse to the 'mystical'. But there can in fact be a fruitful porosity between the practices under consideration in this book and some spiritual disciplines that are also sometimes called 'practices'. Various practices of meditation, for example, aim at a stilling of the over-active mind or the distracting ego (though 'aim at' contains a paradox to be resolved only in the very practice). 'Mindfulness' is a concept now accorded greater recognition (especially in the practice of psychotherapy), though we need to recognise that it includes an enhanced kind of *embodiedness*. It is mostly from the greater currency of Eastern practices, especially Zen Buddhist ones, that this recognition has come. But Western philosophy, too, has included a similar emphasis, albeit in authors and traditions too little recognised in the academy – for example, Simone Weil, for whom 'attention' was both the way and the end of all genuine intellectual work, and phenomenology as a kind of philosophical exercise, sensitised by bodily comportment, in which one seeks accurate perception and just response (Weil, 1977; Merleau-Ponty, 1962).

The Fabric of Practice as Determining the Form of Rationality

As between the technical and the practical kinds of knowledge-orientation that I have just outlined, the technical has an inter-related set of attractions.

The kind of objectivity that it aspires to seems to protect it against intrusions of the merely subjective. The transparency of its procedures seems to free it from reliance on personal gifts or inarticulate intuitions. The replicability of its operations and the generalisability of its findings seem to ensure a universal reach beyond the local or occasional. The prediction and control that it seems to promise provide clear-cut criteria for assessing success and establishing accountability – thereby providing escape from inadjudicable arguments or interminable contests of interpretation. Against these advantages, knowledge with an irreducible core of judgement can be made to appear makeshift, unreliable, elitist and unaccountable. Still, a large question remains as to the competence of technical rationality to deal with the actual fabric of many practical domains. It is a cardinal point for Aristotle that the fabric will determine the kind of activity we are engaged in, which in turn will determine the kind of knowledge that we require and the type of rationality that is appropriate.

The fabric of the material world – say wood, concrete or metal – lends itself to the activity of making, fabrication or production, where a form can be imposed on these materials to yield a substantial, durable product. It was in reflecting on this kind of activity, on this kind of material, that the classical Greek philosophers first elaborated their conception of *techne*. In this conception, they put priority on offering an explicit verbal account of the how and why of the making process, elaborating a set of conceptual dualities that still remain with us, for example form and matter, ends and means, planning and execution, and not least, 'mind' and 'body'. This conception of *techne* might well be claimed to have laid down the dominant paradigm of Western rationality. And the great achievements of modern science have not so much recast it as allowed it all the more to come into its own. For, ironically, the philosophical conception of *techne* did not accurately reflect much of what actually went on in some of the crafts of fabrication – think, for example, of a potter and of the amount of know-how in his or her hands that is irrecoverable in any explicit propositions. But with the increasing marginalisation of genuine craft skill, modern science gives us the kind of general, law-like knowledge that was already anticipated in the concept of *techne* (even though, to be sure, the Greek thinkers had not envisaged the kind of bold experimentation and exploitation of mathematics that came only with the scientific revolution of the seventeenth century). Moreover, the *instrumental* structure of *techne* is not only retained but reinforced in our scientific age: deep-structure knowledge of materials opens a huge field of possibilities within which we can contrive new ends – while at the same time providing just the kind of predictive control that enables us to mobilise means towards their achievement reliably. (What I say here is not at odds with my earlier point that, as practices of inquiry, the sciences do not subscribe to a technicist logic. Rather, it is only when their enquiries have *already* established reliable findings or results that these latter can then be used within a technicist framework.)

What, then, of those other activities that are *not* captured by this technicist paradigm, including, conspicuously, the practices of special concern in this book – as well as some activities that the Greeks themselves knew well and valued highly, such as rhetoric, military strategy and politics or statecraft? The 'fabric' of these practices contains volatile combinations of human passions and motivations. And the skilled practitioner is not imposing a design on stable materials in order to bring about an end-product so much as intervening in a field of forces or immersing herself or himself in a medium in which she or he seeks to bring about a propitious result. In such intervention or immersion, the practitioner is always responding to something that is already going on, and exposed to the play of chance and the vagaries of timing, needs adaptability and a talent for improvisation.

The kind of 'fabric' that I am trying to elaborate here may be illuminated by illustrative reference to the particular practice with which I am most closely engaged: education within the institutional frame of a school. A classroom teacher has to deal with – even if not fully aware of – the countless number of ways in which students may be distant from, resistant to or at sea with what the teacher is trying to teach – and the perhaps no less numerous ways, direct and indirect, by which they might be brought towards it. It is not just that students may not understand the material, but that they may not be engaged by it at all, or may have their relationship to it mediated through varying intensities of interest, dreaminess, apathy or antagonism. The teacher has to confront not only the emotional-imaginative tonality of the whole class, but also different ways in which this may influence and be influenced by the shifting moods of many diverse individual students. What needs to be captured here is the complexity of the teaching situation, the fluctuating forces at work in it, and hence the dynamic character of what it puts in play between teacher and students. There is always something at stake for the teacher and the students, so that success is never guaranteed (or even easily defined in advance). Haunted by the ever-present possibility of failure, teachers succeed only when their activity has the character of an *event* through which students' attention and energy are drawn into and focused by the particular subject-matter, so that, for example, they gain insights, develop competencies and experience a kind of satisfaction that can encourage further interest.

This event-like character is something close to what Hannah Arendt characterises as 'natality', the capacity of action to bring forth what could not have been reliably predicted, so that agents are realised and disclosed to themselves and to each other in new ways (Arendt, 1999; Dunne, 2009). Each action is inserted in a web of interaction, with its own power conditioned by its capacity to mesh with – without manipulating – the actions of *other* agents in the same space. Related to event is *story*. Teaching a class (for an hour or a year) is an *enacted* story. Incidents and episodes cumulate into an unfolding story-line which further incidents and episodes sustain, disrupt or redirect. Teacher and students become characters who contribute to and are constructed by this story-line. It is for this reason that research into teaching is well served by narrative modes of inquiry: the intelligibility of teaching lies not so much in a predictable chain of causality as in the plot of a story that can be narrated only retrospectively.

To acknowledge all this is to recognise the frailty and intricacy of human affairs – or what amounts to much the same thing, the non-sovereignty of the single agent or practitioner; it is also to highlight the dialogical contexts within which every practitioner is set – contexts that are shaped by the practice itself as a historically constructed space of communal collaboration. It is a feature of teaching – as of the other practices addressed in this book – that it does not escape this frailty, intricacy and non-sovereignty, even in its proper concern with successful accomplishment, standards of good practice and the effective achievement of its own proper ends. It is not in order to deny that teaching has definable ends towards which teachers know that they must try to steer their course that I stress the eventful character of teaching; rather, eventfulness is unavoidable precisely because of *the kind* of ends to which teaching is committed. 'Much learning', according to a Buddhist saying, 'is like a poor man counting someone else's coins.' It is just because this kind of learning is *not* an adequate end of educative teaching – just because students must themselves be significantly changed – that the teacher cannot avoid eventful action and the rewards and perils it puts at stake.

My aim here is to capture the intricacy of the fabric of school-teaching as a practice and to argue that no decision on the kind of knowledge (or knowledges) required by an accomplished teacher can be made independently of this fact. And what is true of teaching also holds, *mutatis mutandis*, for other examples of what might be called the 'people practices'. On my analysis, it is in the nature of the kind of ends to which these practices are committed, and of the kind of eventful action that they entail, that they often present us with a problematic situation in which there is no discrete problem already clearly discernible as such – so that we might better speak of a difficulty or *predicament* rather than a problem. A predicament is a point of intersection of several lines of consideration and priority that, though pulling in different directions, are interwoven tightly in a complex web. Attempts to unravel any one of these strands singly (the classic task of analysis) may only introduce greater tangles in others. To return for a moment to my own sphere of education, a teacher may face a situation in which academic standards, psychological needs, considerations of safety, and the demands of social equity, in relation to a diverse group of students, pull in contrary directions – but in which one must make some judgement and decision. In attempting to do so, one is not calculating the efficiency of different possible means towards an already determined end. Rather, one is often deliberating about the end itself – about what would count as the best or a satisfactory (or at least not entirely unsatisfactory) outcome in this particular situation. This will entail a kind of pondering – though some imponderables may not be entirely eliminable from the reckoning. It may indeed only be through action, and not in the end by any purely deliberative process, that this reckoning can finally be carried through. When one judges first and then acts, one is in the more secure reaches of a practice; but sometimes judgement is possible only *in* or even *after* action. One does not only know in order to act, but also acts in order to know – or at least hoping to learn. While strategically directed action will provide new feedback, it also, of course, sets off its own chain of unexpected and unintended consequences; one is involved in an experimental process. Experimentation in these practical fields, however, is subject to constraints that do not obtain in a scientific laboratory – a fact that must itself be factored in to practical judgement. For whereas a 'negative' or disconfirming result may be celebrated by the sceptical spirit of the scientist as a forward step in the onward march of knowledge (Popper, 1972), in the fields I have been investigating here it may have to be recognised simply as an over-costly error. And yet the situation may be such that to hazard *no* experimental probe is itself an error, if not an outright impossibility. It is especially in situations such as this that practical wisdom is the necessary source of judgement.

Conclusion

Earlier in this chapter, I distinguished two kinds of internal goods of a practice: the characteristic outcomes that it seeks to achieve, and the qualities required of good practitioners if they are actually to achieve these outcomes. I hope it is now apparent in the case of the sort of practices considered here that because the first set of goods is of the kind that it is, the second set must include practical wisdom. The analysis has been directed against a particular conception of professionalism which is powerfully entrenched in our contemporary culture and the malign consequences of which we urgently need to combat. My critical aim, of course, has not been to deplore the use of the term 'professional', but only to contest some of the connotations that, given the current ascendancy of technicist modes of thinking, so easily accrete around it. When it connotes the kind of practical judgement outlined above, 'professional wisdom' has real purchase.

In my analysis, professional wisdom has a wide scope. But this does not offset the fact that it must incorporate a recognition of the *limits* of one's understanding and power – and thus an avoidance of the *hubris* attendant on the absence of such recognition. This is where MacIntyrean (1984 [1981]) practice, as an enclave of specifically focused expertise in one delimited domain, cannot in the end be insulated from Aristotelian *praxis* as co-extensive with the living of a person's (or indeed a community's or society's) whole life. Two points can be noted briefly here. First, it is integral to the 'people professions' that although their specific competence is circumscribed, in the lives and narratives of the people with whom they deal this circumscription can never be fully secure: the specific goods achievable for them through the ministrations of a particular practice have to find their place among other different, and perhaps even conflicting, goods to which they are responsive in their whole lives. Second, the limits indicated here are related to the 'eventfulness' and 'frailty' of human affairs already mentioned – or to what might better be called the finitude of human life itself, especially as manifested in the inescapability of death. This is where *professional* wisdom most fully participates simply in *wisdom*.

I cannot explore here the wider ethical issues that arise at the limits of professional practice just indicated. I shall conclude, rather, with two qualifications that may be needed because of the whole direction of the analysis in this chapter and the extent to which, in profiling practical wisdom, I have used *techne* as a foil. First, I acknowledge that technical rationality has its own proper competence in certain circumscribed arenas of operation, and hence that it is right to technicise – even in practical domains – everything that can, without loss, be technicised. For example, if there are routine or systematically categorisable tasks that can be processed by computer software, such processing clearly brings advantage (by economising on time and other probably scarce resources). Still, the main point remains: advantage accrues only if we can reliably recognise those tasks that can and those that can *not* be so programmed, and only if our overall priority is to free our most precious resource (which, on the present analysis, is precisely good practical judgement) to do what only it can do well – rather than to try to supplant it or make it obsolete.

Second, as outlined above, professional wisdom brings an attunement to the fabric of the particular field of practice – a tutored attunement, to be sure, but one that still enables good practitioners intuitively, perhaps even effortlessly, to home in on what is salient and needful. (In Dreyfus and Dreyfus's [1980] well-known analysis, it is characteristic of the 'expert', as distinct from the 'novice', to be able to engage in demanding tasks of a practice without need of effortful analysis or deliberation – as, in the case of the concert pianist, all the earlier struggle with scales, all the hours and years of 'practice', have disappeared into accomplished performance.) This sense of easy attunement lends itself to a picture of the wise as composed and self-possessed. But it may be significantly through experiences of *dis*composure and *dis*possession that wisdom is acquired – just as it is in situations of disruption, even irruption, that it may be most urgently required (here again, particular images of teaching-situations come readily to mind). Moreover, Aristotle's picture of the growth of *phronesis* may suggest a too smooth process of assimilation (see Gadamer, 1990, 350–58), and we should bear in mind also what he says more generally about virtue: that one gets it right only against the background of countless ways of getting it *wrong*. (In relation to teaching, specifically, this point is well made by Raimond Gaita: 'The power of fine teaching is delicately nuanced through its disciplined perception of its many possible corruptions'; Gaita, 2000, 231–2). Often one is aware not of being right, but with a necessary tolerance for what is tentative and halting, of making one's way out of or through what is *not* right: 'That's not right', 'It isn't this', 'No, that doesn't quite get it, either', 'This is nearer, but …'. Here we are reminded that, for Socrates, the knowing that resides in wisdom is largely a knowing that we do *not* know – what might be called learned nescience rather than mere ignorance. This emerges in his notoriously frequent disclaimers that he possesses any answers, even as he pursues his relentless questioning. But it can also be related to his high valuation of the *daimon* that directed him *away* from available options or courses of action that were *not* good. This itself was his *good daimon*. The Greek word for well-being or flourishing is *eudaimonia*, which etymologically means 'having a well-disposed [*eu*] *daimon*' – the Socratic twist on 'well-disposed' here emphasising the ubiquitous background of what potentially deceives, damages or subverts, and against which wisdom, or rather philosophy as the *search* for wisdom, enforces a constant vigilance.

References

Arendt, H. (1999), *The Human Condition*, 2nd edn, Chicago, IL: University of Chicago Press.

Aristotle (1976), *Nicomachean Ethics*, trans. J.A.K. Thompson, Harmondsworth: Penguin.

Dewey, J. (1997 [1938]), *Experience and Education*, New York: Touchstone.

Dreyfus, S.E. and Dreyfus, H.L. (1980), *A Five-stage Model of the Mental Activities Involved in Directed Skill Acquisition*, Berkeley, CA: University of California at Berkeley Operations Research Center.

Dunne, J. (2004), 'Arguing for teaching as a practice: A reply to Alasdair MacIntyre', *Journal of Philosophy of Education*, 37(2), 353–69.

—— (2005), 'An intricate fabric: Understanding the rationality of practice', *Pedagogy, Culture and Society*, 13(3), 367–89.

—— (2009), *Back to Rough Ground: Practical Judgment and the Lure of Technique*, Notre Dame, IN and London: University of Notre Dame Press.

Gadamer, H.G. (1990), *Truth and Method*, 2nd edn, New York: Crossroad.

Gaita, R. (2000), *A Common Humanity: Thinking about Love and Truth and Justice*, London: Routledge.

MacIntyre, A. (1984 [1981]), *After Virtue: A Study in Moral Theory*, 2nd edn, London: Duckworth.

Merleau-Ponty, M. (1962), *The Phenomenology of Perception*, London: Routledge and Kegan Paul.

Murdoch, I. (1970), *The Sovereignty of Good*, London: Routledge and Kegan Paul.

Popper, K. (1972), *Conjectures and Refutations*, London: Routledge and Kegan Paul.

Weil, S. (1977), *Waiting on God*, London: HarperCollins.

2 Expertise – Initiation into Learning, Not Knowing

Michael Luntley

Experienced practitioners across a wide range of professions seem to know a lot. It is because they know a lot that they perform so well. Their practice is a knowing practice. It is what they know that makes them expert professionals. Knowledge matters for professional practice. Experienced nurses who can perform advanced bandaging techniques do so because of what they know. Experienced social workers who manage their clients with care and subtly nuanced interventions and support do so because of what they know about their clients' needs across a spectrum of emotional, psychological, financial, social, housing and other concerns. It is knowledge that informs practice and makes it wise.

However, to a great many writers it has seemed that in order to make sense of all this knowledge, we need to countenance types of knowing that are distinct from ordinary propositional knowledge. This view is now orthodox in the literature on professional wisdom (Dreyfus and Dreyfus, 1986; Dreyfus and Dreyfus, 2005; Benner, 1984; Eraut, 1994; Eraut, 2000). Whatever the details of this orthodoxy, its key move is to proliferate types of knowing. Some of these non-propositional types of knowing are almost ineffable. In the Dreyfus and Dreyfus taxonomy of the trajectory from novice to expert, the final stage of expert knowing is 'intuitive knowledge'. The literature is, however, quite profligate, and includes: experiential knowing, craft knowing, know-how, tacit knowing and personal knowing (Dreyfus, 2005; Dreyfus, 2007; McDowell, 2007). Central to this proliferation is the thesis that propositional knowledge does not suffice to capture the knowledge that informs practice. The key claim in this chapter is that this thesis is wrong: there is no need to proliferate types of knowing.

I call the position that I defend *epistemic conservatism*: ordinary propositional knowledge suffices for an account of the knowledge that informs practice across a wide range of professional activities (Luntley, 2009). We do not need the categories of 'know-how', 'tacit knowledge', 'personal knowledge' or 'intuitive knowledge'. Good old-fashioned

27

propositional knowledge will do. Furthermore, not only will propositional knowledge suffice, it is the only type of knowledge fit for the purpose of making sense of the idea that it is knowledge that makes practice wise.

A key element of my argument will involve clarification of the concept of propositional knowledge. The epistemic conservatism that I defend will seem so unorthodox that it is almost bound to offend. I suspect that is mostly because the literature to date on professional knowledge has operated with an impoverished concept of a proposition. No one has taken time out to ask, 'What is a proposition?' But until that is done, there is no basis for dismissing knowledge of propositions as the model for professional wisdom. I shall show how propositions can themselves be the sorts of things constituted by our perceptual and manipulative engagements with the environment. Propositions are not just things that fill books; they can be things that fill the forms of our actual real engagements with the physical, social, emotional and ethical environments that we manage. It is a mistake to restrict propositions to the clearly articulate structures that fill our heads and our books; they can include the conceptual forms of our active engagements with things, forms whose structure can only be articulated in the context of engagement. Thinking in the moment is still propositional thinking (there is no other kind that makes performance reasonable), but it is thinking with timely and contextually engaged propositions.

The structure of my argument will be as follows. First, I will outline the case for epistemic conservatism; then I will provide a diagnosis of why the virtues of epistemic conservatism have been missed due to a failure to clarify the sense in which expert knowledge can be difficult to codify, and lastly I will outline the case for saying that limits on codifiability support a sense in which the knowledge used by experts can fall outside the normal rules and protocols for performance. There are important ways in which propositional knowledge can resist codification because of the complex social and experiential conditions that need to be in place to for it to exist. This does not make the knowledge non-propositional; it just makes it difficult to articulate independently of our real engagements with the worldly domains that we manage. And it means that there is scope to acknowledge a real creative developmental responsibility that is part of the wisdom of professionals.

Further to the core outline and defence of epistemic conservatism, there are two further themes running through my argument. The first of these concerns the concept of initiation. The proliferation of types of knowing can make it unclear what rigour is left to the idea of non-propositional types of knowing. And if we are not clear what this stuff is, then the complex business of initiating new members into professional practice can too easily elide into mere socialisation of behaviour. I think it is important that the concept of initiation amounts to more than a descriptive tag for something that is otherwise left inarticulate beyond a vague sense of learning the ropes (Luntley, 2010).

Secondly, my defence of epistemic conservatism challenges the view of the relationship between novice and expert found in the orthodox account. The orthodox view treats the role of the expert as the exception, something to be contrasted with the everyday epistemic of the novice. It can then be tempting to look for something very distinctive and out of the ordinary in the epistemology of expertise. Hence the appeal of seeing expert knowledge as intuitive, an almost intangible form of know-how that is so embedded in the subject's engagement with the moment that it cannot survive the attempt to render it in propositions. For reasons that I will rehearse in the next section, I think this is epistemologically reckless and it is also topsy-turvy.

According to this topsy-turvy view, the novice is the ordinary subject who deals in familiar learnt routines and carefully articulated rules and propositions. They have a headful of book learning and a handful of trained routines, and they act according to the scripts encoded in this learning and routinisation. In contrast, the expert is the excitingly different; experts occupy an epistemic standpoint that is an achievement out of the ordinary. This, I claim, is what is topsy-turvy. According to my model, it is the expert who is ordinary and the novice who is the extraordinary construct. Recognising that expertise can be rendered into propositional knowledge helps us recover a key insight: grasp of propositional ways of knowing constituted by our active engagement with the environment is part of our common epistemic heritage. It needs to be acknowledged as ordinary. Our obsession with book learning has helped us forget how engaged our propositions can be. There is an important remembering about the conditions of ordinary propositional knowing that we need to recover. In contrast, it is the regimentation and commoditisation of knowledge that has constructed the peculiar rigidity of the novice as standardly conceived. The idea of the novice is the extraordinary construct. It is an idea of an epistemology that is, I suspect, in large part the result of a managerialist imposition, a regimentation of thought and knowing to provide an industrialised component of work. We miss too big a trick by complying with the ideology that has the expert as the extraordinary, for we then give the lie to the corruption that takes routinised propositional knowledge as the common core to our wisdom and diverts us from acknowledging the ways that propositional knowledge can escape the bounds of book learning. Getting things the right way up does not require novel, special non-propositional knowing. It requires only that we see aright what is involved in how our thought (our propositions) can engage directly the world on which we act.

Epistemic Conservatism and Engaging Propositions

We are interested in the epistemic standing of experts, for it is knowledge that legitimises their performance. To say that what the expert knows justifies their performance is to say that what they know gives reason for their action. Possession of knowledge makes performance reasonable; what is known bears upon action. To say that what is known bears upon action means that what is known can be shown to stand in some reason-giving relation to what is done. We need no specific theory of what the reason-giving relation is like. For now, it is enough to say:

> **K**: What is known bears upon what is done.

I know of no way of making sense of **K** other than by acknowledging that what is picked out by the phrase 'what is known' is something with a conceptual structure. The idea of 'what is known' picks out the content of knowledge. It is a content that, in virtue of its structure, stands in the relation of 'bearing upon' what is done. Similarly, whatever else is picked out by the phrase 'what is done', it is something that can be represented as an intentional action, something that falls under concepts for the actor. This is not to deny that there may be all sorts of other illuminating characterisations of what is done that identify it in ways that might be quite alien to the actor, for example describing the action by its location in a causal chain of happenings. The point is only that in so far as what is done is the sort of thing that is justified in the light of what is known, then it must be, like the latter, the sort of thing that can be located in a conceptual space. It is the sort of thing that can be represented with concepts.

We do not need to say any more to have the main thrust of the argument for epistemic conservatism. If what is known bears upon what is done, it does so by virtue of some shared conceptual structure between what is known and what is done. What is known and what is done are, for purposes of seeing how the former justifies the latter, appropriately represented with propositions. So what is known must be capable of being represented as propositional knowledge or else it is not the sort of thing that is suitable to stand in the relation of bearing upon what is done.

Let me go through this argument a little more slowly and identify with a bit more detail what is doing the work. Two things need to be addressed: (a) what concepts are, and (b) how the notion of 'what is known' relates to the phenomenology of the performing subject. I will start with concepts.

Concepts are the components of propositions. They are the components whose configuration shows what is at issue with a proposition – what it is for the proposition to be true or false. Some concepts are easy to identify. They can be tagged with words. In the proposition

(1) The car is red

it is easy to spot the concept '… is red'. It is a component that recurs in the proposition

(2) The box is red.

The way that the concept '… is red' figures in these propositions is constitutive of the way that they stand or fall together in being true or false. If (1) is true, then it follows that if the box looks the same as the car, then (2) must also be true. If not, there must be some difference in the way these two items look. This basic integration of belief (the way that one being true bears on the truth of another) is made possible by the sharing of concepts. A related point applies with other cognitive states. If I desire to see something red, then if (1) is true, looking at the car will satisfy my desire. Concepts are ways of discriminating things, and concepts populate beliefs, desires and other such states. They do so in ways that systematically integrate those states with respect to how they are evaluated; being true or false for beliefs, being satisfied or thwarted for desires. Whatever else we say about concepts, we must at least say this much.

Saying this much about the notion of a concept makes no commitment to how concepts are articulated in language. There are some concepts that are highly articulated in language – theoretical concepts in science are the obvious case, or concepts like being red, for which we have agreed names in ordinary language. But there are many concepts that are at best only partially expressible in language. They are none the worse for that in being concepts. Clear examples are concepts whose individuation is dependent on ways in which we engage with the environment, for example in perception and in action. We can think of a colour shade for which we have no specific name as 'that sort of red' or even just 'that colour' as we point to it. And what shows that this is a concept is that it is a component of a representation that can be true or false. Like the simple '… is red', it is a component of belief and desire that integrates these states.

If you are looking at colour samples for decorating and you say things like

(3) That red doesn't look right alongside that one.

while pointing to different samples, you are talking and thinking about shades of colour, and doing so in a way that enables you to keep track of shades for sufficient time for the thinking to integrate in the way you adjust your views

– your beliefs and desires about the colour you are trying to select. There is thinking going on. It might be quite short-lived, but it is thinking and it bears on action, for it is thinking with a conceptual structure that exploits the repeatable components of belief and desire made available by your perceptual attention on the shade and thinking of it as 'that red' or 'that colour'. These are concepts, even if they are only partially clothed in language.

Extraordinary sophistication in thought and action with respect to colours can be enabled by such concepts without their ever acquiring stable names or descriptions. They might become stable components of thinking in virtue of your acquiring a recognitional capacity to spot precisely that shade again and again. When that happens, there is no need for you to develop a name or description for the shade. When that happens, we have a case of sophisticated and nuanced thinking whose structure is manifest in the capacity for detailed manipulation of our perceptual engagement with and action upon colour shades.

The development of such ways of thinking is common across a wide range of activities whose details outrun the expressive power of ordinary language. Even when a specialised jargon is developed, the language is typically metaphorical and its meaning cannot be grasped without first acquiring a detailed experience of perceiving and manipulating the discriminations at issue. So even when the language is extended to record such concepts, the language is still secondary to the experience of the appropriate kind of detailed engagement with things that is required to grasp the concept. The people professions provide many examples of such modes of thinking. Consider the experienced nurse whose discrimination of fine shades of performance in advanced bandaging techniques is articulated in the concept of a 'bandaging like this' as he or she demonstrates the technique. This is a concept. The nurse is employing propositional knowledge when he or she tells a student not to 'do it like that', but 'do it like this', even though the proposition cannot be fully tagged in language. You need to be there, witnessing and very often taking part in the procedure to grasp the knowledge involved (see Luntley, 2011).[1]

---

1   Other examples are legion, and easy to spot once you get the idea. Think of the fine shades of discrimination of performance, such as a social worker engaging clients in subtly different ways depending on their needs, their particular state of mind at the time, the efficacy of their mediation and so on. Subtle variations in mode of engagement can be talked of when reflecting on consultations even though the variations are barely visible in language alone – when, for example, a social worker commends a colleague for the 'way they handled' a difficult situation. There is no need for us to have agreed vocabulary for cataloguing all the differences in our modes of engagement in order for those differences to be things that we can talk about and discuss in activity-dependent concepts as 'the way you calmed him down'. The

I shall call such concepts *activity-dependent concepts*. They are concepts which require subtle activities of perception and manipulation to grasp them. You cannot acquire them by book learning alone. You need to see and handle things. Once you see the point of activity-dependent concepts, there is no need to proliferate ways of knowing. Propositional knowing-that can capture the fine-grained subtleties of what people come to know in virtue of the detail of their perceptual and active engagements in the environment.

With book learning, the conceptual content of what we know is, in practice, fully codifiable linguistically. You practise your learning by manipulating language: you write essays, give presentations and so on. You deploy such knowledge by manipulating the words that codify it; you transmit the knowledge by passing words to other people. But with knowledge whose content includes activity-dependent concepts, this linguistic display and transfer is not enough. Where ways of thinking depend on perception and manipulation of the environment, you practise your knowledge not by manipulating words alone, but by manipulating linguistic and environmental combinations. To get someone to understand what you mean when you say 'Do it like this,' you need to execute the action in addition to saying the words. And they have to see, and often participate in, the action to understand what it is you know. To put the point very simply, we reason by manipulating concepts, but with activity-dependent concepts, the manipulations of reason include the manipulation of things.

But now, you might ask, how does this knowing-that relate to the phenomenology of expertise and the sometimes quite inarticulate sense of what they're doing that experts can display? There is something bizarre in taking the phenomenology of expertise as reported in the moment by the expert as a benchmark for the adequacy of our account of what they know. The fact that people find it hard to articulate in the moment what it is that they know that bears on what they are doing ought to be irrelevant to what makes it the case that what they do makes sense because of what they know. The idea that what they know should be answerable to whatever, if anything, they can tell us about what they know in the moment betrays an uncritical Cartesian privileging of the subject's first-person authority. It amounts to assuming that what a subject knows at a point in time that bears upon action is answerable to what they can say at that time. Unless we are prepared to endorse the Cartesian idea that the subject's self-knowledge is transparent through and through to introspection, it is quite unclear on what grounds credence should be given to this.

The task before us is to give an account of how what experts know bears upon what they do. The task is not to describe, in the subject's own terms,

---

language alone tells us very little about what you did, but if you witnessed it, there is much that can be said with these words. What is said is a proposition.

what it is like to know something in the moment and to act upon it. The answer to the latter might be, and typically is, no more than the linguistically uninformative 'It's a bit like this'. As a set of words, that tells us little. If we take the language of expert self-ascription as the guide to their knowledge, we will be short-changed. But that is to miss the point of activity-dependent knowledge. We need to see this language in the context of the appropriate details of the perceptual and manipulative engagement with things. That is how we get a grip on activity-dependent concepts. Furthermore, there is no reason to suppose that this account of language in context is something that will be transparent to the actor at the time. There is therefore no good reason for thinking that a descriptive phenomenology of expertise gives us the authoritative account of what the subject knows and how what they know bears on action.[2]

Coupled with the first point that we need a notion of what is known that can bear upon what is done and that this requires a conceptually structured propositional knowing-that, the inarticulacy of what the subject can offer in the moment is clearly very often a bad guide to what is known.

Codifiability

One of the aspects that has made phenomenological accounts of expertise attractive is the emphasis they place on the idea that expert wisdom is not fully codifiable. There are a number of theses that might be captured by saying that expert wisdom is at best partially codifiable. They need to be distinguished. First, the lack of codifiability might amount to the idea that experts deploy knowledge that cannot be abstracted from their engagement with things. Call this *the embeddedness thesis*:

---

2   This is not to deny that there should be some constraint on what knowledge we ascribe to subjects in order to make sense of what they do. We do not have licence to ascribe just any old knowledge that renders their performance intelligible and reasonable. A constraint to the effect that the knowledge we ascribe must be knowledge that the subject would acknowledge is in the right area, but much needs to be said about how such a constraint is to be enforced. For now, the point is simply that there is no good reason to think that the operation of such a constraint should go by way of the requirement that what they would acknowledge amounts to 'what they are able to articulate in the moment'. In other words, some answerability to capturing what it is like for the subject might be in order, but we should not assume that what it is like is the same as what they report in the moment.

Embeddedness: Some of what is known by experts cannot be individuated in abstraction from the expert's engagement with the environment.

If you characterise what is known with propositional knowledge containing activity-dependent concepts, embeddedness will come out true. It is the point that underpins the idea that much of what experts know cannot be acquired by book learning. (Of course, much can be delivered by book learning; the point is only that not everything can be so delivered.) Second, the lack of codifiability might be intended in the sense that what is known is not capable of being articulated in advance of the knower's engagement with the environment. But it is not clear that this adds anything to embeddedness, for if some of what is known is not abstractable from engagement with the environment, then clearly it cannot be articulated in advance of such engagement. There is, however, a separate point that might be intended by saying that what is known cannot be articulated in advance of engagement. Perhaps what is really intended is the claim that in advance of engagement, what is known does not provide general principles that prescribe performance? We might call this *the particularist thesis*:

Particularism: What the expert knows does not provide general principles that can be articulated in advance of engagement and used to prescribe performance.

As formulated, this is a very weak thesis. It is compatible with the defining commitment of generalism about reasons that holds that it is constitutive of what it is for a subject to act on reasons that the reasons bear upon their action in a way that instantiates a general rule. As I have formulated it, all that particularism says is that such principles cannot be articulated in advance of the engagement with the environment. It is only with such engagement that we grasp the conceptual content that figures in both what is known and under which what is done is undertaken intentionally. Particularism formulated in this way is compatible with the thought that whenever an agent does something with reason, there must be a general pattern to the way that their reasons bear upon what they do. It is quite another matter whether that pattern is salient to the agent at the time of action or whether it can be articulated as a general pattern in advance of the actions, beliefs and desires that instantiate it.

I suspect that many who have been concerned to press the lack of codifiability of expert knowledge – indeed, many particularists in ethics – have had in mind a stronger thesis than particularism as defined above (for standard treatments of particularism, see Dancy, 1993; Dancy, 2004; McNaughton, 1988). But if so, it is difficult to see what a defensible stronger thesis might amount to. Perhaps it is the thought that expert knowledge is so ineffable that it is in principle impossible to codify into knowledge whose content stands in general patterns of bearing upon action that make the latter reasonable? There are two pressure points in this idea. First, if the idea is that expert knowledge is so ineffable that it has no codifiable content at all, then the claim owes us an account of just what kind of knowledge this could be. Without something that can be captured in a conceptual content, it is unclear how this could be something that could 'bear upon' action at all. I have argued that we have no model of what it is for what is known to bear upon what is done that does not treat both as falling under concepts. So perhaps the particularist has something else in mind.

Perhaps the claim is that whatever the content of what is known, it is something that can bear upon what is done without its doing so instantiating a general pattern? This is the idea that there is a conceptual content to what is known, and what is done is something that also falls under concepts, but the fact that the former bears upon the latter does not require that there be any general pattern to the way it does so. This is an extraordinarily radical thesis. It requires that we make sense of the idea that a conceptual content of knowledge (a proposition) have a content composed of a combination of concepts, and that the way that this content in tandem with various other contents bears upon the reasonableness of an action is utterly singular. It commits us to the idea that there is nothing about the way that the proposition, in tandem with other states, bears upon the action that makes it suitable for it to bear upon relevantly similar actions, or that relevantly similar beliefs bear upon the same action. Indeed, this particularism amounts to the claim that there is no such thing as relevantly similar belief and action sets. Although some particularists in ethics sometimes seem to endorse such a position, many writers find it literally incredible (Jackson et al., 2000). I agree.

I suspect that what lies behind the motivation to endorse particularism is the concern that general rules codified in advance of practice and deployed to prescribe practice run the risk of missing some of the fine details which must be attended to for properly nuanced practice. But if so, that is a minor epistemological point, even if in policy terms it is important in the context of a management culture that tries to specify all performance targets in advance of practice. Endorsing a radical particularism just to draw attention to a problematic management epistemology is overkill, and introduces incoherence into the characterisation of expertise. Let us note the motivation at play here as the injunction to acknowledge rule-breaking. Novices follow rules laid out in advance; they are technicians executing pre-determined procedures. In contrast, the expert possesses a wisdom that licenses performance that falls outwith the prescribed rules. There is something right about this thought, something that undermines the prescriptive management culture that has come to dominate many arenas of expert professional practice. It is to the task of saying just what is right about this idea that I now want to turn.

Rule-breaking

In what sense is it right to say that expert understanding falls outside the rules? One sense would be to endorse the sort of radical particularism mentioned in the previous section. That is the overkill strategy, and it is arguably incoherent. Another sense in which expert understanding can fall outside the rules is a function of ignorance, in so far as at the time of the expert performance, we do not have a full account of the rules by which to judge of the reasonableness of action. In such cases, it might turn out that expert practice brings to light rules and discriminations hitherto missed. Once the action has been taken and the relevant pattern discriminated, the new rule is added to the armoury of generalisations to be followed.

The report into the British Airways crash at London Heathrow in 2009 showed that a catastrophic loss of life was avoided by the pilot breaking the rules for landing procedures (Department for Transport, 2010). The aircraft suffered sudden engine failure on final approach. The pilot doubted that it would clear the built-up area outside the airport perimeter, and judged that all on board would die, as would many on the ground. Protocols on final approach make clear that you should never retract the wing flaps on final approach, for that would result in sudden and disastrous loss of altitude. However, given the engine failure, the pilot reasoned that without a sudden increase in airspeed, the aircraft would not make it to the airport anyway. Against the rulebook, he retracted the wing flaps. The plane lost altitude rapidly, but also rapidly picked up speed. As a consequence the plane narrowly cleared the perimeter fence and made a safe emergency crash landing just within the airport perimeter. No lives were lost.

The case is relatively simple. The pilot was in possession of information regarding details of the parameters of potential altitude loss set against speed gain that had not been previously discriminated. This is not surprising, for he was dealing with a novel emergency concerning engine failure very late in final approach. Although his breaching of the normal rules was radical, in the highly particular circumstances, it is also obvious why it was the right thing to do. The gain in speed compensated for the altitude loss to just the right degree to save the lives of all involved.

The performance of the pilot brings to light a generalisation that is obvious once it is discriminated. One would not hesitate to endorse a new rule being written in the light of this episode; for one would want any future pilot placed in similar circumstances to know that the option of retracting the flaps is one to be considered if the trade-off between altitude loss and speed gain would avert a serious incident.[3] Such rule-breaking is important, but it is only a case of breaking the extant rules because we have not got around to thinking of all the potential factors that might bear upon our decisions. Note also, in giving the account of how the pilot adapted the rules, there is no need to ascribe to the pilot anything other than propositional know-that. What matters is that the pilot was attentively engaged with the environment in terms of perceptual tracking of the position and speed of the plane relative to the ground, and that this enabled him to know that by forfeiting just *that much altitude*, he stood a fair chance of reaching *that far point* over the perimeter fence. His way of thinking of altitude and distance was most likely an embedded way of thinking composed of activity-dependent concepts for the distances, speed and momentum at play, but it is still a form of know-that, not know-how.

Call this *epistemic rule-breaking*. It is modest. The pilot's innovation is due to the relative poverty of prior attempts to catalogue the relevant factors in selecting the best way to land a plane. Epistemic rule-breaking reflects the unfinished business in cataloguing the environment and arriving at the optimum taxonomy of what is going on. The example is limiting, for there is no reason to suppose that in finding a new pattern salient, the pilot needed to deploy concepts other than those already available to him. He already had the resources to conceptually discriminate different airspeeds and altitude variations; what was novel was spotting the significance of a range of dependency between these not previously encountered. In contrast, consider the option of cases in which the expert uncovers new propositional knowledge that depends on making discriminations with new concepts.

In cases involving conceptual development, we encounter a different kind of rule-breaking phenomenon. If the expert's experience provides a discrimination that leads to conceptual development, the deployment of the new concept breaches previous rules simply because no such rules employing the concept had been formulated. In such cases, the expert discrimination does not employ a novel type of knowledge, but in adding to the stock of knowledge relevant for the organisation of performance, it exemplifies an important sense in which the learning produced by the expert can shape our ongoing notions of best performance.

When experts learn by developing new concepts, the knowledge they exhibit is still propositional knowledge, including propositions composed with activity-dependent concepts. As such, this propositional knowledge

---

3   To endorse such a new rule is to endorse a generalism about reasons that requires the existence of relevant similarity or groupings of beliefs and desires whenever one provides a reason for another. It is such generalism that is opposed by radical particularism.

exploits concepts that reach right out to the manipulation of things in the environment, for example ways of thinking about specialist bandaging techniques in nursing (Luntley, 2011). But if conceptual development is in play, there must be more to the expert's capacities for manipulating the environment than the conceptually organised modes of manipulation. There must be modes of manipulation and discrimination prior to those that are picked up by, for example, short-lived activity-dependent concepts, or there would be nothing to be picked up. In short, even though the expert's knowledge that bears upon what is done is conceptual through and through, we need to acknowledge modes of discriminating and manipulating things that make such concepts available. This significantly shapes how we should understand initiation into expert performance.

Initiation into expertise is not just a matter of coming to share expert knowledge. Even when we accept the idea of propositional knowledge that is thoroughly embedded in our engagement with the environment because it is composed of activity-dependent concepts, it is not enough to think that the process of initiation is one of initiation into knowledge. And even though initiation into such knowledge has to involve initiation into discriminations and manipulations, for the concepts involved include activity-dependent concepts, still initiation has to be broader than that. It has to include initiation into the modes of discrimination and manipulation that make groupings of things salient and that provide the basic engagement with things that are picked up and classified by activity-dependent concepts. Therefore, initiation has to include initiation into modes of experience and activity that form the basis for the activity-dependent knowing-that that legitimises expert performance. Once this point is acknowledged, it is clear that the epistemic standpoint of the expert is distinguished not by a special or different kind of knowing, but by the contribution of expert discrimination and manipulation towards the development of our ongoing best sense of how to conceptualise the environment under consideration. Experts are rule-breakers not because they exemplify a radical and arguably incoherent particularism about reasons, but because they are pattern-seekers and they contribute to the growing grasp of the patterns that matter in making sense of things. And once we move away from simple examples dealing with physical environments, whether landing airliners or practising advanced bandaging techniques, to the dynamic environments peopled by agents and managed by experts across the 'people professions', it becomes apparent that experts are often not just pattern-seekers, but pattern-makers.

With airliners and various kinds of medical and nursing techniques, a simple realism about the patterns that we need to track in discrimination and manipulation is in order. We might think that the relevant patterns figure in an exhaustive catalogue that could, in principle, have been scripted in advance; we just did not realise how much of it would be relevant until we started behaving in sophisticated ways with these things. But when the environment that the expert deals with includes interacting agents, and when the expert's own interventions are part of the interaction, then such a simple realism is no longer applicable. We need to acknowledge that some of the patterns we track and shape are patterns that come about in part because of the way we track and shape them. The interactions that classroom teachers track can include combinations of cognitive, affective and behavioural elements of learning needs that simply have not been encountered before.[4] In finding a grouping of such things salient, the expert teacher is not so much breaking the rules through acting outwith the previous prescriptions for performance; the expert teacher is, at this point, a prescriber for performance.[5] And once experts shoulder that burden, initiation into expertise must equip them with the resources to handle this. These will be varied, but centrally are twofold: (a) the cognitive resources for making the sorts of discriminations and manipulations on which activity-dependent concepts draw; (b) the broadly ethical resources for managing the complex interactions and resulting distributions of power and agency.

With regard to the cognitive resources, the bare minimum that needs to be said is something like this: we need to acknowledge the way that our capacities for consciously attending to things can help explain how things become salient for us and ripe for picking up with activity-dependent concepts. Expertise is marked, in part, by a rich capacity for attending to fine discriminations that, once picked up with concepts, can become the subject matter of propositional knowledge. It is in deploying such attentional skills that the expert does more than merely enact previously learnt routines and follow previously formulated principles no matter how sophisticated these may be. It is the attentional capacities, the preparedness to always see more worthy of thinking about, that marks out the distinctive contribution of expertise to many forms of professional performance. The point should not be over-stated. I do not believe that a distinction between novice and expert is cognitively well founded. That is to say, I do not think that there is a principled differentiation of cognitive skills between workers at these different levels. My suspicion is that the idea of the novice is a construct, someone whose performance has been subjected to organisational constraints that blinker a common and quite natural inquisitiveness that

---

4   For details of a pilot project investigating the expertise of classroom teachers, see Ainley and Luntley (2007a, 2007b).

5   Note that this is compatible with a form of realism about the patterns prescribed. Even though we are pattern-makers, we still need to track the patterns we make. What we are and what we do are part of the environment that we track, and this changes as we track it, because it includes that tracking.

lies at the root of conceptual development. Novices are, if you like, stunted experts, but not normally of their own making.

Theoretically, the appeal to attention as the operation of conscious awareness independent of concepts is enough to provide the materials for a model of conceptual development that explains the creativity, novelty and apparent rule-breaking that phenomenologists find in expert performance. If that were all that we said, then it would suffice for a model of initiation to say that initiation requires not just introduction to activity-dependent knowledge, but also practice in the exercise of attention that equips the expert with the resources to develop new concepts. The point of this approach to the concept of initiation is that it focuses on the question: 'What are the capacities that the initiate requires in order to be apt to be initiated?' This is an important question, one that is typically missed in discussions of initiation (Luntley, 2010). The minimal answer to this is that the initiate expert needs capacities for attention. I suspect that a fuller answer is available.

There is room to acknowledge a variety of modes by which attention can be excited and brought to bear on things. I do not object to the idea of treating attention as a primitive operation of conscious awareness that needs no further scaffolding. Nevertheless, it seems fruitful to consider the possibility that there might be much to say about the ways in which our attention can serve as a scaffold. For example, the scaffolding of attention can include affective states both in our emotional responses to things and in our emotional responses to other subjects as we try to match our performance to theirs. The latter point is the beginnings of a tale about the role of mentors and the way that apprentices mould their performance by working alongside and shadowing the performance of their skilled colleagues. Such mentoring is much more than a facility for sharing knowledge; it is also a facility for acquiring modes of attending that equip the apprentice with the resources to become a concept-generating expert, someone whose performance falls outwith some of the extant rules because they are actively engaged in the interrogation of practice and the development of the contours of its cutting edge.

With regard to the ethical resources, the complexities of initiation rapidly multiply. Once you acknowledge the dynamic of the social interaction, including the effect that expert intervention plays in this dynamic, then expert behaviour carries a heavy ethical burden. In the people professions, the expert is helping to shape environments in which people live who have emotional, social, psychological and health dimensions. As with the cognitive resources, the drive to articulate and codify the shape of these engagements, although valuable, will always run the risk of disguising options and fooling practitioners into thinking that their task is simply to enact procedures, rather than interrogate and, where appropriate, instigate new ways of conceiving of the options they face. And what constitutes 'appropriate' is up for grabs, too.

This is complicated stuff, but notwithstanding all the very great detail that could and should be said about a properly nuanced account of cognitive and ethical initiation, the core point that I have been pressing remains good. No matter how complex and diverse the modes of perceptual and manipulative engagement may be, what they provide for the expert are saliences to be picked up conceptually as components for ordinary propositional knowledge. However detailed our description of initiation needs to become, its upshot is propositional knowledge – the sort of knowing that bears upon what we do.

References

Ainley, J. and Luntley, M. (2007a), 'The role of attention in expert classroom practice', *Journal of Mathematics Teacher Education*, 10(1), 3–22.
—— (2007b), 'Towards an articulation of expert classroom practice', *Teaching and Teacher Education*, 23(7), 1,127–38.
Benner, P. (1984), *From Novice to Expert: Excellence and Power in Clinical Nursing Practice*, London: Addison Wesley.
Dancy, J. (1993), *Moral Reasons*, Oxford: Blackwell.
—— (2004), *Ethics Without Principles*, Oxford: Clarendon Press.
Department for Transport (2010), *Report on the Accident to Boeing 777-236ER, G-YMMM, at London Heathrow Airport on 17 January 2008*, <http://www.aaib.gov.uk/sites/aaib/publications/formal_reports/1_2010_g_ymmm.cfm (accessed 25 March 2011).
Dreyfus, H. (2005), 'Overcoming the myth of the mental: How philosophers can profit from the phenomenology of everyday expertise', *Proceedings and Addresses of the American Philosophical Association*, 79(2), 47–65.
—— (2007), 'The return of the myth of the mental', *Inquiry*, 50(4), 352–65.
—— and Dreyfus, S. (1986), *Mind over Machine: The Power of Human Intuition and Expertise in the Era of the Computer*, Oxford: Blackwell.
—— and Dreyfus, S. (2005), 'Expertise in real world contexts', *Organization Studies*, 26(5), 779–92.
Eraut, M. (1994), *Developing Professional Knowledge and Competence*, London: The Falmer Press.
—— (2000), 'Non-formal learning and tacit knowledge in professional work', *British Journal of Educational Psychology*, 70(1), 113–36.
Jackson, F., Pettit, P. and Smith, M. (2000), 'Ethical Particularism and Patterns', in B. Hooker and M. Little (ed.), *Moral Particularism*, Oxford: Oxford University Press, 79–99.

Luntley, M. (2009), 'Understanding expertise', *Journal of Applied Philosophy*, 26(4), 356–70.

—— (2010), 'On education and initiation', *Journal of Philosophy of Education*, special edn in honour of R.S. Peters' 80th birthday.

—— (2011), 'What do nurses know?', *Nursing Philosophy*, 12(1), 22–33.

McDowell, J. (2007), 'What myth?', *Inquiry*, 50(4), 338–51.

McNaughton, D. (1988), *Moral Vision*, Oxford: Blackwell.

3 Evidence-based Practice and Professional Wisdom

Chris Clark

What is 'Evidence-based Practice', and Why is it Controversial?

In several fields of applied professional knowledge including health, social care, education and criminal justice, the drift of much recent public policy has been to seek to ensure that only intervention methods and treatments of scientifically demonstrable efficacy and safety are adopted by service agencies and used by practitioners (see, for example, Davies et al., 2000; Nutley et al., 2007). A substantial body of academic researchers in these fields has also joined in with the claims that chosen methods and programmes ought to be based on high-quality scientific research. The fundamental premise of evidence-based practice is that professional interventions ought to be guided and informed by documented, publicly available, scientifically valid, reproducible and transmittable knowledge (Pawson et al., 2003). It is widely held that such a basis for action is both a practical and an ethical necessity (see, for example, Gambrill, 2007).

Evidence-based practice (EBP) is used as general term applicable in all human service fields; it represents a wider application of the outlook and concepts originally developed under the umbrella of evidence-based medicine. EBP shares a common orientation with its close relative, evidence-based policy, the latter having its main focus on public policy and organisational issues, while EBP foregrounds the perspective of the individual practitioner. This chapter is primarily concerned with evidence-based practice from the practitioner's viewpoint, and will refer chiefly to the literature of medicine and social care. It will also draw on the literature about evidence-based policy where relevant.

At first glance, the idea that professionals ought to base their interventions on scientific knowledge might seem obviously, even trivially, incontrovertible. It is generally taken to be a defining characteristic of modern professionals that they act on objectively defensible grounds, and not from mere custom, prejudice or whim. It would appear completely untenable to sanction the possibility that practitioners might ignore relevant evidence. As Goldenberg puts it: 'the term "evidence-based medicine" has a ring of obviousness to it, as few physicians, one suspects, would claim that they do not attempt to base their clinical decision-making on available evidence' (Goldenberg, 2006, 2,621). Furthermore, is not the astonishing development of medicine, especially, over the last couple of centuries directly attributable to the advance and application of scientific knowledge and its displacement of tradition and superstition? Yet the contemporary debate shows that the seemingly obvious legitimacy of evidence can by no means be taken for granted. To understand why 'evidence-based' policy and practice have in fact excited so much controversy, it will be useful to examine the nature of the evidence they invoke.

Evidence to inform practice can be analysed in two contrasting ways: it can be classified according its source, and it can be appraised according to the various standards of scientific validity. Sources may include academic research, clinical trials, user experience and so forth. In the field of social care, Pawson et al. (2003) show that the classification of sources is a question of some complexity. They identify over 12 diverse 'forms of knowledge', but decide, on largely pragmatic grounds of simplicity and clarity, to utilise a primary classification of five source types by community of origin: organisational knowledge, practitioner knowledge, user knowledge, research knowledge and policy community knowledge.

The second mode of analysis is epistemological: it hinges on the standards of validity for appraising claimed knowledge. It is here that the argument about evidence acquires the most notoriety. In the classic methodology now associated with the Cochrane Collaboration in medicine, there is a hierarchy of validity of research evidence, with randomised control trials at the top of the scale of rigour and anecdote at the bottom. Table 3.1 is a typical example of such a hierarchy.

Evidence relevant to practice and policy in a particular area of social need will come, of course, from multiple sources and will be of variable scientific value. The acknowledged means of transmitting the results of multiple research studies and sources of experience to the rank-and-file practitioner is the systematic review (but see Pawson (2006) for a radical critique of the systematic review). Systematic reviews combine the research and experience from multiple sources, and aim to produce succinct and authoritative findings accompanied with clear ratings of their dependability. Since comprehensive systematic reviews are complex and weighty projects in their own right, their conclusions are commonly translated into clinical guidelines, treatment protocols, simplified classifications, rules of procedure

Table 3.1   Hierarchies of evidence

I-1	Systematic review and meta-analysis of two or more double-blind randomised controlled trials
I-2	One or more large double-blind randomised controlled trials
II-1	One or more well-conducted cohort studies
II-2	One or more well-conducted case-control studies
II-3	A dramatic uncontrolled experiment
III	Expert committee sitting in review; peer leader opinion
IV	Personal experience

Source: Davies et al. (2000), 48.

and so forth, all designed to be readily portable and easily assimilated by practitioners and managers who do not have the leisure or expertise to carry out their own reviews of research. These secondary or derivative summaries of evidence for practice are widely disseminated by government ministries, charitable research organisations and quasi-independent bodies such as the National Institute for Health and Clinical Excellence (NICE) and the Social Care Institute for Excellence (SCIE); they are the main vehicles for delivering the evidence in evidence-based practice.

Since all of this may seem quite unexceptional, why is evidence-based practice so controversial? The problem is that the entirely general and apparently uncontroversial notion of *evidence* was publicly appropriated by schools of thought which in fact adopted a rather particular and restricted conception of valid evidence for practice. The evidence in the original manifestations of evidence-based practice was predominantly evidence as understood from a positivist point of view. To avoid an arduous journey through the badlands of philosophy of science, by 'positivism' I will mean here that point of view which regards all human and social phenomena as in principle entirely comprehensible from the standpoint of an assumed detached and objective observer, in a manner in principle identical to the aspirational objectivity of the natural scientist towards the phenomena of the material world. Positivism in this sense sees no place in any true science for the interpretation of the essentially unobservable meanings and values attributed by human beings to the social world. The characteristic goal of positivist social science is to find law-like regularities that lead to usable, if not altogether watertight, predictions; its characteristic tools are validated and reliable measurements that could be reproduced by any relevantly competent practitioner. (For further discussion, see, for example, Crotty (1998) and Benton (1977)). So, for instance, in a document entitled 'How to read a paper: Assessing the methodological quality of published papers' (Greenhalgh, 1997), the *British Medical Journal* recommended readers to consider two fundamental questions:

1. What specific intervention or other manoeuvre was being considered, and what was it being compared with?
2. What outcome was measured, and how?

Although the discourse of evidence-based practice has broadened in scope and increased in theoretical diversity as it has grown vastly in volume, it remains predominantly informed by a positivist outlook. Nevertheless, it will not do to assert, as Thyer (2008) does of American social work, that 'we are all positivists', and thus hope to paper over significant differences in espoused standards of scientific validity and relevance. In the world of evidence-based practice, the dominant *sources* and the ruling *standards* are not in fact unrelated to each other; on the contrary, they share common roots. The dominant research sources for evidence-based practice are informed by a positivist outlook, while research from other paradigms is relegated to a position of inferiority or even illegitimacy.

The Critique of Evidence-based Practice

We have seen that when the territory of evidence-based policy and practice was newly identified, it was first occupied by colonists of a broadly positivist outlook. In its early days there appears to have been a polarisation of views about it. Advocates of evidence-based practice held that nothing but practice founded on hard science was in principle ultimately defensible, while its opponents – and others who were simply unconvinced – felt that it was based on a conception of evidence that was inadequate, both as description and prescription, to inform practice with infinitely variable, knowing human actors in the uncertain and essentially contested spheres of health, education or social care.

With the passage of time, there has been some softening of positions. Nutley et al. (2007), while recognising that the evidence-based policy and practice movements may have begun with rather narrow, scientistic conceptions of what constitutes valid evidence, argue that the debate has since broadened to admit a more diverse range of viewpoints. These concern

Table 3.2   Limitations of evidence-based medicine identified in the critical literature

1	Incommensurate nature of population evidence and individual patient profiles
2	Bias towards individualised interventions
3	Exclusion of clinical skills from medical practice
4	Production of formulaic guidelines
5	Failure to consider patient views and narratives
6	Difficulties in disseminating and implementing evidence into practice

Source: Lambert (2006), Table 1, 2,634.

both evidence itself and the processes whereby it affects, and is affected by, political pressures and values. There is increasing recognition of the power and legitimacy of practice knowledge and practitioner judgement embedded in practitioner communities. Lambert (2006) provides a picture of the evolution of evidence-based medicine in which six major limitations identified in the critical literature have been progressively accommodated by a broadening and loosening process (see Table 3.2).

In the process of evolution, evidence-based medicine has thus retreated from some of the more thoroughgoing claims of its fundamentalist advocates, and has perhaps even achieved a degree of domestication whereby the notion of *evidence* is not necessarily regarded with hostility by those not of a positivist outlook. Nevertheless, evidence-based practice remains a controversial concept. Here we will briefly sample some of the critiques. They range more or less across a spectrum, from those who accept the founding assumptions of evidence-based practice as understood from a positivist standpoint but see a need for refinements and enhancements, to those who reject it on fundamental epistemological or political grounds.

Clarification, Redefinition and Development of Knowledge

A large number of apologists for evidence-based practice have argued that while it is based (as sketched above) on fundamentally incontrovertible first principles, its meaning needs to be clarified. If there are difficulties about accepting or implementing the basic idea, they are based on misunderstanding or the present lack of well-developed methodologies for applying scientific evidence to clinical and service practice. Such difficulties can be addressed by more careful definition and by developing improved practical means for enabling practitioners to utilise hard evidence. Olson, for example, considers some different examples in order to show that '"evidence-based practice" is not a homogeneous concept' (Olson, 2007, 282), but that there are few contradictions between the conceptualisations. Magill offers an overview of the gradual infiltration into social work of concepts of evidence-based practice borrowed from medicine. It is suggested that: 'Effective utilization of the EBP framework will require guidelines connecting a range of social work treatment questions with the appropriate methodologies to address them' (Magill, 2006, 105). McNeil (2006) offers a compromise view that would accept the strengths of evidence-based practice while seeking to preserve social work's traditional values, while Pollio (2006), Graybeal (2007) and Cnaan and Dichter (2008) are among the many who want to incorporate the *science* of evidence-based practice while preserving the traditional *art* of social work. Varying this theme, Walter (2003) proposes that social work occupies a 'third space' between art and science, and links professional practice to theatrical improvisation.

A point accepted by virtually all commentators is that the range of good research evidence available to serve as a foundation for practice is still too limited. As Magill observes about social work, 'a more immediate concern is the absence of a valid and applicable framework for guiding practice decisions' (Magill, 2006, 106). Even in the most comprehensively researched areas of medicine, where EBP is supported by thoroughgoing and well-publicised systematic reviews of extensive high-quality research, we have the familiar experience of yesterday's authoritative clinical guidance and advice to patients being all too rapidly superseded by the results of today's new research. In large areas of the social services, it is generally accepted that the available research base is manifestly inadequate. However, although it is uncontroversial that more research is always needed, the very inevitability of this feature does begin to raise some more fundamental suspicions: for if the research base is *always* going to be inadequate, might it be that the whole notion of basing practice on research is fundamentally flawed? This is one stimulus for critiques that will be explored further below.

Can Evidence Actually Influence Policy and Practice?

Although some advocates of evidence-based policy and practice seem to assume that the superiority of their doctrine is indeed self-evident and incontestable, other analysts have reflexively (and somewhat disarmingly) noticed that according to their own standards of validity, evidence-based approaches are no more exempt from the need to demonstrate their effectiveness than any other school of thought.

Reviewing the introduction and development of evidence-based policy-making, Boaz (2008) identifies six unresolved issues in bringing evidence to bear more effectively on policy and practice. The first of these turns on the nature of evidence: it is not as solid or immutable as the metaphor of a *base* implies, but it is constantly changing in a context which is also constantly changing: 'evidence does change in its relevance and reliability over time' (Boaz, 2008, 241). For this reason, the term 'evidence-informed' is preferred over 'evidence-based'. Nutley et al. likewise 'prefer the term "evidence informed", "evidence influenced" or even "evidence aware" to the more usual – and over-egged – tag of "evidence based"' (Nutley et al., 2007, 30).

This conclusion about the fluidity of evidence chimes with Campbell's observation in a study of policy-makers' views of evidence-based policy. Campbell concludes that:

> evidence, in itself, rarely provides policy options or leads directly to policy decisions. All available information, pressures and resources have to be weighed up and a balanced response developed, a skill summed up by the term 'judgement' or 'pragmatism' by some of the officials interviewed. (Campbell, 2007, 16)

Oakley et al. reflect on the experience of the Evidence for Policy and Practice Information and Co-ordinating Centre (EPPI-Centre) at the Institute of Education at the University of London, whose 'main business is conducting and supporting systematic reviews of social science research relevant to different areas of public policy' (Oakley et al., 2005, 6). They see evidence-based approaches as constituting particular challenges to social science, including 'the culture of academia, and research funding practices that militate against the building of a cumulative evidence base' (Oakley et al., 2005, 5). Culture clash has its counterpart in the agencies, too; Johnson and Austin (2008) are among the many writers who find the lack of an appropriate organisational culture in service agencies as a challenge to evidence-based practice.

Evidence-based Approaches as Falsely Representing Clinical and Practical Reasoning

While the revisionist views of evidence-based practice described above envisage a constructive accommodation between crude positivism and the manifold complexities of the real world, a more radical stream of criticism has it that a preoccupation with supposedly scientific evidence misunderstands the nature of practical reasoning in clinical or professional practice. Scientific evidence and knowledge are incapable of rendering the individual, improvisatory, fluid and artistic aspects of practice. These are not to be seen as defects, but on the contrary, as vital characteristics of effective and humane practice. Schön's (1983) work *The Reflective Practitioner: How Professionals Think in Action* is justly famous for originating this line of inquiry long before 'evidence-based practice' became a catchword.

Floersch (2004) is one of many writers to adopt Schön's distinction between technical-rational knowledge and knowledge-in-action. Ethnographic approaches capturing oral discourse are essential to discover knowledge-in-action. In a series of studies, Taylor and White (2006) have likewise argued that ethnography, narrative and discourse analysis, among other forms of interpretive social science, provide the route to understanding clinical judgement and decision-making in practice (see White and Stancombe, 2003; Taylor, 2006). Munro (2004) observes the difficulties of applying the concepts of audit – a pre-eminently technical-rational pursuit – to social work, which comprises individualistic practice within a humanistic tradition. The poor theoretical development of social work makes it difficult to identify meaningful indicators of good practice. Blom (2009) wants to argue that a state of 'un-knowing' better characterises the position of the social worker than the traditional representation of the professional as the bearer of expert knowledge. Un-knowing is an approach that recognises that we can never accurately predict what will happen in social life.

It is unsurprising to find the perennial theme of the limited reach and insight of hard scientific knowledge into the many complexities of individual lives in the literature of social work. There can be no doubt, moreover, that the volume of good scientific evidence in biomedical research vastly outweighs what is presently available in social work and allied services. Nevertheless, it would be wrong to see the emphasis on clinical art and practical judgement in social work as stemming from some fundamental difference between it and scientific medicine: for in medicine, too, we find the repeated theme that clinical judgement is a complex, many-faceted activity that must centrally address dealing with uncertainty (Dowie and Elstein, 1988). The insights of interpretive social science and hermeneutics are just as relevant to medicine as they are to social work.

Evidence-based Practice as Falsely Rejecting Alternative Theories of Knowledge

The claim that evidence-based practice fails to capture, explain or elucidate the true nature of clinical reasoning in the therapeutic encounter is often supported via a complementary argument (or series of arguments) about theories of knowledge. There are two distinguishable, but often closely related, aspects. The first is to criticise the empiricist philosophy of science which evidence-based practice embodies. The second goes a stage further to make the argument that evidence-based practice, far from being an ideologically neutral pursuit of scientific truth and unquestionable practical effectiveness, is actually a political project designed to maintain the power of ruling interests. Much of the debate thus resembles the paradigm wars that have animated the social sciences over the last 50 years or more.

Goldenberg (2006) squarely locates evidence-based medicine as the progeny of positivism. It thus fails to learn from feminism and phenomenology, among other developments in post-positivist philosophy of science. This is also a political project: 'the configuration of policy considerations and clinical standards into questions of evidence conveniently transform [*sic*] normative questions into technical ones' (Goldenberg, 2006, 2,630). In the same issue of *Social Science and Medicine*, Barry (2006) contrasts anthropological notions of evidence with the standard assumptions of evidence-based medicine and argues that the latter is hostile to the application and evaluation of alternative therapies: 'evidence is used not only to assess the efficacy of therapies, but also in political ways to influence how alternative medicine is integrated, assimilated or blocked from entry into the biomedical system' (Barry, 2006, 2,655).

In social work, Houston (2005) is not against positivist methods, but in application of Bhaskar's critical realism, calls for a more inclusive stance that also admits retroductive approaches that allow for the possibility of unseen causal mechanisms. Here Houston develops a line suggested by Sheppard (1995, 1998). In somewhat similar vein, Gould (2006) recognises the contribution of randomised controlled trials to the knowledge base for mental health services, but wants to make a place for qualitative research and practitioner and user knowledge. Butler et al. (2007) also draw on experience in mental health services to contrast evidence-based with traditional relationship-based ways of doing social work, and they call for complementarity between process or relationship and outcome-focused approaches.

Glasby and Beresford (2006) are fundamentally critical of what they see as the bias in the whole project of evidence-based practice in social care, arguing that:

1. Objectivity is not a prerequisite for valid evidence (and can even be harmful in some circumstances).
2. There is no such thing as a hierarchy of evidence.
3. There is much greater scope for literature reviews that include a much broader range of material than would usually be the case in traditional systematic reviews. (Glasby and Beresford, 2006, 271)

In particular, they criticise how evidence-based practice excludes as valid knowledge the wisdom of practitioners and the experience of users. Elsewhere, Beresford (2007) develops the argument for taking service user knowledge and experience seriously. His review of user-controlled research concludes that it has a:

> valid and particular contribution to make to the generation of knowledge. It can not only help in the development of new knowledge, but can also make possible the creation of knowledge in areas that might otherwise be overlooked and engage a wider range of user perspectives and analysis than might otherwise be the case. (Beresford, 2007, 339)

As the examples above already illustrate, the critique of evidence-based practice on epistemological grounds shades almost imperceptibly into critique on ideological or political grounds. Adopting Freidson's (1970) and Larson's (1977) sociological perspective of the professional project, McDonald (2003) views the adoption of evidence-based practice in social work as a tool of professional self-advancement.

Many writers have observed that evidence-based practice has been conscripted as a tool of Labour's 'modernisation' of government (see, for example, Newman (2000) on managerialism and modernising public services). Government has borrowed the seemingly unchallengeable authority of scientific evidence to enforce and legitimise a particular view of the relationship between itself and citizens in health, welfare and other fields. Foucault's concept of governmentality illuminates the processes whereby government procures compliance with its political projects not by the direct exercise of forcible authority, but by controlling the discourse of power and changing the way we think. Rose and Miller (1992) describe it thus:

> Government is a *problematizing* activity: it poses the obligations of rulers in terms of the problems they seek to address. The ideals of government are intrinsically linked to the problems around which it circulates, the failings it seeks to rectify, the ills it seeks to cure …. It is around these difficulties and failures that programmes of government have been elaborated. (Rose and Miller, 1992, 174; original emphasis)

Hence:

> Knowledge is thus central to [the] objectives of government and to the very formation of its objects, for government is a domain of cognition, calculation, experimentation and evaluation. And, we argue, government is intrinsically linked to the activities of expertise. (Rose and Miller, 1992, 175)

Sommerfeld (2005) is one writer who considers that evidence-based practice should be seen as part of the apparatus of governmentality in social work, while Winch et al. (2002) provide a much fuller version of a similar argument as it applies to nursing.

The Domains of Knowing for Practice

How shall we picture the mind of the professional faced with a problem to address? This is a slightly more specific variant of the general question of how we are to grasp practical reasoning in action, and that is as vast as the history of human self-understanding. Nevertheless the following broad general schema, which owes much to Polanyi (1962) and Schön (1983, 1987), seems to be as serviceable in this context as any other. I will speak of three domains of the actor's knowing and understanding, and emphasise here that the contents of these domains are individually specific: in principle, each individual has their own profile in the three domains.

The first domain, which I shall term *background knowledge*, comprises the individual's knowledge and understanding of the world at large. It is developed through life as a sediment of experience. Some of this may be acquired through formal instruction and structured learning, but most is probably built up subconsciously without any specially focused or directed effort. It includes naturalistic knowledge of the world, symbolic and cultural understanding, and also normative beliefs about what is good and right, valuable and important, reprehensible and wrong. Such knowledge functions constantly in the background, and is frequently not explicitly accessible to its owner; it tends to be called into consciousness only when circumstances create a specific stimulus. Characteristically, individuals are unable to cite convincing authority for their background knowledge even when it would be widely accepted as true. As Polanyi (1962) expresses it:

> Only a small fragment of his own culture is directly visible to any of its adherents. Large parts of it are altogether buried in books, paintings, musical scores etc., which remain mostly unread, unseen, unperformed. The messages of these records live, even in the minds best informed about them, only in their awareness of having access to them and of being able to evoke their voices and understand them. (Polanyi, 1962, 375)

Detailed rehearsal of the basis and justification of knowledge held in the background is mostly limited to the special contexts of academic, legal and religious discourse.

The second domain, which I shall term *foreground tools*, refers to the instruments and models, both tangible and abstract, that the problem-solver has at their immediate disposal. This covers everything from the ordinary object of daily use (a knife to cut the bread) to sets of abstract directions (instructions, rules and schedules of every description) to sophisticated guides to addressing complex problems and cases (diagnosing and treating cancer). What is characteristic of foreground tools is that the problem-solver is clearly aware of their availability and understands their utility; they are in the problem-solver's hands or available on the shelf, whether literally or metaphorically, and their purpose and function is well understood. While models and methods for practice may traditionally have been the province of textbooks, increasingly in the UK it is government or government-sponsored agencies that issue such materials in the health and welfare fields. For example, the current set of policies for childcare in Scotland presented under the generic title 'Getting It Right for Every Child' proposes eight areas of well-being that practitioners and agencies should attend to. The practice model further comprises the 'My World Triangle' – 'a mental map that helps practitioners understand a child or young person's whole world' – and the 'Resilience Matrix', which can be plotted 'on a blank matrix so that the balance between vulnerability and resilience, and adversity and protective factors can be weighed' (Scottish Government, 2008). The guidance is replete throughout with checklists and specific instructions.

Background knowledge and foreground tools are, in principle, capable of public expression in symbolic terms. The third domain is not so much a realm of publicly expressible knowledge as a faculty of the individual: it is the capacity for *practical reasoning* in the face of concrete problems in the real world. It denotes the ability to utilise acquired knowledge, past experience and current data to pursue a solution to the situation in hand. Schön calls this 'knowing-in-action': 'we reveal it by our spontaneous, skilful execution of the performance' (Schön, 1987, 25).

As noted above, many writers invoke the idea of artistry in skilful performance, and suggest that fully accomplished professional practice consists in the blending of advanced specialised knowledge with the intuitive, tacit skill needed to apply it both speedily and aptly. In consummate professional, craft or artistic performance, this application of knowledge and skill to the issue in hand seems to the observer almost effortless, but of course it requires great effort to achieve this capacity. Polanyi (1962) observes 'the well-known fact that *the aim of a skilful performance is achieved by the observance of a set of rules which are not known as such to the person following them*' (Polanyi, 1962, 49; original emphasis).

The examples below, drawn from social work, further illustrate conceptions of how knowledge is applied in practice. Social work is instructive in this context because much of the basis of its expertise lies beyond the remit of hard science, drawing as it does on the understanding of human cultures and the putting into effect of normative values for which scientific evidence offers no undisputed warrant. The latter point is thematic in a recent textbook that critiques the 'mechanical' approach of evidence-based practice, re-emphasising the 'humanistic' values of health and social care (McCarthy and Rose, 2010).

A number of writers have emphasised the similarity between practical inquiry in social work and the epistemology of qualitative research (for example, Sheppard, 1995; Riemann, 2005; White and Stancombe, 2003). Sheppard more specifically addresses the question: 'How can social workers go about thinking and reasoning about situations they confront in practice?' (Sheppard, 2006, 198) and develops a model emphasising (philosophical) realism, reflexivity in reaching decisions, the capacity to generate alternative hypotheses, and the necessity of avoiding confirmation bias.

It remains, however, a persistent and evergreen theme in the literature that decision-making in professional practice can never be entirely captured by prescriptive models: there will always be a necessary element of practice wisdom – that readily recognisable but elusive and ineffable quality that distinguishes the deeply skilled, highly regarded professional from the merely adequate functionary. Van de Luitgaarden (2009) casts doubt on the relevance of algorithmic rational choice models that are said to underlie evidence-based practice, proposing instead that social work and like fields require a more naturalistic style of decision-making. O'Sullivan aims to rehabilitate practice wisdom, seen as 'the ability to base sound judgements on deep understandings in conditions of uncertainty' (O'Sullivan, 2005, 222). Taylor and White (2006) place particular emphasis on 'educating for humane judgement', where the emphasis on educating social workers should be to equip them 'with the skills to exercise "wise judgement under conditions of uncertainty"' (Taylor and White, 2006, 937) – a phrase they take from Eraut (1994).

Conclusion

Despite its superficial plausibility as a foundational principle for effective intervention, many writers have shown that evidence-based practice is not the scientifically objective and value-neutral enterprise that it is often claimed to be. On the contrary, it embodies a particular philosophy of science that has been widely criticised for its intrinsic inability to render meaningful accounts of human living. This failure in particular extends to its inadequacy both as account and prescription for the application of knowledge and expertise in all kinds of human service practice, a failure rooted in the fact that the essential human insights needed for practice in fields such as social work and medicine are not comprehended by positivist empirical research. Although evidence-based practice claims the superior authority of science, it has been shown as actually still rather weak in its scientific understanding of human reasoning in the application of knowledge where such knowledge is extensive but still partial, often pointing to conflicting prescriptions for action, and practically incapable of being fully tested and validated in the fleeting moment of application. Furthermore, evidence-based practice has been recruited to a political project of control of the human services and the citizens who use them.

There is, nevertheless, something to be learnt from evidence-based practice. Using a conception of knowledge in practical action in the tradition of Polanyi and Schön, I have proposed that it is useful to apply a distinction between our background knowledge of the world, which resides largely out of our present awareness, and what I termed the foreground tools that we more or less consciously pick up when we deliberately address some practical end. Evidence-based practice is indeed a valuable source of foreground tools. When we seek a means to grapple with a complex problem, it would manifestly be foolish to ignore the findings, methods and protocols that have been carefully fashioned out of extensive research and clinical and service experience. Such tools are valuable safeguards against the ever-present dangers of partial knowledge of relevant research, unconscious bias and fallible memory, which every practitioner should guard against. They can promote effectiveness, accountability and the expansion of systematised experience. We should certainly welcome the rigorous systematic review that sifts and accumulates experience in a comprehensive manner that would never be possible for every individual practitioner faced with a similar kind of problem.

Professional wisdom, however, recognises and teaches that evidence-based practice will never cover all of the issues that the individual practitioner or the service organisation encounter in an average day. The extent of our well-based scientific knowledge is fated to be always less than our perception of the needs and issues that require to be addressed. Furthermore, professional wisdom gives full scope to the ineluctably individual character of professional expertise. Every practitioner uses tools in a slightly different way, just as every child uses their voice in a subtly different way even while learning the common language of the community. It is these individualities that evidence-based practice is largely unable to account for, and that are so widely expressed in terms borrowed from the world of artistic expression rather than the world of hard science. Foreground tools, however useful, cannot supplant practical reason, that irreplaceable and indispensable interface between our constant need to achieve practical ends and the unfathomable uncertainty of the real world. Professional wisdom, we might therefore say, means making use of the foreground tools that evidence-based practice may have to offer, while exercising all due scientific scepticism and discrimination. At the same time, professional wisdom understands that evidence-based practice can never provide all the practical answers that we need. It cannot give us much help in developing the skills to apply general precepts to particular moments and cases. Even more tellingly, evidence-based practice is mute on the moral and political ends of the human service professions, without an understanding of which they are ultimately meaningless. Evidence-based practice must be the servant of practical reason, and practical wisdom means understanding both its strengths and its limitations.

References

Barry, C.A. (2006), 'The role of evidence in alternative medicine: Contrasting biomedical and anthropological approaches', *Social Science and Medicine*, 62(11), 2,646–57.

Benton, T. (1977), *Philosophical Foundations of the Three Sociologies*, London: Routledge and Kegan Paul.

Beresford, P. (2007), 'The role of service user research in generating knowledge-based health and social care: From conflict to contribution', *Evidence and Policy*, 3(3), 329–41.

Blom, B. (2009), 'Knowing or un-knowing? That is the question: In the era of evidence-based social work practice', *Journal of Social Work*, 9(2), 158–77.

Boaz, A. (2008), 'Does evidence-based policy work? Learning from the UK experience', *Evidence and Policy*, 4(2), 233–52.

Butler, A., Ford, D. and Tregaskis, C. (2007), 'Who do we think we are? Self and reflexivity in social work practice', *Qualitative Social Work*, 6(3), 281–99.

Campbell, S. (2007), *Analysis for Policy: Evidence-based Policy in Practice*, London: H.M. Treasury.

Cnaan, R.A. and Dichter, M.A. (2008), 'Thoughts on the use of knowledge in social work practice', *Research on Social Work Practice*, 18(4), 278–84.

Crotty, M. (1998), *The Foundations of Social Research*, London: Sage.

Davies, H.T.O., Nutley, S.M. and Smith, P.C. (ed.) (2000), *What Works? Evidence-based Policy and Practice in Public Services*, Bristol: The Policy Press.

Dowie, J. and Elstein, A. (ed.) (1988), *Professional Judgment: A Reader in Clinical Decision Making*, Cambridge: Cambridge University Press.

Eraut, M. (1994), *Developing Professional Knowledge and Competence*, London: Falmer Press.

Floersch, J. (2004), 'A method for investigating practitioner use of theory in practice', *Qualitative Social Work*, 3(2), 161–77.

Freidson, E. (1970), *The Profession of Medicine: A Study of the Sociology of Applied Knowledge*, New York: Dodd, Mead & Co.

Gambrill, E. (2007), 'Views of evidence-based practice: Social workers' code of ethics and accreditation standards as guides for choice', *Journal of Social Work Education*, 43(3), 447–62.

Glasby, J. and Beresford, P. (2006), 'Who knows best? Evidence-based practice and the service user contribution', *Critical Social Policy*, 26(1), 268–84.

Goldenberg, M.J. (2006), 'On evidence and evidence-based medicine: Lessons from the philosophy of science', *Social Science and Medicine*, 62(11), 2,621–31.

Gould, N. (2006), 'An inclusive approach to knowledge for mental health social work practice and policy', *British Journal of Social Work*, 36(1), 109–25.

Graybeal, C.T. (2007), 'Evidence for the art of social work', *Families in Society*, 88(44), 213–24.

Greenhalgh, T. (1997), 'How to read a paper: Assessing the methodological quality of published papers', *British Medical Journal*, 315, 305–8.

Houston, S. (2005), 'Philosophy, theory and method in social work: Challenging empiricism's claim on evidence-based practice', *Journal of Social Work*, 5(1), 7–20.

Johnson, M. and Austin, M.J. (2008), 'Evidence-based practice in the social services: Implications for organizational change', *Journal of Evidence-Based Social Work*, 5(1), 239–69.

Lambert, H. (2006), 'Accounting for EBM: Notions of evidence in medicine', *Social Science and Medicine*, 62(11), 2,633–45.

Larson, M.S. (1977), *The Rise of Professionalism: A Sociological Analysis*, Berkeley, CA: University of California Press.

Magill, M. (2006), 'The future of evidence in evidence-based practice', *Journal of Social Work*, 6(2), 101–15.

McCarthy, J. and Rose, P. (ed.) (2010), *Values-based Health and Social Care: Beyond Evidence-based Practice*, London: Sage.

McDonald, C. (2003), 'Forward via the past? Evidence-based practice as strategy in social work', *The Drawing Board: An Australian Review of Public Affairs*, 2(3), 123–42.

McNeil, T. (2006), 'Evidence-based practice in an age of relativism: Toward a model for practice', *Social Work*, 5(12), 147–56.

Munro, E. (2004), 'The impact of audit on social work practice', *British Journal of Social Work*, 34(8), 1,075–95.

Newman, J. (2000), 'Beyond the New Public Management? Modernizing Public Services', in J. Clarke, S. Gewirtz and E. McLaughlin (ed.), *New Managerialism, New Welfare?*, London: Sage, 45–61.

Nutley, S.M., Walter, I. and Davies, H.T.O. (2007), *Using Evidence: How Research Can Inform Public Services*, Bristol: The Policy Press.

Oakley, A., Gough, D., Oliver, S. and Thomas, J. (2005), 'The policy of evidence and methodology: Lessons from the EPPI-Centre', *Evidence and Policy*, 1(1), 5–31.

Olson, T.M. (2007), 'Reconstructing evidence-based practice: An investigation of three conceptualisations of EBP', *Evidence and Policy*, 3(2), 271–85.

O'Sullivan, T. (2005), 'Some theoretical propositions on the nature of practice wisdom', *Journal of Social Work*, 5(2), 221–42.

Pawson, R. (2006), *Evidence-based Policy: A Realist Perspective*, London: Sage.

——, Boaz, A., Grayson, L., Long, A. and Barnes, C. (2003), *Types and Quality of Knowledge in Social Care*, London: Social Care Institute for Excellence.

Polanyi, M. (1962), *Personal Knowledge: Towards a Post-critical Philosophy*, 2nd edn, London: Routledge and Kegan Paul.

Pollio, D.E. (2006), 'The art of evidence-based practice', *Research on Social Work Practice*, 16(2), 224–32.

Riemann, G. (2005), 'Ethnographies of practice–practising ethnography: Resources for self-reflective social work', *Journal of Social Work Practice*, 19(1), 87.

Rose, N. and Miller, P. (1992), 'Political power beyond the state: Problematics of government', *British Journal of Sociology*, 43(2), 173–205.

Schön, D.A. (1983), *The Reflective Practitioner: How Professionals Think in Action*, London: Temple Smith.

—— (1987), *Educating the Reflective Practitioner*, San Francisco, CA: Jossey-Bass.

Scottish Government (2008), *A Guide to Getting it Right for Every Child*, 1st edn, Version 1, Edinburgh: Scottish Government.

Sheppard, M. (1995), 'Social work, social science and practice wisdom', *British Journal of Social Work*, 25(3), 265–93.

—— (1998), 'Practice validity, reflexivity and knowledge for social work', *British Journal of Social Work*, 28, 763–81.

—— (2006), *Social Work and Social Exclusion: The Idea of Practice*, Aldershot: Ashgate.

Sommerfeld, P. (2005), 'Introduction', in P. Sommerfeld and P. Herzog (ed.), *Evidence-based Social Work: Towards a New Professionalism?*, Bern: Peter Lang, 7–29.

Taylor, C. (2006), 'Narrating significant experience: Reflective accounts and the production of (self) knowledge', *British Journal of Social Work*, 36 (2), 189–206.

—— and White, S. (2006), 'Knowledge and reasoning in social work: Educating for humane judgement', *British Journal of Social Work*, 36(6), 937–54.

Thyer, B.A. (2008), 'The quest for evidence-based practice? We are all positivists!', *Research on Social Work Practice*, 18(4), 339–45.

Van de Luitgaarden, G.M.J. (2009), 'Evidence-based practice in social work: Lessons from judgment and decision-making theory', *British Journal of Social Work*, 29(2), 243–60.

Walter, U.M. (2003), 'Toward a third space: Improvisation and professionalism in social work', *Families in Society*, 84(3), 317–22.

White, S. and Stancombe, J. (2003), *Clinical Judgement in the Health and Welfare Professions: Extending the Evidence Base*, Maidenhead: Open University Press.

Winch, S., Creedy, D. and Chaboyer, A.W. (2002), 'Governing nursing conduct: The rise of evidence-based practice', *Nursing Inquiry*, 9(3), 156–61.

4 Intuition and Professional Wisdom: Can We Teach Moral Discernment?

Daniel Vokey and Jeannie Kerr

Introduction

Professionals must make sound judgements in the complex contexts of contemporary practice in order to fulfil their manifold responsibilities to their clients, their colleagues, their employers and society at large (Nash, 2002; Trotman, 2008). Accordingly, those responsible for programmes of professional education should undertake to help both prospective and practising professionals – teachers, nurses, counsellors, social workers, doctors, clergy, police officers and so forth – to enhance their ability to make sound practical judgements as a key condition of responsible action (Shulman, 2007). A partial or inaccurate understanding of the nature and development of the capabilities required for sound judgement and responsible action will limit the effectiveness of professional education initiatives; conversely, those designing and implementing programmes of professional education should draw upon a comprehensive and defensible account both of what is involved in sound practical judgement and responsible action, and of how those capabilities are cultivated. Our intent in this chapter is to contribute to such an account by investigating how attention to the intuitive dimensions of practical judgement can complement the focus upon analytical reasoning characteristic of most existing approaches to professional ethics education for 'human service' professionals (Atkinson, 2000, 69; Claxton, 2000, 40; Atkinson and Claxton, 2000, 1; Vokey, 2005). Mindful of how both professional work and professional education are inherently moral practices, we focus upon understanding forms of *moral intuition* and their proper contributions to moral judgement.

A Preliminary Clarification of Terms

As we use the terms, *practical judgements* are choices among possible courses of action in particular situations, and *practical wisdom* refers to the capabilities exercised in making sound practical judgements. By extension, we speak of *professional judgement* and *professional wisdom* when the contexts requiring decision and action are those of professional practice. Some practical judgements are *moral judgements*, understood as choices in contexts with moral issues or dimensions such that moral considerations necessarily play a role in arriving at sound decisions about what to do. To define moral judgements in this way is, of course, to leave many important questions open for further discussion. Given the religious, philosophical and cultural pluralism characteristic of modern liberal democracies, we cannot assume a common understanding of how *moral* and *non-moral* considerations should be distinguished, or of the sense in which a moral judgement can be 'sound'.[1] Moreover, this definition does not specify what characterises decisions that properly count as *judgements*. We take up this latter topic below when considering whether or not a choice must issue from conscious deliberation in order to count as a judgement.

Why Investigate Intuition?

These questions about the nature of moral judgement are related to two problems that explain our current focus upon moral intuition – problems that we have encountered while studying the cultivation of practical wisdom from the perspective of neo-Aristotelian virtue ethics (Kerr, 2007; Vokey, 2001; Vokey, 2005). The first problem is to identify what should serve as *evidence* in learning to make better choices when moral values are at stake. If practical wisdom is to develop through the experience of making and reflecting upon practical judgements, then those decisions – including moral judgements – must, in principle and in practice, be open to correction. What evidence or grounds should we use to assess moral decisions and actions as better or worse? How should we explain and defend our moral commitments when they are challenged from different moral points of view?

---

1   Both the authors reside in Vancouver, BC, where, in addition to the very multicultural immigrant and settler population, the presence of First Nations peoples and cultures brings home MacIntyre's (1988) point that there is no neutral moral language or tradition-independent way to engage in moral inquiry and practice.

John Rawls introduced the idea that both particular moral judgements and general moral principles should be tested through a dialectical process of seeking *reflective equilibrium* between them (Huemer, 2008, 369; Daniels, 2008). This understanding of moral assessment and justification subsequently appears in the work of prominent authors in professional ethics for educators (Coombs, 1998, 563, 567). To endorse using the method of reflective equilibrium for moral justification, we must believe that it is reasonable to have confidence in and give epistemic weight to our considered convictions that particular actions or events are morally right (or morally wrong), even when those convictions conflict with general moral principles or conventions. Such confidence only makes sense if we believe humans have a faculty or sense – a kind of 'moral compass' – that can apprehend moral truth. Recently, moral philosophers such as Michael Huemer (2005, 2008) have renewed arguments in support of this metaethical position by defending ethical intuitionism. Huemer is also representative in allowing that our intuitions can be partially or wholly wrong for a 'menagerie' of reasons – including bias, miscalculation and confusion – that can also confound deliberative forms of reasoning (Huemer, 2005, 137–9). Positing that some unspecified cognitive capacity can help us arrive at moral truth, but is no more infallible than any other form of human cognition, is good reason to seek to understand moral intuition well enough to determine how education can make it as reliable as possible, in part by addressing potential sources of error.[2]

The second problem we have encountered is complexity: the high number and wide range of considerations that bear upon practical judgement and responsible action. It has been long recognised that interpreting the implications for practice in particular circumstances of commitment to a moral principle requires a 'moral capacity', and this particular cognitive capacity is often named 'judgement' (Blum, 1994). 'Judgement' is also the name typically given to the ability to determine correctly *which* moral principles are relevant to a particular situation, and to arbitrate between them when they conflict (Coombs, 1998, 556). Some similar cognitive capacity will be necessary, then, when the considerations relevant to a practical or professional decision include not only a wide range of general moral principles, but also one's personal beliefs and ideals as well as the stated and unstated expectations of the workplace (Vokey, 2009, 349). Because inferential reasoning from general principles cannot yield a definitive answer under such conditions, we must posit some form or forms

---

2   Haidt (2001, 185) makes a similar point: 'A correct understanding of the intuitive basis of moral judgment may be useful in helping decision makers avoid mistakes and in helping educators design programs (and environments) to improve the quality of moral judgment and behavior.'

of non-inferential cognition that enable us to arrive at a sound decision. Following Gustafson, we will use the term *discernment* to refer to the ability to arrive intuitively at a sound moral judgement in the face of complexity in a way that can incorporate, without being limited to, analytical or deliberative forms of human cognition:

> The final discernment is an informed intuition; it is not the conclusion of a formally logical argument, a strict deduction from a single moral principle, or an absolutely certain result from the exercises of human "reason" alone. There is a final moment of perception that sees the parts in relation to a whole, expresses sensibilities as well as reasoning, and is made in the condition of human finitude. In complex circumstances it is not without risk. (James M. Gustafson, cited in Nash, 2002, 168)

Responses to the two problems of evidence and complexity must be part of any comprehensive and defensible account of how practical wisdom can be cultivated. The solutions offered above posit non-inferential forms of knowing or judgement, but do not specify in what these cognitive capacities consist or how they can be improved. Accordingly, we address the following two questions:

1. How can the different senses in which the terms *moral intuition* and *moral judgement* are used be clarified by identifying the different capabilities involved in responding adequately to situations in which moral matters are at stake?
2. In what senses and in what ways can the different forms of moral intuition (and, thereby, moral judgement) be improved through education?

In the first section below, we present a response to the first question that we developed by reviewing conceptual work on moral perception in the light of recent empirical research that highlights the role of intuition in moral decision-making (Haidt, 2007; Haidt, 2008). In the second section, we present a summary of the picture of moral agency emerging from that literature to consider what general implications can be drawn for professional education. In the third section, we identify important philosophical and educational questions that the empirical research on moral intuition leaves unaddressed. We then present our conclusions concerning what additional inquiries must be undertaken and how the results should be integrated in order to develop an adequate theoretical framework for cultivating professional wisdom.

Moral Intuition and Moral Judgement

Intuition is generally understood to mean *immediate, non-inferential cognition.* Beyond that minimum, however, there is no consensus on a definition among those studying it empirically. Eraut (2000, 255) observes that researchers do not agree on the range of phenomena that can be properly described as intuitive. Similarly, Hogarth (2001, 6) points out that the concept of intuition is not well-defined in the psychological literature, and may in fact be covering too many phenomena; and Hodgkinson et al. (2008, 1) argue that the empirical research on intuition is conceptually underdeveloped despite its potential contributions to many lines of inquiry. To differentiate the different senses when the terms *moral intuition* and *moral judgement* are used, we found Lawrence Blum's (1994) discussion of moral perception a helpful point of departure, particularly the 'cab driver' scenario he constructs to illustrate the variety of 'psychological operations' involved in moral agency. Embellished for our purposes, the scenario goes like this:

> Tim, a white businessman, is trying to hail a cab. It is a dark, rainy, windy and chilly night. The street is full of traffic and the sounds of rush hour. Tim has had a long day at work and wants to get a taxi as quickly as possible so that he can get out of the rain and get home for dinner with his family on time. Tim is very focused on looking for a cab as he shields himself from the wind and rain with his umbrella. He partially registers that a black woman (Clarice) is holding a small child in her arms about 20 metres up the street. She also seems to be trying to hail a taxi while coping with the weather and managing her child. A cab comes down the street and the driver, Kurt, passes by Clarice and stops for Tim. Tim, feeling pleasure at the prospect of getting out of the rain, gets in without thinking of Clarice at that moment. Once in the back seat Tim notices a leaflet titled Stop Immigration Now. He then looks up to Kurt's rear view mirror and sees that Kurt is a white man. The image of Clarice arises unbidden from Tim's memory and he imagines how discouraged and angry she must have felt to see the cab pass her by and stop for him, because Tim now sees the cab driver's action as a form of racial discrimination. Moved by what he takes to be a grievous affront to the dignity of Clarice, Tim tells Kurt to wait and tries to get Clarice's attention to come and take the cab in his stead.

Tim's action results in part from how he constructs elements of his experience as a particular kind of situation with particular kinds of moral relevance. We consider this interpretive act a form of insight – that is, a grasp of intelligible relationships among particular ideas and/or events (Lonergan, 1958). Tim's action also results from his immediate 'felt apprehension' of Kurt's action as morally wrong, both in motivation and in likely consequences; coupled with Tim's disposition to care enough about such moral harms to try to put them right. Clarice and her child's physical discomfort as well as Clarice's likely emotional distress have, in Blum's terms, *moral salience* for Tim, as does Kurt's apparent refusal to stop for Clarice. In his emotional response and subsequent action, Tim's empathic imagination is spontaneously engaged, as well as his intellectual understanding of systemic injustice. Tim's instruction to Kurt follows directly from his interpretive grasp of the situation and his emotional response to it, and does not involve *deliberation* in the sense of *a conscious assessment of reasons for and against alternative courses of action*.

Tim's instruction to Kurt and attempt to engage with Clarice is, of course, only one possible response out of many others. Tim could direct Kurt to take him home, repressing his concern for Clarice and/or rationalising the decision to give priority to his own objectives (get out of the rain and get home) and responsibilities (show up for dinner on time). Or Tim could ask Kurt why he did not stop, either to check his interpretation of Kurt's action or to initiate a lecture to Kurt on the evils of racially motivated discrimination. If Tim's interpretation of the situation is mistaken in one or more respects, then the appropriateness of his action is likely compromised as a result. Perhaps Clarice had turned away to attend to her child as Kurt passed, with the consequence that he did not notice her, and so racism might have played no role in Kurt's stopping for Tim, who might have simply missed this element of the situation. Tim might have reason to reinterpret the situation as he interacts with Kurt and Clarice and to take additional action in that new light.

Understanding *moral intuition* broadly as non-inferential moral cognition, we can identify three different forms in the 'cab driver' scenario: Tim's *interpretive construction* of the situation, his immediate *felt apprehension* of Kurt's action and its likely consequences as morally wrong, and Tim's *non-inferential assessment* of what he might and should do that resulted in his action. Such cases illustrate the kind of everyday 'coping' that is more characteristic of our moral agency than conscious deliberation in the face of moral dilemmas (Dreyfus and Dreyfus, 2004; Varela, 1999, 23). Even those who emphasise the important contributions of discursive reasoning to moral judgement agree that 'much of human information processing occurs automatically, including processes that lead to moral action' (Narvaez, 2010, 165). Accordingly, we find it reasonable to stipulate that a decision need not involve conscious deliberation – much less reasoning with reference to universalisable moral principles – in order to count as a moral judgement.

To observe that moral choice and action – *moral agency* for short – does not necessarily involve conscious deliberation is not to say that this is ideal. Under what conditions, if at all, the contributions of moral intuition to ethical action should be subject to review by moral reasoning is still open to debate. We take up this topic in the course of addressing our second question, which is concerned with how professional and other educational initiatives might promote practical wisdom by helping participants improve moral intuition in its various forms.

Implications for Educating Moral Intuition

Contemporary empirical research on moral intuition centres on Haidt's (2001, 2007, 2008) *social intuitionist model* of moral judgement (SIM) that many other theorists rely upon to support their versions of moral intuitionism (Narvaez, 2010, 164–5; Musschenga, 2008, 2). The SIM emerged in the 1990s as an alternative to the rationalist model that dominated mainstream Western academic moral psychology from the 1960s to the 1980s, 'in which moral judgement is thought to be caused by moral reasoning' (Haidt, 2001, 814). One consequence of Haidt's and similar research is that moral psychology now generally describes mature moral agency in terms, not of Kohlberg's Stage Six principled reasoning, but of contextually situated *ethical expertise*, in which the different forms of intuition identified above play an integral role. Presenting the general implications for professional education of recent empirical work on moral intuition therefore begins with a closer look at how mature moral agency is described in these terms.

Moral Intuition, Moral Reasoning and Ethical Expertise

The 'cab driver' scenario above illustrates how responsible moral agency must begin with an accurate interpretive construction of events as a situation in which one or more kinds of moral value are at stake. Because such interpretation is a form of insight, ethical expertise includes *moral intelligence* – that is, a capacity to grasp correctly the moral significance of a sequence or pattern of events. Because interpreting events accurately presupposes awareness of relevant particulars, ethical expertise includes *attentiveness* coupled with *dispositions to care* about moral matters so particulars have the correct moral salience. The 'cab driver' scenario also illustrates the important contributions to moral judgement and action of *ethical and political theory*; ethical expertise thus includes both knowledge of general moral concepts such as *injustice* and the ability to determine correctly what properly counts as particular instances of those concepts. The immediate 'felt apprehension' of actions or events as morally good or bad is the form of moral intuition that is the 'heart' of SIM: 'One sees or hears about an event and one instantly feels approval or disapproval' (Haidt, 2001, 818).[3] Ethical

3   In the literature, such immediate felt responses are sometimes referred to

expertise thus includes the capacity to be appropriately moved such that the 'gut feelings' of the mature moral agent correctly identify which actions merit moral praise, and which deserve moral censure.

Blum refers collectively to these initial elements of ethical expertise as *moral perception*, defined as 'anything contributing to, or encompassed within, the agent's salience-perception of the situation before he deliberates about what action to take' (Blum, 1994, 37). Part of the ethical expertise of the mature moral agent is that, under normal circumstances for that person, his or her moral perception is accurate and sensitive enough to yield a correct intuitive assessment of the right thing to do and the motivation to follow through: 'normally an expert … neither reasons nor acts deliberately. He or she simply spontaneously does what has normally worked and, naturally, it normally works' (Dreyfus and Dreyfus, 2004, 253). According to SIM, then, moral judgement and action properly originate in intuition much more often than reasoning. Even so, SIM's proponents believe that some situations do call for moral deliberation, such as 'when intuitions conflict, or when the social situation demands thorough examination of all facets of a scenario' (Haidt, 2001, 820; see also Dreyfus and Dreyfus, 2004, 256). Like moral perception, moral deliberation understood on the social intuitionist model involves a complex interaction of feeling, imagination, insight, intellectual understanding and intention in which each of sensory perceptions, emotions, images, concepts and objectives affects the rest. One key difference between moral perception and moral deliberation, as with intuition and discursive reasoning more generally, is that the operations involved in the latter are available to consciousness, while those involved in the former are not: 'only results enter awareness' (Haidt, 2001, 818; see also Gigerenzer, 2007, 192).

As in rationalist models of moral judgement, moral deliberation in SIM involves imagining both what various courses of action are possible in a given situation and how different responses would affect the different parties involved; thus capacities for *empathy* and *role-taking* are both important elements of ethical expertise. Equally important to deliberation is the mature moral agent's willingness and ability to 'stand back' and review his or her initial intuitions in a critical light. Haidt observes that in rare cases, the ethical expert might have to 'reason their way to a judgment by sheer force of logic, overriding their initial intuition', when (as one example) role-taking gives rise to a second and equally compelling 'felt apprehension' about what is morally at stake. Consequently, notwithstanding the limited ability of conscious thinking to handle complex problems compared to intuitive

---

as *intuitive moral judgements*. Although we consider these kinds of moral intuitions to be cognitive acts, we do not refer to them as 'judgements' because *felt apprehensions* do not necessarily result in decision and action.

perception (Musschenga, 2008, 4; Musschenga, 2009, 599), the capabilities involved in careful analytical reasoning are a recognised component of ethical expertise, and appeals to abstract, universalisable principles can be decisive in deliberations of this kind. Much more frequently, however, the ethical expert 'will deliberate over their intuitions, not their principles' (Dreyfus and Dreyfus, 2004, 261).

In the SIM model, analytical reasoning and non-inferential intuition are *both* subject to various forms of bias that the mature moral agent must be willing and able to identify and redress (Musschenga, 2008, 20). Ethical expertise thus includes a good measure of *self-knowledge*, since the source of bias can be personal (Blum, 1994; Dreyfus and Dreyfus, 2004, 256) as well as cultural and even biological (Huemer, 2008, 381–2). Ethical expertise also includes *communicative competence* reflecting the *social* side of the SIM:

> … ever since Plato wrote his Dialogues, philosophers have recognized that moral reasoning naturally occurs in a social setting, between people who can challenge each other's arguments and trigger new intuitions. … The social intuitionist model avoids the traditional focus on conscious private reasoning and draws attention to the role of moral intuitions, and of other people, in shaping moral judgements. (Haidt, 2001, 820; see also Haidt, 2007, 999; Musschenga, 2009, 609–10)

From even this brief summary, it is evident that the ethical expertise of the mature moral agent consists in a complex interaction of perceptual, emotional, intuitive, intellectual, and volitional capabilities. How are these virtues acquired? How (if at all) can they be taught?

Professional Education for Ethical Expertise

When first presenting his theory, Haidt remarked that because much of the evidence he cites is from research outside the domain of moral judgement, 'the social intuitionist model is presented here only as a plausible alternative approach to moral psychology, not as an established fact' (Haidt, 2001, 815). If our foray into its recent literature is any indication, moral psychology currently accepts that mature moral agency requires a combination of intuition and discursive reasoning, but is less sure which of the two is the 'senior partner' and deserves corresponding priority in education (Haidt, 2008; Narvaez, 2010; Musschenga, 2009). These cautions notwithstanding, the picture of mature moral agency emerging from recent empirical research has significant implications for professional education; implications that follow from conceiving moral education on the model of a 'novice-to-expert' progression (Dreyfus and Dreyfus, 2004; Narvaez, 2010). The path to expertise in any craft, discipline, profession or field is one of gradual initiation into the shared beliefs, attitudes, interests, norms and priorities that define members of that particular community of practitioners and are embodied in its activities. By definition, full membership in such a community means being able to contribute to the ongoing development of its explicit and implicit standards of assessment. Ethical expertise is no different: the range of capabilities involved in sound practical judgement and responsible action are acquired or enhanced in the process of becoming a full member of one or more healthy communities – and corresponding traditions – of moral inquiry and practice (Varela, 1999, 24; MacIntyre, 1988; MacIntyre, 1990). It is through participation in such a community's ways of life that the perceptual, affective, intuitive, deliberative, volitional and communicative competencies of mature moral agency are developed, thanks in significant part to the guidance and inspiration provided by the words and deeds of the individuals esteemed as exemplars within that group (Vokey, 2001, 261–73).

That communities and role models are important to moral education is, of course, not a realisation that is unique to contemporary moral psychologists:

> Education for practical reasoning is ... best done within a community whose members understand and appreciate the importance of honing the intellectual and moral skills upon which good judgment depends. Developing the capacity for such judgment lies at the heart of professional preparation. ... This is the formative dimension of education. There are few educational tasks more urgent, or more demanding, than this. (Shulman, 2007, 562)

On this view, in order to help prospective and practising professionals enhance their capacities for sound judgement and responsible action, instructors in programmes of professional education would form communities of moral inquiry and practice alongside their counterparts working 'in the field'. Courses in professional ethics would complement, but not substitute for, initiation into and multiple forms of mentoring within such a community.

Generally speaking, we are sympathetic to the descriptions of mature moral agency and of the development of ethical expertise emerging from the empirical study of intuition within contemporary moral psychology. We look forward to investigating further its contributions to understanding practical judgement, such as the notion of deliberating over intuitions both in solitary reflection and in social contexts. At the same time, we find that the social intuitionist model raises questions that moral psychology cannot address on its own – questions that must have at least provisional answers before programmes in professional education can responsibly educate moral intuition. Accordingly, the nature of these questions, and the way forward to address them, is the topic of our final section.

Professional Education and the 'Wisdom' Traditions

By our definition, *discernment* is the capacity that meets the challenge of complexity. Let us further stipulate that, in part by finding the proper mean between rashness and timidity in moral judgement, discernment enables those who possess ethical expertise to know when moral deliberation is and is not required *and* when they have deliberated both long and well enough to be rightly confident in their decisions. In other words, it is the possession of discernment that distinguishes those who rightly have confidence in their moral judgements, whether deliberative or immediate, from those who do not. Remarks recognising that something like discernment is required to know *when* to deliberate (Musschenga, 2009, 609) and *when* it is time to bring deliberation to an end do appear in the SIM literature: 'We use conscious reflection to mull over a problem *until one side feels right*. Then we stop' (Haidt, 2001, 829; emphasis added), and also 'when faced with a dilemma, the expert does not seek principles but rather reflects on and tries to sharpen his or her spontaneous intuitions by getting more information *until one decision emerges as obvious*' (Dreyfus and Dreyfus, 2004, 258; emphasis added). Such remarks notwithstanding, relatively little attention has been given to the following questions: In what does such discernment consist? And, how (if at all) can it be learned or taught?

The key question is the second one. As an intuitive process of assessment, discernment can be heuristically defined as a cognitive capacity possessed by those who have become genuinely virtuous and wise (Varella, 1999, 4) by cultivating over time many of the perceptual, affective, intuitive, intellectual, volitional and communicative excellences of which humans are capable. Once discernment is characterised in this way, it becomes important to professional education to know the practices through which and the conditions under which experience matures into wisdom. This point reveals an important connection between the problem of complexity and the problem of evidence. As noted above, affirming the possibility that practical wisdom can develop through a dialectical interplay of experience and reflection presupposes that we are right to take seriously our felt apprehensions that particular actions or events are morally right or morally wrong. Are we justified in having confidence in, and giving epistemic weight to, this form of moral intuition?

Moral psychology can only go so far in answering this question because, as an empirical science, it is descriptive, not prescriptive: one cannot validly argue from an empirical 'is' to a normative 'ought' without additional premises. Musschenga (2008, 2009) reinforces this point when he argues that the validity and reliability of moral intuition cannot be established in the same way as other kinds, because the truth or rightness of moral judgements cannot be established independently by empirical research. The same epistemological issue arises as soon as the development of ethical expertise is located within particular communities of moral inquiry and practice because different communities profess and enact very different beliefs about what is morally right and wrong, and there is no strictly empirical way to decide between them (Dreyfus and Dreyfus, 2004, 262–3). One indication of this moral pluralism and the educational challenges it represents is the difficulty that many professional faculties, associations and governing bodies have in reaching agreement on substantive criteria for assessing professional conduct (Robertson, 2010).

For any form of moral or character education to be defensible in pluralistic secular societies, there must be grounds for assessing moral judgements other than the authority of tradition and custom. Post-conventional thinking is often considered epistemologically superior to conventional reasoning in moral as well as other cognitive domains, which serves to highlight the need to give ethics a basis other than uncritical or dogmatic belief. Moral psychology once looked to impartial reason to provide such grounds in the form of either universal or universalisable moral principles, but this puts more weight on logic than it can bear (Dreyfus and Dreyfus, 2004, 262). There are indications in the SIM literature that moral psychology now looks to evolutionary theory for grounds that will enable it to avoid cultural moral relativism (Haidt, 2007, 1,001; Narvaez, 2010, 172). We would certainly agree that ethical expertise is desirable in part for its essential role in human flourishing, and that we are well advised to seek common ground with people representing different religious, philosophical, political and cultural traditions by comparing ideas about which ways of life do and do not conduce to human well-being. At the same time, we are persuaded by arguments (for example, Huemer, 2005) that reductionist moral theories, evolutionary or otherwise, ultimately fail to provide an adequate alternative to moral relativism once they attempt to ground moral convictions on non-moral 'facts'. We are similarly persuaded that assigning 'felt apprehensions' an important cognitive role in ethical expertise requires a different world view than the strictly materialist one typically associated with evolutionary theory. While moral psychology is becoming more interdisciplinary, the research that it integrates is scientific or social-scientific: Haidt presents SIM as 'more consistent than rationalist models with recent findings in social, cultural, evolutionary, and biological psychology, as well as in anthropology and primatology' (Haidt, 2001, 814). This limited scope is sufficient for research undertaking to formulate a theory of moral judgement that best 'fits the data'. However, the means and ends of professional education must be justified in normative as well as pragmatic or instrumental terms.

Our general point is that moral psychology must be complemented by other forms of inquiry, including moral philosophy, to develop defensible rationales and frameworks for programmes of professional education.

Community, Tradition, and the Cultivation of Wisdom

If we are to develop our potential for practical and professional wisdom by becoming full members of communities of moral inquiry and practice, they will have to be communities and corresponding traditions that are both dedicated to and successful in cultivating wisdom. The general implication we draw from our inquiry into moral intuition is that those who share responsibility for the design and implementation of programmes of professional education need to investigate what higher education can learn from philosophical and religious 'wisdom' traditions about how the full range of perceptual, affective, intuitive, intellectual, volitional, and communicative virtues can be cultivated. That Western philosophical traditions have much to offer is illustrated by many examples such as the work on literature, moral perception and the virtues by Nussbaum (1986, 1987, 1988), on intrinsic value and the visual arts by Carr (2004), and on judgement and professional practice by Dunne (1993, 1999, 2005). There is also much to be learned from the many living traditions that understand practical wisdom to be the fruition of a 'holistic' educational path with spiritual and/or contemplative dimensions (Archibald, 2008; Mipham, 2005; Palmer, 1998; Varella, 1999; Walker, 1987). For one reason, we see very important links between, on the one hand, the recognised need to identify and redress different forms of error and *bias*, and on the other hand, time-tested teachings on how the insight to know and the compassion to do 'the right thing' arises from transcending self-attachment (Glassman, 1998; Lonergan, 1973). Appreciating what the world's wisdom traditions have to offer contemporary programmes in higher education requires a personal engagement with them that, while remaining non-dogmatic, goes beyond simply reading their texts. This is because there are limits to what one can learn about a moral community from the outside looking in.[4]

---

4   The value of integrating 'first-person' experience of contemplative practices with 'third-person' study is affirmed in a variety of contemporary academic initiatives such as the 2010 Mind and Life Summer Research Institute at the Garrison Institute, Garrison, NY, 14–20 June 2010 on 'Education, Developmental Neuroscience and Contemplative Practices: Questions, Challenges, and Opportunities' <http://www.mindandlife.org/research-initiatives/sri/sri10>; see also Naropa University (2008).

Conclusion

Discernment, defined heuristically as what distinguishes those who rightly have confidence in their practical judgements, involves the integration of perceptual, affective, intuitive, intellectual, volitional and communicative capabilities. Such practical wisdom involves different forms of moral intuition, defined broadly as non-inferential moral cognition. Discernment can be cultivated through a dialectic of experience and reflection, but as yet there is no consensus on exactly how. In particular, the proper role of analytical reasoning within the education of moral choice and action is a topic of ongoing discussion and debate. Recognising the crucial roles of mentorship, community and tradition in education for practical and professional wisdom underlines the importance of articulating an alternative to moral relativism that does justice to the facts of moral pluralism. Accordingly, a comprehensive and defensible account both of what is involved in sound practical judgement and responsible action and of how those capabilities are cultivated must establish what kinds of evidence properly ground moral and other normative claims, which will require that empirical research be complemented by other forms of inquiry, including moral philosophy.

References

Archibald, J. (2008), *Indigenous Storywork: Educating the Heart, Mind, Body and Spirit*, Vancouver: UBC Press.

Atkinson, T. (2000), 'Learning to Teach: Intuitive Skills and Reasoned Objectivity', in T. Atkinson and G. Claxton (ed.), *The Intuitive Practitioner: On the Value of Not Always Knowing What One is Doing*, Buckingham: Open University Press, 69–83.

Atkinson, T. and Claxton, G. (ed.) (2000), *The Intuitive Practitioner: On the Value of Not Always Knowing What One is Doing*, Buckingham: Open University Press.

Blum, L.A. (1994), *Moral Perception and Particularity*, New York: Cambridge University Press.

Carr, D. (2004), 'Moral values and the arts in environmental education: Towards an ethics of aesthetic appreciation', *Journal of Philosophy of Education*, 38(2), 221–39.

Claxton, G. (2000), 'The Anatomy of Intuition', in T. Atkinson and G. Claxton (ed.), *The Intuitive Practitioner: On the Value of Not Always Knowing What One is Doing*, Buckingham: Open University Press, 32–52.

Coombs, J. (1998), 'Educational ethics: Are we on the right track?', *Educational Theory*, 48(4), 555–69.

Daniels, N. (2008), 'Reflective Equilibrium', in Edward N. Zalta (ed.), *The Stanford Encyclopedia of Philosophy*, Fall edn, <http://plato.stanford.edu/archives/fall2008/entries/reflective-equilibrium> (accessed 25 March 2011).

Dreyfus, H.L. and Dreyfus, S.E. (2004), 'The ethical implications of the five-stage skill-acquisition model', *Bulletin of Science, Technology and Society*, 24(3), 251–64.

Dunne, J. (1993), *Back to the Rough Ground: Practical Judgment and the Lure of Technique*, Notre Dame, IN: University of Notre Dame Press.

—— (1999), 'Virtue, Phronesis and Learning', in D. Carr and J. Steutel (ed.), *Virtue Ethics and Moral Education*, London: Routledge, 49–64.

—— (2005), 'An intricate fabric: Understanding the rationality of practice', *Pedagogy, Culture and Society*, 13(3), 367–89.

Eraut, M. (2000), 'The Intuitive Practitioner: A Critical Overview', in T. Atkinson and G. Claxton (ed.), *The Intuitive Practitioner: On the Value of Not Always Knowing What One is Doing*, Buckingham: Open University Press, 255–68.

Gigerenzer, G. (2007), *Gut Feelings: The Intelligence of the Unconscious*, New York: Viking/Penguin.

Glassman, B. (1998), *Bearing Witness: A Zen Master's Lessons in Making Peace*, New York: Bell Tower.

Haidt, J. (2001), 'The emotional dog and its rational tail: A social intuitionist approach to moral judgment', *Psychological Review*, 108(4), 814–34.

—— (2007), 'The new synthesis in moral psychology', *Science*, 316(5,287), 998–1,002.

—— (2008), 'Morality', *Perspectives on Psychological Science*, 3(65), <http://pps.sagepub.com/content/3/1/65> (accessed 25 March 2011).

Hodgkinson, G.P., Langan-Fox, J. and Sadler-Smith, E. (2008), 'Intuition: A fundamental bridging construct in the behavioural sciences', *British Journal of Psychology*, 99(1), 1–27.

Hogarth, R.M. (2001), *Educating Intuition*, Chicago, IL and London: University of Chicago Press.

Huemer, M. (2005), *Ethical Intuitionism*, New York: Palgrave Macmillan.

—— (2008), 'Revisionary intuitionism', *Social Philosophy and Policy*, 25(1), 368–92.

Kerr, J.A. (2007), 'Educating Heart and Mind: Fostering Ethical Emotional Learning in Elementary Schools', master's thesis, Vancouver: University of British Columbia.

Lonergan, B.J.F. (1958), *Insight: A Study in Human Understanding*, revised student edn, San Francisco, CA: Harper and Row.

—— (1973), *Method in Theology*, 2nd edn, London: Dartman, Longman and Todd.

MacIntyre, A. (1988), *Whose Justice? Which Rationality?*, Notre Dame, IN: University of Notre Dame Press.

—— (1990), *Three Rival Versions of Moral Inquiry: Encyclopaedia, Genealogy, and Tradition*, Notre Dame, IN: University of Notre Dame Press.

Mipham, S. (2005), *Ruling Your World: Ancient Strategies for Modern Life*, New York: Broadway.

Musschenga, A.W. (2008), 'The epistemic value of intuitive moral judgements', *Philosophical Explanations*, <http://vu-nl.academia.edu/ BertMusschenga/Papers/131892/The_epistemic_value_of_intuitive_ moral_judgements> (accessed 25 March 2011).

—— (2009), 'Moral intuitions, moral expertise and moral reasoning', *Journal of Philosophy of Education*, 43(4), 597–613.

Naropa University (2008), *Contemplative Education*, <http://www.naropa. edu/conted> (accessed 25 March 2011).

Narvaez, D. (2010), 'Moral complexity: The fatal attraction of truthiness and the importance of mature moral functioning', *Perspectives on Psychological Science*, 5(2), 163–81.

Nash, R. (2002), *'Real World' Ethics: Frameworks for Educators and Human Service Professionals*, 2nd edn, New York: Teachers College Press.

Nussbaum, M.C. (1986), 'The discernment of perception: An Aristotelian conception of private and public rationality', in J.C. Cleary (ed.), *Boston Area Colloquium in Ancient Philosophy*, Lanham, MD: University Press of America, 155–201.

—— (1987), 'Finely aware and richly responsible: Literature and the moral imagination', in A.J. Cascardi, *Literature and the Question of Philosophy*, Baltimore, MD: John Hopkins University Press, 167–91.

—— (1988), 'Non-relative virtues: An Aristotelian approach', *Midwest Studies in Philosophy*, 13(1), 32–53.

Palmer, P. (1998), *The Courage to Teach: Exploring the Inner Landscape of a Teacher's Life*, San Francisco, CA: Jossey-Bass.

Robertson, J. (2010), 'Addressing Professional Suitability in Social Work Education: The Experience and Approach of Field Education Coordinators', unpublished doctoral dissertation, Vancouver: University of British Columbia, <https://circle.ubc.ca/bitstream/handle/2429/23031/ ubc_2010_spring_robertson_jeanette.pdf?sequence=1> (accessed 25 March 2011).

Shulman, L.S. (2007), 'Practical wisdom in the service of professional practice', *Educational Researcher*, 36(9), 560–63.

Trotman, D. (2008), 'Liberating the Wise Educator: Cultivating Professional Judgment in Educational Practice', in A. Craft, G. Gardner and G. Claxton (ed.), *Creativity, Wisdom, and Trusteeship: Exploring the Role of Education*, Thousand Oaks, CA: Corwin Press, 158–66.

Varela, F.J. (1999), *Ethical Know-how: Action, Wisdom, and Cognition*, Palo Alto, CA: Stanford University Press.

Vokey, D. (2001), *Moral Discourse in a Pluralistic World*, Notre Dame, IN: University of Notre Dame Press.

—— (2005), 'Teaching Professional Ethics to Educators: Assessing the "Multiple Ethical Languages" Approach', in K. Howe (ed.), *Philosophy of Education 2005*, Urbana, IL: Philosophy of Education Society, 125–33.

—— (2007), Hearing, Contemplating, Meditating: In Search of the Transformative Integration of Heart and Mind, in C. Eppert and H. Wang (ed.), *Cross-cultural Studies in Curriculum: Eastern Thought, Educational Insights*, Hillsdale, NJ: Lawrence Erlbaum, 287–312.

—— (2009), '"Anything you can do I can do better": Dialectical argument in philosophy of education', *Journal of Philosophy of Education*, 43(3), 339–55.

Walker, S. (ed) (1987), *Speaking of Silence: Christians and Buddhists on the Contemplative Way*, New York: Paulist Press.

5 Teacher Education as a Missed Opportunity in the Professional Preparation of Ethical Practitioners

Elizabeth Campbell

The Cultivation of Ethical Knowledge:
An Introduction

In response to the question of whether or not higher education has the capacity to foster in students enhanced moral and ethical sensibilities, Derek Bok famously argued:

> Skeptics will reply that courses in moral reasoning have no effect on behaviour, but this criticism seems overdrawn. To be sure, no instruction can suffice to turn a scoundrel into a virtuous human being. But most young people arrive at the university with decent instincts and a genuine concern for others. For them, courses that foster an ability to detect ethical issues more perceptively, to think about them more carefully, to understand more clearly the reasons for acting morally seem likely not only to train their minds but to have a positive effect on their behaviour as well. (Bok, 1988, 7)

More than 20 years later, this question, with its ancient roots invoking consideration of whether virtue can be taught, continues to be relevant and open to debate. While Bok was concerned with university students in a broad sense, the question takes on particular significance for those enrolled in professional preparation programmes, such as medicine, law, business, engineering, and especially the 'people professions' such as those addressed in this book – teaching, social work, nursing, ministry and counselling – for their educative potential is not only restricted to the moral cultivation of individual character for some general purpose of societal benefit. Rather, there is an expectation for such programmes that those who graduate from them will emerge as morally accountable practitioners, well grounded in the ethical dimensions, responsibilities and standards inherent in their respective professions.

In the discipline of education, which is the focus of this chapter, professional ethics are intricately woven into the very essence of teaching as a moral profession. Central to much of the relevant scholarship in the field is the teacher as a moral agent, one who exemplifies in all aspects of his or her conduct and practice a range of 'dispositions' (Sockett, 2006) or virtuous qualities that reflect one's professional 'manner' (Richardson and Fenstermacher, 2001). The teacher's choices, judgements, actions, inclinations and intentions not only illuminate the moral aspects of the curricular, pedagogical, evaluative and interpersonal work in which teachers engage on a daily basis (Buzzelli and Johnston, 2002; Jackson et al., 1993; Simon, 2001), but also reflect the ethical imperatives that underlie the professional role of the teacher (Campbell, 2008b; Carr, 2000). They also make visible the ethical tensions and dilemmas that challenge teachers regularly as they juggle competing responsibilities to individual students, as well as to groups of students, colleagues, parents, administrators and other stakeholders, and as they weigh ethical principles such as the duty of care and the duty of justice that can frequently collide in the context of classroom dynamics.

Consequently, professional ethics in education should not be seen solely as a narrow set of rules, laws or standards; while they necessarily connect to more formalised codes, the ethics of teaching also transcend them to embody the moral nuances of the practitioner's professional world. Those teachers who have a keen appreciation of such nuances have been successful in cultivating what I have defined previously as 'ethical knowledge' (Campbell, 2003). Ethical knowledge is a personal and professional capacity that compels teachers to examine their own conduct and question their own intentions and actions. It requires them to anticipate and understand how moral and ethical values such as justice and fairness, honesty and integrity, kindness and compassion, empathy and respect for others can be either upheld or violated by seemingly routine and normative practices. Such practices may be formal or informal, planned or spontaneous; they may relate to:

> ... teachers' use of pedagogical techniques or classroom management strategies, their choices of curriculum and teaching materials, their methods of assessment and evaluation, their interpersonal exchanges with students and others on behalf of students, or any other aspect of their daily practice that has the potential to influence student wellbeing emotionally, intellectually, and physically. Ethical

knowledge may be recognized in the tone of voice a teacher uses to address students, the care a teacher takes with students' work, the substance of a lesson taught, the casual remarks a teacher makes, the way a teacher arranges groups or adjudicates among the sometimes conflicting needs and interests of students. (Campbell, 2008a, 4)

For those of us who believe that ethical knowledge is at the core of good teaching, it would seem logical that the starting point for its cultivation would be in pre-service teacher education programmes. Student teachers, or teacher candidates, are unlikely to enter such programmes lacking some kind of moral and ethical foundation as human beings. The key, however, is to enable them to make reflective and knowledgeable connections of both a conceptual and a practical nature between intuitive wisdom and the professional realities of teaching. For some time now, scholarship in the field has been insistent on the need for teacher education to fulfil a mandate to acquaint future teachers with the moral and ethical intricacies of their chosen profession. Regrettably, however, it has also acknowledged that teacher education, in contrast to other professions, has traditionally neglected this essential component of pre-service preparation (Bull, 1993; Joseph, 2003; Nash, 1996; Strike and Ternasky, 1993).

Following from the consistent and generalised critique of teacher education for its collective failure to acquaint student teachers with the ethics of teaching, I recently conducted a research project that sought to investigate qualitatively whether and how programmes in some Canadian schools of education offer experiences that could contribute to an appreciation on the part of student teachers of applied professional ethics and, more broadly, the moral dimensions of teaching that are infused and embedded in teachers' work.[1] As well as analysing documentary evidence gathered from a wide variety of programmes and courses, the study involved the interviewing of 45 student teachers at the end of their programmes from three faculties of education, 15 beginning teachers who recently graduated from five faculties, and five teacher educators from two faculties. While key findings have been reported elsewhere (Campbell, 2008a), empirical synopses from the study are integrated throughout this chapter to illustrate and supplement the theoretical arguments presented.

The subsequent section of this chapter introduces the idea of professional ethics as a missing foundation in teacher education. It considers what is taught by way of inadequate, and in some cases alarming, substitutes for the rigorous exposure to morally and ethically defensible teaching

---

1   I gratefully acknowledge the Social Sciences and Humanities Research Council of Canada for its support of this research project, entitled 'The Cultivation of Ethical Knowledge in Teaching'.

practices. The chapter further addresses the perceived value of personal background and practical experience as contributing to the development of ethical sensitivity in ways that ironically seem to render pre-service teacher education irrelevant.

The Missing Foundation

Teacher education programmes are traditionally and typically brief in duration and dense in curriculum coverage. In order to maximise the limited capacity of many programmes, content in the components not directly related to curriculum and instructional methods or clinical/practical preparation is frequently conflated into a range of 'foundations' courses that offer at the very least an introductory overview of various disciplines considered influential in teaching. Educational psychology courses focus on theories of child development, learning models, multiple intelligences and cognitive growth. Sociological foundations consider the place of schooling and education generally in the context of the larger society, and adopt various socio-political orientations to the promotion of cultural studies. Foundational approaches to the history and philosophy of education may concentrate on pivotal educators of the past and their theories that have had enduring effects on how we conceptualise curricula and pedagogy. And more generic foundations of teaching components tend to centre on practice-based issues such as classroom management, assessment, school law and, occasionally, professionalism.

It is not difficult to see how the instruction of professional ethics within the context of the moral and ethical dimensions of teaching could be infused across such foundational areas, especially the latter one, as well as in the curriculum and methods components of teacher education. And in some cases, this may indeed be the case. However, embedding the teaching of ethics across other curricular areas may be comparable in reality to hiding it. It is certainly not the same as presenting it as a focused, integral, non-elective and essential 'foundation' of teaching in and of itself. Courses or components that prioritise the ethics of teaching as applied to the individually accountable practices of professional teachers and that offer a depth of experience intended to hone the ethical judgement of student teachers are rare.

My own research with elementary and secondary teacher candidates and new teachers is consistent with the argument that pre-service teacher education does not contribute adequately to enhancing the ethical knowledge of future teachers. Common responses from the participants to the question of whether they were engaged in work related to the ethics of teaching tended to be vague and uncertain in tone. In their words, even if an issue occasionally 'did come up', it never seemed planned and was often in reaction to a student-initiated question. There was consensus among all participants that they 'were not overly certain as to which components of the programme were ethically related', especially in so far as the connection to daily practice is concerned. Several participants expressed a desire for more direct exposure to the ethical dimensions of routine practice and the need to recognise them as such. As one stated:

> I would have liked to know more about ethics on the basic day-to-day level. Little things like decision making that really affect most teachers more so than the big huge dilemma problems (like suspecting child abuse) that are sometimes encountered. While that's important, I would have liked it if they'd have covered some of the smaller seemingly less important things to do with ethics as well – like just being aware of how you speak to students. It was addressed but it wasn't talked about in terms of ethics and how that makes you an ethical teacher or not. So, unless you're introspective, you wouldn't really catch on.

Despite an expressed need for a 'better foundation in ethics', 'just to set clear lines of what is appropriate and what is inappropriate', other participants speculated that it would be challenging to identify such a concrete foundation because 'a lot of ethical rules are unwritten' and 'when you're working in a very social job, situations are very different every day'. It was difficult for them to envision a focused course, unit or component on professional ethics that could be taught explicitly. Instead, they guessed that issues of some ethical relevance were 'streamlined' or integrated and embedded throughout their programme as a kind of 'unspoken curriculum', to quote one participant. When asked whether lessons on ethics were part of a core foundations course on educational professionalism, history, philosophy and law, one teacher educator responded: 'No, I don't think it [ethics] is consciously part of the thread; it's there because it's naturally there.' However, examples of embedded ethics were very dimly remembered by the students, if at all, and there appears to have been no lasting impression made about the moral and ethical aspects of teaching and their daily enactment in schools.

So what did these teacher candidates learn from the implicit curriculum that, in the words of one of them, 'kinda relates to ethics'? Even though their recollections are tentative and fuzzy, and they still distinguish between their experiences and what one might normally consider professional ethics education, they did identify aspects of their programmes that can be seen as having something to say about the moral and ethical dimensions of teaching, even if they are not represented in this context. Their accounts generally fall into three broad thematic areas: (1) standards and laws, (2) social justice education and (3) negative modelling from the field. Even collectively, they constitute an inadequate substitution for more explicit education that would engage students in some depth in thoughtful reflection on the moral complexities that they would shortly assume.

In their interdisciplinary text on the elements of ethics for professionals, Johnson and Ridley (2008) note that:

> Much like laws, ethics codes often are concerned with minimum standards of practice, and, like laws, they vary across jurisdictions and professions. Ethical excellence requires more than adherence to minimum standards. It demands a deeper commitment to live according to bedrock virtues and aspire to timeless principles. (Johnson and Ridley, 2008, xvi)

While I share their sentiment, which echoes many criticisms of formalised ethical codes or standards in education, I would also expect that new teachers should, at the very least, be conversant with the ethical standards that officially govern their practice. The participants in my study all came from a jurisdiction that has a professional college of teachers and an associated statement of ethical standards. Yet during the interviews, most of the participants did not refer to the ethical standards until they were prompted to do so, and even then, their responses conveyed a complete lack of interest in or knowledge and understanding of this professional code.

By contrast, what did seem to linger for the participants was what several of them referred to as 'scare tactics' and certain 'do's and don'ts' to protect oneself as a teacher that emanated from discussions of school law, specifically related to teacher misconduct regulations (for example, sexual misconduct, the duty to report child abuse), controversy over such practices as hugging children, and union-crafted rules around collegial relations governing normative expectations of solidarity and loyalty. They expressed concern about being fired, sued, reprimanded or jailed – all extremely unlikely outcomes for the vast majority of teachers – and any potential to consider the actual realities of ethical practice seems to have been overshadowed by unhelpful warnings and curtailed by superficial nods to unexamined and unexplained standards.

Increasingly, schools of education are introducing courses of a socio-political nature, oriented towards issues of social justice, equity and diversity (Ayers, 2004; Beyer, 1997; Slattery and Rapp, 2003). Based on ideological principles of critical theory, such courses conceptualise the teacher's moral role as being that of a social activist, societal change agent and disrupter of the educational status quo, rather than as an individual professional publicly endorsed and accountable for his or her own ethical conduct in relation to the direct well-being of pupils in his or her care. As one teacher educator commented, ethical issues in his programme constitute 'social and political ethics rather than individual ethics in classrooms'. In this more macro approach to ethical responsibility, which uses the language of politics more than the language of ethics, student teachers are implicitly urged to critique and resist societal and institutional norms and values, rather than uphold those 'bedrock virtues' and 'timeless principles', to recall Johnson and Ridley (2008), most typically associated with professional ethics. I have previously criticised this conceptualisation of ethics as being a misguided and potentially doctrinaire distraction from professional ethics education (Campbell, 2008a; Campbell, 2008b). Most of the participants had experienced some version of social justice education, and while some referred to it in connection to ethical issues in a general sociological sense, most were clear in distinguishing it from professional ethics and the moral dimensions of teaching as they are addressed in this chapter.

The third thematic category of experiences in teacher education that the participants described as being ethically educative relates to situations they witnessed in schools during the practice teaching or clinical/practicum components of their programmes. In fact, most believed that they encountered moral and ethical issues in teaching within this context more than any other. While some referred to an occasional positive example of teachers being caring and fair, respectful and attentive to the cognitive and emotional well-being of their pupils, alarmingly, most accounts overwhelmingly illustrate unethical classroom practices of their supervising teachers and other experienced practitioners in schools. This is not to suggest that there may not have been many more unreported experiences of a positive nature that students simply did not necessarily recognise as 'ethical' practice. On the other hand, unethical lessons are often far more obvious and easy to identify. The most illuminating lessons the participants learned as student teachers were negative lessons – shocking examples of often taken-for-granted daily practices such as 'teachers gossiping about students and their families, treating students unfairly, engaging in dishonest assessment practises, subverting school policies, neglecting students as well as curricular expectations, disparaging colleagues and administrators, and publicly frightening, ridiculing, or embarrassing students' (Campbell, 2008a, 12). Participants who spoke of such negative occurrences relied on their own intuitive moral and ethical sensibilities to identify them as wrong, unprofessional and unethical; they did not recall aspects of their formal teacher education that would lead them to such a judgement.

Some of the more disturbing stories the participants recounted reflected levels of negligence and cruelty that defy the perception of teaching as a moral profession. One spoke of an elementary teacher who disciplined a student by sticking the boy's lollipop, which he had brought to class against the rules, to his forehead and making him sit still with it attached for the duration of the class: 'and everybody in the class laughed and laughed, and he just let them laugh at the kid. It was unreal ... and then he told the other teachers in the staff room afterwards and they were laughing too'. Another spoke of an experienced kindergarten teacher who yelled at and humiliated children every day, played games of favouritism and neglected others; her comments to the student teacher included public references to a little girl who seemed quite needy ('If I hear her whiney little voice any more I'm going to wring her neck'), a child with autism ('Why waste your time? He's an idiot, he's never going to be anything but a burden on society'), and an English as a second-language student who, according to the student teacher, 'spoke not one word of English and she [the teacher] never even acknowledged him. She would just shake her head and say "he's slow, he's so slow" and she never modified the curriculum or accommodated him once.'

The participants who recounted such practical experiences were clearly alarmed by them, as well as by their own feelings of powerlessness to defend the students and speak out against such treatment. Furthermore, their moral outrage at what they knew to be unethical conduct was never addressed or harnessed in a positive way to help cultivate the ethical knowledge they would need as teachers who at some future point might have to face similarly unethical teachers as colleagues. On the contrary, in their programmes they were taught a lesson that is hard to see as anything but a corruption of the idea of collegial 'professionalism', as they were advised by faculty instructors to keep quiet, go along with whatever the supervising teachers did, and never 'break ranks' with colleagues.

The participants in my study confirm what the research literature has been arguing for some time – that professional ethics in teaching is a neglected area of formal study in many faculties of teacher education. In addition, the examples of what they did learn implicitly or haphazardly are of highly questionable benefit in contributing to enhanced ethical knowledge. As well as being indicative of a missing foundation, this gap also raises understandable doubts that, during their initial preparation, teachers are being primed to reflect on how the choices they make, the actions they take, the language and attitudes they adopt, have moral and ethical significance on a daily basis. From the routine, even mundane, exchanges in classrooms and schools to more extreme and challenging situations that confront teachers with practical dilemmas, conceptualisations of professional behaviour inevitably rely on the teacher's well-honed moral and ethical judgement. It does not appear that teacher candidates, at least those involved in my project, had much opportunity to cultivate such judgement, or develop their ethical knowledge, during their induction into the profession.

Teacher Education as Too Late and Too Early

Although many of my study's participants claimed that they would have wanted greater exposure to the moral and ethical complexities in teaching by way of explicit instruction in professional ethics, some also expressed resistance to a stand-alone course on the topic, especially if it were too philosophical or theoretical at the expense of studying practical and experientially based case studies. They also questioned whether it would ultimately be effective as a way of cultivating what is discussed here as ethical knowledge. As one teacher candidate said:

> I see a lot of lack here in this area [professional ethics], but I also feel it needs to come from within first, and then we need to be exposed and maybe trained to hone it better, I guess. But unless I am ethical and believe that integrity is something that I need to stick to, I don't think that any amount of faculty training is going to help me get there.

So if ethical knowledge, as a kind of professional wisdom, does not come from formal education – especially if it consists of abstract, philosophical and theoretical ideas or superficial exposure to rules, codes, laws and regulations – from where does it come? The participants were quite assertive in claiming that professional ethics is a matter of personal character and 'common sense', a term quite a few participants used, that is developed by virtue of life experiences, family upbringing and teaching experience gleaned over the years once one joins the profession. They seemed to regard professional ethics as an extension of general ethics that are cultivated during the formative years of one's development. If they are correct in this assumption, and the related hope that many expressed that teachers are naturally good people, then this would suggest that by the time student teachers arrive at a faculty of education, it is too late to exert any notable influence on the moral and ethical sensibilities they will bring to their practice as teachers. However, many scholars have pointed out that professional ethics in teaching, while essentially inclusive of core moral principles such as fairness, integrity, honesty, compassion, courage and patience, also extends beyond these to reflect what some call professional virtues, as well as competence and service ideals rooted at least partly in the principles of beneficence, non-maleficence, justice and autonomy (Haynes, 1998; Lovat, 1998; Sockett, 1993).

It is hoped that experience enhances one's awareness of professional virtue, and hence augments ethical knowledge. Indeed, ethical knowledge is experientially based, in terms of enabling conceptual and practical connections to be made between abstract virtues or moral principles and the particular details of one's own professional behaviour and conduct. However, there seems to be ample evidence that experience alone cannot be assumed to lead to enhanced ethical knowledge, or indeed to better behaviour (Campbell, 2003; Colnerud, 1997; Tirri, 1999).

None the less, most of the participants expressed the hope, if not the assumption, that despite their lack of formal ethics education in their pre-service programmes, a clear understanding of professional ethics would emerge once they got out on their own into schools and became more experienced teachers. Indeed, some argued that knowledge of the ethical dimensions of teaching depends on such experience, and could not likely be gleaned beforehand. Consequently, the conclusion to be drawn is that the point at which student teachers are enrolled in their pre-service programmes is too premature, too early to expect them to develop a keener sense of the ethical dimensions of teaching. How can they know these until they actually experience them for themselves? Practice teaching and other clinical components offer some valuable reference points, but the real learning takes place once they enter their own classrooms and are responsible for their own students. Many participants believed that it is at this point that ethical awareness and professional judgement are fostered. A second-year new teacher, reflecting on her teacher education programme as compared to what she had learned since graduation, summarised what many participants claimed:

> I think maybe it's probably only over the last couple of years that I have really started thinking about, am I being really fair with the kids? ... I don't know if at that point [teacher education], ethics are something teachers are thinking about. Do they think about what it means to be ethical? I think not, because at that point they haven't been put into situations where their ethics were tested. It's only when you teach a couple of years and you're put into situations where you really need to think about whether you are treating a student in the most fair manner, whether or not you are completely professional in speaking to a colleague, whether or not you are professional speaking to a parent. So, it's hard to teach ethics that no one has really applied yet.

The belief that the lack of student teachers' practical experience in classrooms necessarily restricts the capacity of teacher education programmes to address the ethical dimensions of teaching practice, combined with a kind of unproven faith in the inherent goodness and intuitive moral judgement of the teacher candidates themselves, creates a clear tension and a rather perplexing paradox. Expressive of a 'too late, too early' sentiment, it regards the cultivation of moral and ethical judgement as occurring *before* one enters a teacher education programme, as a result of one's early upbringing, and then complemented by practical professional experiences garnered *after* one graduates from a teacher education programme. The apparent conclusion to be drawn thus renders teacher education irrelevant to the development of professional ethics and ethical knowledge.

Yet such a conclusion contradicts not only an obvious consensus in the scholarly literature, but also a 'commonsense' assumption that professional preparation programmes are exactly the correct context for initiating students into an appreciation of the moral and ethical dimensions, standards, complexities and responsibilities they will face in their future careers. After all, being an ethical person does not automatically guarantee that one will become an ethical professional. An intuitive moral sense is naturally important. However, professionals need to cultivate their ethical knowledge by recognising and making practice-based connections between conceptual perspectives on ethics or virtues and the intricacies of the practitioner's work itself, knowledge of which is not necessarily intuitive. And if we wait until teachers are more experienced before provoking them to consider the ethical nature of their own practice, it may be that they have become socialised by the norms of their colleagues and schools, and become too well versed in behaving in a certain way to change. Experience does not suffice. Professionals need to evaluate this experience through the lens of ethical awareness and make difficult judgements about their own intentions and actions.

Conclusion

It is truly unfortunate that the tendency in teacher education programmes is to miss the so obvious opportunity to engage students in the ethical imperatives that will define their own professionalism. I do not accept that the tension or paradox discussed above justifies the continued negligence of our discipline. We should therefore not abandon the idea of making teacher education the pivotal context for the initial cultivation of ethical knowledge. We just need to approach this challenge in a more focused, deliberate, direct and consistent way. A concentrated and intentional attempt on the part of teacher education programmes is needed, not simply to teach abstract versions of professionalism, but also to demonstrate vividly how moral and ethical judgement and sensitivity, combined with a rigorous understanding of relevant standards and underlying theoretical principles, are played out in the actual details of practice. This is how to initiate the cultivation of ethical knowledge in teaching.

While I have believed in the value of integrating and embedding such lessons in professional ethics and the moral dimensions of teaching across the teacher education curriculum, I am no longer confident that such an approach on its own can be trusted to achieve adequate pedagogical goals in this area. While, ideally, integrative attention to professional ethics could still be woven through the programme, a more focused commitment to explicating this important topic as being 'foundational' is necessary as well. This commitment could take the form of a separate course on ethics or a specific unit carved into a mandatory component of the programme with obvious connections to examples of 'real life' practices in teaching. A clear pedagogy should be applied (case study analysis seems to be a favoured instructional method to engage student interest), and student teachers should be evaluated in some form on their understanding. We should not assume that ethics, and by extension professional ethics, is a matter of intuitive judgement that teachers as inherently moral people will come to appreciate and apply on their own once they become experienced practitioners. If teacher education programmes neglect to make professional ethics education an intentional and central aspect of their curricula, then they will continue to miss a significant opportunity to try to influence the collective ethical knowledge of the profession.

References

Ayers, W. (2004), *Teaching the Personal and the Political: Essays on Hope and Justice*, New York: Teachers College Press.

Beyer, L.E. (1997), 'The moral contours of teacher education', *Journal of Teacher Education*, 48(4), 245–54.

Bok, D. (1988), 'Can higher education foster higher morals?', *Business and Society Review*, 66, 4–12.

Bull, B. (1993), 'Ethics in the Preservice Curriculum', in K.A. Strike and P.L. Ternasky (ed.), *Ethics for Professionals in Education: Perspectives for Preparation and Practice*, New York: Teachers College Press, 69–83.

Buzzelli, C.A. and Johnston, B. (2002), *The Moral Dimensions of Teaching: Language, Power, and Culture in Classroom Interaction*, New York and London: Routledge Falmer.

Campbell, E. (2003), *The Ethical Teacher*, Maidenhead: Open University Press/McGraw-Hill.

—— (2008a), 'Preparing Ethical Professionals as a Challenge for Teacher Education', in K. Tirri (ed.), *Educating Moral Sensibilities in Urban Schools*, Rotterdam: Sense Publishers, 3–18.

—— (2008b), 'Teaching Ethically as a Moral Condition of Professionalism', in L. Nucci and D. Narváez (ed.), *The International Handbook of Moral and Character Education*, New York: Routledge, 601–17.

Carr, D. (2000), *Professionalism and Ethics in Teaching*, London: Routledge.

Colnerud, G. (1997), 'Ethical conflicts in teaching', *Teaching and Teacher Education*, 13(6), 627–35.

Haynes, F. (1998), *The Ethical School*, London: Routledge.

Jackson, P.W., Boostrom, R.E. and Hansen, D.T. (1993), *The Moral Life of Schools*, San Francisco, CA: Jossey-Bass.

Johnson, W.B. and Ridley, C.R. (2008), *The Elements of Ethics for Professionals*, New York: Palgrave Macmillan.

Joseph, P.B. (2003), 'Teaching about the moral classroom: Infusing the moral imagination into teacher education', *Asia-Pacific Journal of Teacher Education*, 31(1), 7–20.

Lovat, T.J. (1998), 'Ethics and ethics education: Professional and curricular best practice', *Curriculum Perspectives*, 18(1), 1–7.

Nash, R.J. (1996), *'Real World' Ethics: Frameworks for Educators and Human Service Professionals*, New York: Teachers College Press.

Richardson, V. and Fenstermacher, G.D. (2001), 'Manner in teaching: The study in four parts', *Journal of Curriculum Studies*, 33(6), 631–7.

Simon, K.G. (2001), *Moral Questions in the Classroom*, New Haven, CT and London: Yale University Press.

Slattery, P. and Rapp, D. (2003), *Ethics and the Foundations of Education: Teaching Convictions in a Postmodern World*, Boston, MA: Pearson Education.

Sockett, H. (1993), *The Moral Base for Teacher Professionalism*, New York: Teachers College Press.

—— (2006), *Teacher Dispositions: Building a Teacher Education Framework of Moral Standards*, Washington, DC: American Association of Colleges of Teacher Education.

Strike, K.A. and Ternasky, P.L. (1993), *Ethics for Professionals in Education: Perspectives for Preparation and Practice*, New York: Teachers College Press.

Tirri, K. (1999), 'Teachers' perceptions of moral dilemmas at school', *Journal of Moral Education*, 28(1), 31–47.

Part II

The Personal and Affective Dimension of Professional Engagement

6 Virtue, Character and Emotion in People Professions: Towards a Virtue Ethics of Interpersonal Professional Conduct

David Carr

Professions and Professional Values

While such terms as 'profession', 'professional' and 'professionalism' are implicated in a fairly tangled and unruly web of usage (see Carr, 1999; Carr, 2000), it is conceptually prudent to observe some rough distinctions. To begin with, whereas to characterise a task as 'professionally' executed may mean that it conforms to certain occupational standards, to describe an individual as a 'professional' may just mean that they get paid for what they do. But one should also beware of taking the term 'professional standards' to mean 'standards of a profession' – since we may talk of the high professional standards of a plumber or joiner, without supposing that plumbing or cabinet making are professions, or for that matter, of the lack of professional standards of such members of time-honoured professions as lawyers or general practitioners. Broadly speaking, whereas the adjective 'professional' is a general term of normative appraisal – so that the conduct of any human occupation might be described as 'professional' or 'unprofessional' – the term 'profession' refers more to a particular category of human occupation.

But then what kinds of human occupations are professions, and what kinds of professional standards are appropriate to them? While this partly

97

depends on the kinds of occupations in question – so that while law would presumably require legal expertise, surgery would need surgical skills – I have previously argued that occupations commonly referred to as 'professions' are generally enmeshed in certain levels of moral principle often also defined or embodied in codes of ethical conduct. This does go some way towards distinguishing professions from those trades and other services to which ethical rather than technical or commercial standards may not always apply: thus, someone may well be described as a *good* builder or plumber, even though they do not do business in a particularly fair or honest way. Indeed, it would seem that even where commercial enterprises do operate according to ethical codes, such codes may only be extrinsically related to business practice: it may be the primary concern of so-called 'ethical' consumer services to increase profit rather than to deal fairly. On the other hand, there is a good case for regarding the ethical obligations of medicine and law – to promote the health or legal rights of patients or clients – as *intrinsic* to such occupations. This would be irrespective of the malpractice of particular doctors or lawyers, or even the shortcomings of entire medical or legal institutions and systems: thus, there may appear to be something not just personally but professionally objectionable about doctors who would be willing to leave patients to suffer or die because they stood to profit financially by offering preferential treatment to richer patients.

To be sure, this aspect of professional obligation may also be deontologically construed in terms of something like Kantian moral *duty* (Kant, 1948). On this view, a duty or obligation to meet the relevant needs of clients would or should be central to the professional values or standards of members of such professions as medicine or law. Indeed, something like Kantian deontology would appear to make reasonably good sense of key aspects of professional ethics – notably those that enjoin universally equitable treatment from practitioners. However, in so far as the traditional professions such as medicine and law are implicated in the provision of such fundamental conditions of human flourishing as health or freedom from oppression or ignorance, it seems appropriate to think of general healthcare, due process and education as universal human *rights*, and of general practitioners, lawyers and teachers as therefore morally and professionally *obligated* to recognise and satisfy such rights. On the other hand, it makes less sense to talk of a client's right to a meal in an expensive restaurant or to a Rolls-Royce car, and it is not obvious that salespersons should feel obligated to supply a motor car to someone who cannot pay for it. On this view, withholding a car from someone who cannot pay for it would not make someone a bad car salesperson, but there would seem to be a very real sense in which any doctor who deliberately withheld aid from the destitute and suffering – for reasons of profit or personal advantage – would be less than a professionally good doctor. Much the same would seem to apply, *mutatis mutandis*, to teachers, nurses, social workers or ministers.

Such universal obligation, however, is also commonly expressed in terms of the idea of *impartial* treatment or of treating others without, as it were, fear or favour. While this may not be equivalent of treating others exactly alike, it is certainly often understood (in something like Kantian terms) to imply treating patients or clients *impersonally*. Thus, it will be said, to reveal one's personal feelings or (worse still) individual preferences in professional contexts is to be partial in one's dealing with them, and hence to conduct oneself unprofessionally. But this may seem to raise problems for some occupations often referred to as professions, such as ministry, teaching, nursing, social work and counselling. To be sure, the professional status of such occupations has often been subject to qualification by the use of such terms as 'people profession', 'semi-profession' or 'vocation' (see, for example, Etzioni, 1969). That said, such vocations or people professions would appear nevertheless liable to the same impartiality requirements as other more commonly recognised professions. In this regard, 'professionally exemplary' teachers would seem to be those who treat pupils impartially – which might also appear to mean with some personal detachment – rather than those who allow personal considerations or relationships to influence their professional judgements or decisions.

Personal and Affective Dimensions of 'People Professions'

The problem which this chapter addresses is that while there would appear to be something like a *prima facie* obligation to such detached or disinterested professional impartiality in the case of such 'people professions' as teaching, social work, nursing and religious ministry, there would also appear to be a deep sense in which really good teachers, nurses, ministers, social workers and so on precisely *are* those who are able to engage in relationships with pupils, patients and clients in a more *personal* – in the sense of emotionally committed – way. Of course, there are obviously proper and improper ways of so engaging. In the case of all professions or occupations charged with the care of vulnerable or immature persons – such as teaching, social work or nursing – there are modes of personal relationships or association that are acknowledged to be abusive or exploitative. While this has not always been recognised as well as it might have been – for example, in the case of teaching, where harsh physical and psychological punishment and humiliation were formerly much inflicted in the name of authority and discipline – a very much finer point has certainly been put on the professional inappropriateness of such practices in recent days. So latter-day professionally trained practitioners of teaching, social work or ministry can have little excuse for failing to appreciate that physical or psychological cruelty or the sexual abuse of pupils, parishioners or clients are quite beyond the professional pale to the point of actual suspension or dismissal.

The more difficult question for such professions is that of how to determine the extent of professionally legitimate personal concern for pupils, patients, parishioners or clients, when – to the purpose of promoting the educational, social, spiritual or other flourishing of such constituencies – knowledge of their personal circumstances may have a distinct bearing on satisfactory professional treatment, or such interest or concern may well seem an occupational requirement. Indeed, the general problem here is not only that we should want good teachers, social workers, priests or whatever to be wise, caring, compassionate, sympathetic and empathetic – as well as honest and just – individuals, but that even professional honesty and justice – at least in the realms of 'people professional' practice – are not well captured in the terms of impartiality construed as impersonal or emotionally detached distribution or prescription. As Aristotle (1941b) said of the virtue of justice: it may be no less unjust to treat unequals equally than to treat equals unequally. At the very least, if a teacher wants to do justice to each pupil in his or her class, it may be that this is not a matter of treating all pupils alike. Again, it is not merely that he or she may properly recognise a professional need to give more time or attention to this (less or more able) pupil than to that (more or less able) one, but that a certain degree of warmth or familiarity may seem to be more justified towards this insecure or under-confident child than to that over-confident one. Likewise, ministers or social workers are likely to find that different levels or qualities of personal association are required for dealing satisfactorily with differently placed parishioners or clients.

Thus, the theoretical problem would appear to be that the received predominantly deontological ethics of professional duty or obligation and client or consumer rights does not do adequate justice to the professional practice of such 'people professionals' as social workers, priests and teachers, even if it does much justice to the actual practice of members of such standard professions as medicine and law. In the first place, deontological ethics inclines to the expression of ethical values and principles in terms of fairly rigid and inflexible rules, laws or prescriptions enjoining agents *always* to do X or to avoid doing Y. It cannot, of course, be reasonably doubted that universal prohibitions or imperatives have a significant part to play in any ethical system. So if (as Aristotle says) adultery is always and everywhere wrong, one might no less hold (in any code of professional ethics) that humiliation or sexual abuse of pupils or other clients are always and everywhere wrong. But it is doubtful that *all* the qualities and dispositions that we would want to attribute to professional or other moral association may be formulated in terms of such rules. However, secondly, there would appear to be an affective dimension or component to many of the qualities of moral association that are important to the practice of 'people professions' that is deliberately ruled out of court on Kantian and other deontological or duty-based conceptions of ethics or moral association.

On the one hand, then, although good teachers or social workers may well be those who should feel obligated to address the needs of all in educational or social need, such service cannot be simply a matter of disinterested distributive justice – of ensuring that individual pupils or clients are given neither more nor less attention than others according to some general rule of equal treatment. While it is expected of any satisfactory educational or social service that pupils or clients receive the quality of attention that is peculiarly suited to their needs and interests, such professional attention seems to need a level of personal and interpersonal association sufficient to determine such interests and needs: to know what pupils or clients really need in terms of satisfactory professional provision, practitioners need to get to know them in something like personal terms. However, as each and every personal association has its own peculiar emotional chemistry, the affective or emotional dimensions of professional response will vary accordingly. In this light, any adequate ethics of teaching or social work practice would have to do justice to the emotional dimensions of practitioner-client association – and, to be sure, to offer some means of evaluating such dimensions.

The Ethics of Care

One influential perspective on a professional ethics that focuses directly on the affective or emotional dimensions of moral agency of so-called 'care ethics'. There are in fact many different versions of care ethics: indeed, since care ethics is often reluctant to engage in much clear self-definition, distinctions between care ethics and other ethical positions are prone to unhelpful blurring. Still, on what are widely regarded as defining statements of this view, it has certain key features. The first is the claim that genuine moral or ethical responses are grounded in human affective or emotional rather than cognitive or rational life or experience. From this viewpoint, care ethicists have been inclined to draw inspiration from such philosophers in the 'sentimental' ethical tradition as Hume (1969), rather than from such modern rationalists as Kant (though there may be more rapprochement, given a shared focus on benevolence, with utilitarianism). A key moment of care ethics occurred with the publication of Carole Gilligan's (1982) critique of the even more influential neo-Kantian work of the American psychologist of moral development and education Lawrence Kohlberg (1984). Kohlberg's work was criticised for precisely elevating an essentially deontological account of morality as justice – focused on an exclusively cognitive grasp of moral principles – that deliberately sidelined such apparently affective components of moral response as caring and compassion.

Secondly, it should be emphasised that care ethicists have often – like Hume and his 'emotivist' successors (see Ayer, 1967; Stevenson, 1944) – taken a rather dim view of the place of reason in moral life, and it may not be misleading to characterise much care ethics as a form of 'non-cognitivism' or precisely in more recent terminology 'sentimentalism'. (For recent discussion of relations between care ethics, sentimentalism and other ethical positions such as virtue theory, see the essays by Slote, Noddings, Darwall and others in Curren, 2010.) According to this view, excessive concern with principles of justice – with the rigorously fair distribution of goods and services – may not necessarily enhance and may even serve to impede the kind of positive human association we ought to call moral. It is not that reasonably fair distribution of goods is of no importance to care ethicists, but the moral import of such fairness is not to be located in the universalised prescriptions of individual rational agents or the imposed rules of institutions, but in a more general climate of positive attachment in which, if all goes well, individual agents and institutions are implicated. Thus, for many care ethicists (for example, Noddings, 1984; Noddings, 2002), care and concern are not usefully regarded as personal virtues, individual rational capacities or institutional imperatives, but rather as morally positive qualities of institutions, practices or association: they are properties or qualities of 'ethos' rather than individual agency or capacity. As Noddings (2002, xiii) has said: 'Care ethicists depend more heavily on establishing the conditions and relations that support moral ways of life than on the inculcation of virtues in individuals.' Figuratively speaking, such qualities lie at the heart of moral agency, whereas principles are merely – as it were – of the head.

A third feature of care ethics in the hands of its key advocates is that it has been generally inclined to a *gendered* interpretation of care. The burden of Gilligan's work – evidently influenced by a proto-care ethics of psychoanalytical feminism (see, for example, Chodorow, 1978) – was that Kohlberg's (1984) empirical research on moral development was heavily weighted in favour of male responses. It therefore failed to take into account the very different responses to moral dilemmas of girls who, because of their own very different developmental histories, place much more moral weight on relationships and emotional attachments to others than upon general moral rules and principles. While this gendered interpretation of moral responses is not uncommon in care ethics, it is, however, liable to rather different interpretation and evaluation in the work of different care ethicists. Gilligan (1982) seems to have been inclined (as indicated by the title of her book *In a Different Voice*) to a rather dualist reading of the so-called evidence of different patterns of development – on which view, there would just be different male and female conceptions of morality based (respectively) on principle and attachment. But other care ethicists (especially Noddings, 1984) have been inclined to argue for the greater truth or validity of a so-called feminine ethics of attachment over any male ethics of rule or principle. According to this view, the core ethical project would be presumably to encourage caring attitudes and dispositions rather than observance of moral principles in all would-be moral agents, irrespective of gender.

There can also be no doubt that care ethics has been regarded as highly relevant to professional development – particularly in those 'people professional' contexts in which personal relationships are obviously of particular occupational significance. Indeed, given that the main contribution of the influential care ethicist Nel Noddings has been to educational philosophy, her application of care ethics to issues of the professional training of teachers and the institutional contexts of schooling is hardly surprising. Once again, however, it should be emphasised that Noddings's care ethics focuses not so much on the development of care as a particular professional virtue or rational capacity that might enable individual practitioners to practice care on or towards others. For Noddings, caring is a more general feature of positive human association, and also a morally reciprocal quality or relation. From this viewpoint, it is something that ought to constitute an entire institutional climate or ethos (such as schooling, medical care or social service), and caring for others is actually neither more nor less important than being cared for by others. Thus, in so far as the general position admits of clear articulation, good professional teachers, social workers or nurses would be those who are able to accommodate their practice to some such general climate of professional care and contribute positively to the enhancement of such a climate.

All this, however, obviously raises particular issues about how this might be done, as well as more general questions about care ethics as such. To begin with more general issues, we might first ask what should be made of any gendered interpretation of care ethics. On the one hand, while the idea that morality comes in not one but two versions does at least do justice to the suspicion that moral responses may be grounded in either principle or affect, reason or emotion, there is clearly something unsatisfactory about any idea of one moral convenience for gents and another for ladies. To say that affect is a central feature of moral response would imply that this is just as important for males as females. Indeed, this is presumably the point of those care ethicists who have argued for the moral superiority or greater truth of care ethics over a principled ethics of justice. But this raises questions, at least on those care ethical accounts that are clearly distinguished from other propriety brands of ethics, about the stiff resistance to principles (of distributive justice and so on) that one often finds in key statements of this view. In short, much mainstream care ethics inclines to a moral particularism involving strong denial of the relevance of universal or general rules or precepts to moral life and association. (For contemporary examples of such particularism, see Dancy, 1993; Dancy, 2004.) On this view, circumstances that call for caring responses are highly context-dependent and seldom (if at all) of a kind that might be subsumed under predetermined rules: what is instead called for is a kind of intuitive sympathy or empathy that is more emotionally attuned to the particularities of this or that situation.

While such ethical particularism does not directly entail moral emotivism or non-cognitivism – since particularists may also be moral realists who take moral perceptions or judgements to be cognitively grounded – it may combine with the emotivist tendencies of care ethics to form a potentially lethal subjectivist cocktail. If the moral responses of care ethics are located mainly or exclusively in affective rather than cognitive states and such states cannot even in principle rely for guidance on general moral rules or principles – since moral responses are inevitably linked to this or that situation – then the criteria for deciding that a given caring response is appropriate rather than inappropriate in any circumstance would seem hard to discern. We may well feel sympathy or care for a particular distressed patient or pupil, but what would tell us whether that sympathy is well-grounded or well-measured in this or that situation? We may well agree that it is important to display some degree or level of care or sympathy in professional contexts in which we are dealing with distressed clients, for those incapable of such feeling would hardly be fit to do the job; but it could also be that excessive care or sympathy – construed as unrestricted affective attitudes – might do more harm than good in a teaching or nursing context.

It should not be supposed here that *no* kind of reason is available to caring or other sentimentalist agents or practitioners: on the contrary, the arch-sentimentalist David Hume had a clear concept of reason as 'the slave of the passions' (Hume, 1969, 462). Reason, for Hume, could be used in the service of passion to help the passionate satisfy their passions. However, the key point is that such reasoning would be the instrumental reasoning of morally extrinsic significance, rather than the principled reasoning of intrinsic moral value. Since, on a Humean or other sentimentalist view, moral states are states of affect rather than cognition, they are not *themselves* liable to rational appraisal or justification. Whereas it may therefore be possible to work out in the light of practical reason how such states might be satisfied, reason offers no basis upon which such states of affect might be appraised or judged as morally appropriate or inappropriate. Indeed, such evaluation would depend upon the kind of principled moral reflection towards which care ethics has often appeared so unsympathetic.

Virtue Ethics: Reconciling Principle and Feeling

It might now be suggested that since we cannot account satisfactorily for moral life in terms of either an ethics of principle or an affective ethics of care taken separately, we might look rather to an ethics of principle *and* affect. In that case, might one not attempt to combine the emphasis on principle of a Kantian or Kohlbergian ethics with the emphasis on the emotional attachment of care ethics? Despite the surface appeal of some such strategy, however, it has evident problems. From the side of principle, it is clearly a difficulty that a Kantian or Kohlbergian deontological ethics is not only an ethics of general or universal principle, but that it explicitly regards feelings and emotions as quite morally or ethically irrelevant: judgements based upon feeling rather than rationally established moral precepts or rules simply do not qualify as moral judgements. So although we might admit that the caring of care ethics requires a rational dimension, or that some moral reasons may have general or universal force, it does not seem that a deontological ethics readily accommodates recognition of the affective or particularistic dimensions of moral association. The same applies, *mutatis mutandis*, to any ethics of care that rejects the universal rules or principles of deontological ethics. Ethically speaking, the general difficulty is something like that of trying to combine the moral theories of Hume and Kant – which are plainly in some opposition to each other.

In fact, what is clearly needed is a moral theory – including a theory of professional ethics – that is able to reconcile the affective or emotional with the rational or principled dimensions of moral life and association and that avoids the unhelpful opposition of these implied by both deontological and care ethics. The main features of such a view are, I believe, to be found in the ethics of Aristotle (1941a) – revived in recent times under the heading of 'virtue ethics'. Aristotelian ethics has clearly a place for both feeling or emotion and reason or rational judgement – in both universalistic and particularistic forms – but not as deontological and care ethics construe these. First, Aristotelian or virtue ethics takes the side of care ethics in regarding emotion and emotional attachment – when appropriately developed or cultivated – as morally relevant. In this regard, Aristotle seems at odds with Kant, for whom agency motivated by feeling rather than principle can never count as moral. For Aristotle, a person could not count as, for example, generous or compassionate without appropriately formed feelings of concern or compassion. But while this might seem to bring him closer to Hume, for whom moral action can only be driven by feeling or emotion rather than reason, morally relevant affect needs, for Aristotle, to be properly informed or *cultivated*. So, whereas Hume opposed affect to reason (as the 'slave of the passions'), Aristotelian passion or emotion in the context of moral life and association is itself necessarily rational or cognitive.

Thus, if it is agreed that there can be no complete or coherent account of moral life and association (or of professional ethics) that does not have a place for human feeling and emotion, it should be clear that such an account still requires a *cognitive* theory of emotion – for it is only in such terms that it is possible to see how morally relevant feelings may be educated, refined or cultivated. Such an account plays a central role in Aristotle's (1941a) *Nicomachean Ethics*, and it avoids the modern opposition of reason to feeling, or 'cognition' to 'affect', that seems to overshadow the ethics of both Hume and Kant as well as their various sentimentalist, deontological and care ethical heirs. However, it should probably be said here that Aristotle (and perhaps before him Plato) appears to distinguish between *affect* – the natural and pre-rational states of fear, anger and pleasure of non-human brutes and pre-rational humans – and the *emotions* of rational agents experienced as so-called 'intentional' states. On this view, while emotions are grounded in pre-rational affect – and have therefore a distinct feeling dimension – they are also invariably directed on or cognisant of states of affairs in the manner of judgements or evaluations: thus, anger is usually anger *at* … (this or that offence); fear is fear *of* … (such and such danger); pride is pride *in* … (this or that personal achievement). Indeed, it is mainly in terms of such 'intentionality' – rather than any accompanying physical feelings – that emotional states are identified and distinguished. (For modern cognitive theories of emotion, see Bedford, 1957; Kenny, 1963; Peters and Mace, 1962; Peters, 1963; Nussbaum, 1997; Solomon, 1983; Solomon, 1988.) But it is also by virtue of such intentionality that emotions are educable: it is only in so far as emotions involve judgements or appraisals that one can come to consider them right or mistaken, appropriate or inappropriate, or come to refine or adjust them accordingly.

Thus, while Aristotle is in agreement with care ethics that affective pro-attitudes are essential components of anything worth calling moral engagement or association, such attitudes require rational (cognitive) ordering for the proper development of that virtuous character that he takes to be the main aim of moral life. For Aristotle (1941a), indeed, the cultivation of character is the prime target of moral development, since he is inclined to hold that rather than virtuous agents being those who perform independently established right actions, correct moral actions are those that a truly virtuous agent may be expected to perform. However, the Aristotelian view is basically that moral virtues are more or less equivalent to states of emotion, feeling or appetite ordered in accordance with some deliberative ideal of practical wisdom (Carr, 2009). For Aristotle, then, proper caring could not be just a general quality of positive climate that characterises some associations and institutions – for, on the face of it, the very formation or fostering of such associations or climates surely requires deliberate effort on the part of agents who have cultivated the rational capacity for caring as an individual moral virtue. As a moral virtue, moreover, caring would have to be practised – as Aristotle is himself inclined to put it – at the right times, with reference to the right objects, towards the right people, with the right motive, and in the right way. In short, even if an absence of caring may be considered to be a general defect of human relationships or institutions, there are likely to be wrong or inappropriate no less than right or appropriate ways of expressing, exhibiting or exercising caring or other virtues.

Varieties of Virtuous Principle and the Importance of Character

Inevitably, any such normativity of virtue needs to be determined by appeal to rational principles of one sort or another. Aristotle, like care ethicists, recognises that many if not most of the judgements of virtuous agency are bound to be particularistic in the sense of requiring sensitivity to the peculiar features of particular moral context. Thus, the main principle that for Aristotle governs the exercise of *phronesis*, or practical wisdom (the guiding intellectual virtue of human moral life) – his so-called principle of the *mean* – is one that allows the virtuous agent considerable room for deliberative manoeuvre. Basically, the doctrine of the mean serves to define virtuous conduct only as a mid-point between unacceptable excesses or deficits of emotion. So to begin with, as noted, there could be no virtue of caring in the absence of caring affect or emotion. But, on the other hand, there may be inappropriate excess as well as deficiency of care or sympathy, therefore virtuous agents need to ensure that they are behaving thus or so towards people at the right time, with the right motive, in the right way, and so on. But how might this be determined? Aristotle believes, with most other moral theorists persuaded of the role of reason in moral life and association, that there are objective considerations of human weal and woe that are sufficient to ground general or even universal judgements of moral right or wrong. Thus, for example, he explicitly holds that although an agent may sometimes have to deliberate how to express a given virtuous emotion, there can be no deliberating when, where or with whom to commit adultery, for adultery is *always* wrong.

In this regard, as already noted, there will be certain definite limits on caring conduct – especially in professional contexts. Thus, fairly obviously, even if a schoolteacher or social worker genuinely and deeply cares for a pupil or client, there are limits – usually expressed in professional codes of ethics – to which any natural human expression of such care would be deemed acceptable in professional or other contexts. These are obviously also related to considerations of justice as fairness. For even though Aristotle (1941b) argued that the virtue of justice could not be reduced to treating different people in the same way, he was also clearly aware that distributive justice is a major cornerstone of social and political order, and that therefore any virtuous unequal treatment of others could not be consistent with conduct motivated by fear or favour. So even though good teachers may recognise that this particular deprived, demoralised and vulnerable child – at this particular time in this particular class – may need more of their care, sympathy and attention than that secure, confident or self-assured one, such unequal treatment could not be justified if based on personal preference for the former or it entailed serious disadvantage to the latter. Thus, caring teachers need at all times to reconcile judgements of particular local need with considerations of wider common good and social justice.

In sum, while modern professional and other ethics of deontic principle have rightly acknowledged the significant role of moral rules in human life, and care ethics has recognised the importance of the affective or emotional dimension, it is arguable that only (neo-Aristotelian) virtue ethics offers a satisfactory account of the interplay of (universal and particular) moral reflection and emotion in human conduct – and, by implication, in professional conduct. Essentially, this account is couched in terms of the idea of virtue as moral character: as such, the virtues of character are equivalent to states of emotion, feeling or appetite ordered in accordance with that deliberative capacity to which Aristotle refers as *phronesis*, or practical wisdom. Moreover, this Aristotelian concept of character may be regarded as the vital missing ingredient not only in the deontic ethics of principle and more recent ethics of care, but in any and all other latter-day accounts of professional ethics. In recent years, indeed, it has been common to reduce this or that notion of professional conduct largely to a combination of the mastery of repertoires of technical occupational competence and the observance of professional regulations expressed in terms of obligations and prohibitions. This has often fatally missed what I have argued elsewhere (Carr, 2007) lies at the heart of professional development – and this is precisely the development of character. Indeed, I have previously argued that many of the qualities that have often been regarded as technical skills or competences in the professional literature – such as class management in the case of teaching – are in fact better construed as qualities of character. In short, to whatever extent teachers, nurses, ministers, social workers and counsellors may require skills, it is the cultivation of virtues such as courage, temperance, justice and wisdom that really lie at the heart of exemplary professional conduct, and it is virtue ethics which gives the best available account of these and of how these may be cultivated.

References

Aristotle (1941a), 'Nicomachean Ethics', in R. McKeon (ed.), *The Basic Works of Aristotle*, New York: Random House, 927–1,112.
—— (1941b), 'Politics', in R. McKeon (ed.), *The Basic Works of Aristotle*, New York: Random House, 1,113–16.
Ayer, A.J. (1967), *Language, Truth and Logic*, London: Gollancz.
Bedford, E. (1957), 'Emotions', *Proceedings of the Aristotelian Society*, 57, 283–304.
Carr, D. (1999), 'Professional education and professional ethics', *Journal of Applied Philosophy*, 16(1), 33–46.
 (2000), *Professionalism and Ethics in Teaching*, London: Routledge.
—— (2007), 'Character in teaching', *British Journal of Educational Studies*, 55(4), 369–89.
—— (2009), 'Virtue, mixed emotions and moral ambivalence', *Philosophy*, 84(1), 31–46.
Chodorow, N. (1978), *The Reproduction of Mothering: Psychoanalysis and the Sociology of Gender*, Berkeley, CA: University of California Press.
Curren, R. (ed.) (2010), 'Symposium on Sentimentalist Moral Education', *Theory and Research in Education*, 8(2), 125–97.
Dancy, J. (1993), *Moral Reasons*, Oxford: Clarendon Press.
—— (2004), *Ethics Without Principles*, Oxford: Clarendon Press.
Etzioni, A. (1969), *The Semi-professions and their Organization: Teacher, Nurses and Social Workers*, London: Collier-Macmillan.
Gilligan, C. (1982), *In a Different Voice: Psychological Theory and Women's Development*, Cambridge MA: Harvard University Press.
Hume, D. (1969), *A Treatise of Human Nature*, Harmondsworth: Penguin.
Kant, I. (1948), *Groundwork of the Metaphysic of Morals*, trans. H.J. Paton as *The Moral Law*, London: Hutchinson.
Kenny, A. (1963), *Action, Emotion and Will*, London: Routledge and Kegan Paul.
Kohlberg, L. (1984), *Essays on Moral Development*, vol. I, New York: Harper & Row.
Noddings, N. (1984), *Caring: A Feminist Approach to Ethics*, Berkeley, CA: University of California Press.

—— (2002), *Educating Moral People: A Caring Alternative to Character Education*, New York: Teachers College Press.

Nussbaum, M.C. (1997), 'Emotions as Judgements of Value and Importance', in P. Bilimoria and J.N. Mohanty (ed.), *Relativism, Suffering and Beyond: Essays in Memory of Bimal K. Matilal*, Oxford: Oxford University Press, 231–51.

Peters, R.S. (1963), 'Reason and habit: The paradox of moral education', in W.R. Niblett (ed.), *Moral Education in a Changing Society*, London: Faber and Faber.

—— and Mace, C.A. (1962), 'Emotions and the category of passivity', *Proceedings of the Aristotelian Society*, 62, 117–42.

Solomon, R. (1983), *The Passions: The Myth and Nature of Human Emotion*, Notre Dame, IN: Notre Dame University Press.

—— (1988), 'On emotions as judgements', *American Philosophical Quarterly*, 25, 183–91.

Stevenson, C.L. (1944), *Ethics and Language*, New Haven, CT: Yale University Press.

7 Some Aristotelian Reflections on Teachers' Professional Identities and the Emotional Practice of Teaching

Kristján Kristjánsson

Teachers of Morality – Moral Teachers

Aristotelianism has exerted a powerful influence on moral education during the last quarter of a century. So pervasive has this influence been that two of the most popular trends succeeding Kohlberg's developmentalism are avowedly Aristotelian in origin: *character education*, based broadly on the tenets of virtue ethics, and *social and emotional learning*, derived from the concept of emotional intelligence. Devout Aristotelians, and I include myself among them, may grumble that those trends have rushed off too quickly in their own home-made directions. Character educationists seem at times to be overly concerned with the inculcation of a body of set traits, but too little concerned with the development of critical moral wisdom (*phronesis*), and EQ (emotional intelligence) theorists typically fail to heed Aristotle's warning that emotional competence without moral depth is the mere calculated cleverness of a knave. Nevertheless those two approaches have unleashed an unprecedented interest in practical methods of moral education that clearly deserve to be labelled 'Aristotelian': moral habituation, sentimental education, service learning and the emulation of moral exemplars (see Kristjánsson, 2007).

People sometimes speak of the 'moral dimension of teaching'. In so far as that concept refers to the teaching of morality, then, whether directly (through special classes in such areas as 'moral education', 'citizenship education', 'life skills') or indirectly (by conducting oneself as a moral exemplar to one's students), Aristotelianism has become one of the guiding lights of educational practice. There is, however, another understanding of the 'moral dimension of teaching' that has less to do with didactic moral considerations than with morality in a more basic sense: with the *moral teacher* rather than with the *teacher of morality*. Teachers engage daily in interactions with other persons within their school walls: colleagues, administrators, students, parents. Irrespective of the example they set to their students by the way they behave – critically important as that is – there are surely independent reasons why any good teacher would want those interactions to satisfy the requirements of morality: reasons that have to do with general moral duties to others, professional duties, and last but not least, duties to oneself (in striving to flourish as a human being). It is a matter of some surprise and disappointment that Aristotelianism has not informed recent discussions on this facet of the moral dimension of teaching to the same extent as it has informed the didactic one (for a notable exception, see Carr [2000] and Hansen [2001]). In what follows, I concentrate on teaching-related examples; for Aristotelian influences in other people professions, see, for example, Banks (2006) in social work and Armstrong (2006) in nursing. Before analysing the discursive situation, it is in order to begin with a short illustrative example: the story of 'Runner Fan'.

In the aftermath of the Sichuan earthquake in China on 12 May 2008, many stories of individual heroism emerged. Especially heartening were the stories of brave, selfless teachers using their bodies to protect students as classrooms collapsed around them. One of them, teacher Tan, was found dead with four students alive, shielded under him. In glaring contrast to those tales of heroism was the story of teacher Fan Meizhong – a story he told unrepentantly after the earthquake. As the tremors began, 'Runner Fan', as he came to be known, yelled 'earthquake', abandoned his students and ran for his life. No thanks to Fan, none of the students were hurt. In subsequent interviews, Fan explained that there were no formal legal or ethical obligations on teachers to sacrifice their lives for their students in such situations. He would have sacrificed himself for his one-year-old daughter, Fan argued, but it would be totally unrealistic to expect him (or any normal person) to do the same for what was merely a group of students in a classroom. What upset many people was not so much the act of running away, which Fan could have done spontaneously in the panic of the moment. Rather, they were offended by his relentless insistence that this had been the right thing to do, and the fact that he did not regret his decision. Fan's defiant stance provoked a spate of replies, and for weeks blogs in China and all over Asia were flooded with divisive responses to his argument (Datong, 2008).

Among Asian educators, reflections on Fan's story quickly evolved into discussions of more abstract topics such as the notion of professional versus personal duties and the emotional burdens that the profession of teaching places upon its practitioners. Indeed, this story connects well to at least two recent discursive traditions in education, concerning 'teachers' professional identities' (see, for example, Beijaard et al., 2004) and the 'emotional practice of teaching' (Hargreaves, 1998). My previous comments on the lack of Aristotelian insights referred precisely to the discursive situation that I rue within those two traditions. Not only has the relevant literature been driven by concerns that often neglect the moral dimension of teaching in general and Aristotelian moral theory in particular, but both traditions have become saddled with a dominant paradigm that I consider at once theoretically questionable and practically unwholesome. I call it the *constructivist-cognitive paradigm*, and take serious exception to it in what follows. One must be careful about terminology here, however. By 'constructivist', I am referring not to a plausible if somewhat trite didactic constructivism (according to which teaching is most effective when it connects to students' existing knowledge structures), but rather to a form of anti-realist epistemological constructivism. Similarly, by 'cognitive', I do not mean the sense invoked in such locutions as 'cognitive theories of emotion' (in which the cognitive is also meant to embrace *hot* sentiments), but rather 'cognitive' as narrowly understood to denote *cold* mental processes that exclude the affective.

Prior to further elaboration, two caveats must be entered. The first and more obvious is that my discussion will necessarily touch upon an accumulation of things, not all of which can be accorded full justice in this chapter. I refuse, however, to let those limitations soften the challenging stance that I wish to take. The second caveat is that my aim is not to offer a full-blown Aristotelian alternative to the constructivist-cognitive paradigm. I have a more modest aim: to pave the way for such an alternative and offer some suggestions as to its outcome by exposing the weaknesses of the dominant paradigm. In any event, I hope that my exploration reveals how the problematics of both issues – the professional identities of teachers and the emotionality of teaching – change as we examine them through an Aristotelian lens.

Professional Identities and Selfhood

'Professionalism' has been a buzzword in educational discourse since the mid-1980s. With the idea of teachers' professionalism came the notion that it was tied to certain operationalisable standard-based skills or competences (see, for example, Burke, 1989), and that those skills would have to find their way – through systematic teacher education or through the consciousness-raising of practicing teachers – into the professional identities of teachers. Truly expert teaching was suddenly all about identity development and dedication to continuing self-improvement.

Although the emphasis on standards and measurable outcomes tended to include suggestions about the adoption of ethical codes of practice, by which practitioners were formally instructed, among other things, to allow the interests of their 'clients' (read: students) to come before those of their colleagues, many theorists complained that the so-called professional reforms had reformed much of the moral life out of teaching. Some critics suggested that the language of professional competences was not really applicable to the moral dimension of the teaching practice (Hansen, 2001); others argued that if competence-talk were to be made applicable to the whole of that practice, it should better incorporate moral concerns (Fenstermacher, 1990). Yet others ventured to claim that the notion of the professional teacher should be equated with that of the moral teacher (Sockett, 1993; Carr, 2000; Campbell, 2003). Following those wake-up calls, it seems to have become more widely accepted of late that excluding the moral dimension from teacher professionalism is unadvisedly restrictive, and that professional identities cannot be understood in isolation from moral identities. In general, the professionalism literature regarding teachers and other professionals is becoming more ethically sensitive, and even virtue-oriented (see, for example, Maxwell's (2008) book on compassionate empathy as a professional ideal).

Even if this literature has gradually been relieved of its 'moral problem', a deeper conceptual problem remains. In their extensive meta-analysis of studies during 1988–2000, Beijaard et al. (2004) found the very concept of professional identity to be enveloped in a fog of confusion. Either it was not defined at all, or merely given an un-argued-for stipulative definition. No clear or shared sense of a teacher's professional identity emerged. In the research they reviewed, it tended to be assumed that teacher education would have to begin by exploring the 'teaching self', but whether or not that 'self' was the same as 'identity' remained an enigma. The studies that offered any characterisation of the core concept seemed to rely on an anti-realist notion of a socially constructed self. Within that self – or rather, that constructed identity – we are told, lurked many sub-identities, among which was that elusive professional identity as one voice in a multiple-identity chorus.

How is this sub-identity constructed, then? 'Through narration' was the typical answer found in this meta-analysis: by living out and telling stories about oneself as a teacher (see, for example, Connelly and Clandinin, 1999). No particular epistemological reasons for this answer appear to have been forthcoming. One can guess from subsequent sources, however, what they probably would be: narratives are the only means of understanding teachers' identities because there is no objective truth 'out there' (or, for that matter, 'in here') for us to comprehend. Truth is, in any case, 'a floating value, akin to a swirl'; but in making subjective sense of the chaos of experience, teachers, among others, contrive coherent-like stories about themselves which, in turn, produce their identities (Day and Leitch, 2001). Postmodernists such as Zembylas have a field day with such creation stories: The idea of a singular, stable and permanent selfhood is an Enlightenment myth. People partake in various power-structured language games, however, in which they create their own locally articulated, locally recognised, fleeting, fractured, contextual and multiple identities – or such identities are created for them (Zembylas, 2003b). Ironically, Zembylas thinks that identity-formation can and should have a moral goal: resistance – the struggle to free oneself from subjection. But given the Foucauldian assumption, with which Zembylas whole-heartedly agrees (Zembylas, 2003a), that all aspects of a people's lives are subject to disciplinary formation and that no 'true self' exists underneath all the masks and facades, the clarion call for 'freedom from subjection' does little more than remind us of the postmodernists' penchant for shooting themselves in the foot.

There is good reason to take stock here and pursue a miniature history of ideas. First of all, narrativism about selves is not a single theory. There are at least three distinct versions of it: the hard anti-realist postmodern version that understands 'storied accounts' of identity as feeble and essentially invalid attempts to make sense of truth in 'a swirl'; a soft anti-realist version, according to which storied self-accounts are valid in so far as they satisfy the epistemological conditions of coherence and believability, and a realist version, which claims that narration is the underlying structure of selfhood and that identity stories are valid to the extent that they correspond with this actual structure. Therefore, simply positing that teachers' professional identities are narratively constructed does not help to solve the underlying conceptual problem of what such identities really are. In order to resolve that dilemma, we must come to grips with the notoriously intractable debate between self-realists and self-anti-realists. For the former (such as Aristotle, 1985), selves actually do exist, comprising our deepest traits and commitments. Obviously, identities or constructed self-concepts also exist, but they are either true or false. When they are true (by capturing the self), we possess self-knowledge; when they are false (by missing the self), we are-self-deceived. For self-anti-realists (such as Hume, 1978, Book I; he modifies his position in Book II), no actual selves exist. What we call 'selves' are simply identities or self-concepts: our beliefs about who we are and what we are.

This is not the place even to begin a comprehensive rebuttal of anti-realism (see further in Kristjánsson, 2010). In fact, it must be admitted that Hume marshals some convincing arguments against the notion of substantive realist selfhood – while wanting to preserve the notion of the 'soft' realist self of everyday experience. Although there is something to be said for the view that Hume's scepticism about hard self-realism does not get the better of him, there is nothing to be said for the view that the postmodernists' Hume-on-steroids version of anti-realism does not get the better of them. Unfortunately, it is the latter that seems to have taken captive the discursive tradition on teachers' professional identities – when that tradition actually addresses rather than merely shirks the question of what such identities are. But postmodern anti-realism does not only set ordinary experiences of selfhood utterly at nought, it is unable to make any coherent sense of the difference between self-knowledge and self-deception.

What would be the main ingredients in an Aristotelian paradigm of professional identity? The first observation would be that as important as identities or self-concepts are, actual selfhood is more important. To be sure, one's self-concept does not simply describe and interpret the self without influencing it. Just as noticing a blemish on your face in a photograph may induce you to remove the blemish from your face rather than merely airbrushing it from the photo, so the projection of one's self-concept may prompt one, consciously or unconsciously, to recast any of one's core traits or commitments. In that sense, the identity-construction of teachers is a worthy object of inquiry. But in the end, what matters is that teachers' selves are in order – that they have the proper traits and commitments – not merely that they want to have them, or assume that they have them. The second ingredient, Aristotle would argue, is that one's selfhood and emotions are intimately linked; I return to that point in the following section (see also Kristjánsson, 2010). Third, Aristotle would abide by the 'one-self-to-a-customer' rule (Flanagan, 1996). Each person has one self. Truly multiple selves exist only in pathological cases. Some of the core commitments of teachers' selves will concern their profession. We can refer to those as their 'teacher selves', if you like, although it is slightly misleading, and to their beliefs about those commitments as their 'teacher identities'. Moral persons will seek morally grounded consonance among (a) their various commitments, among (b) their various beliefs about those commitments, and between (a) and (b). The tool that we have at our disposal to do just that – and to resolve any remaining dilemmas – is *phronesis*. That is basically what *phronesis* is for. The upshot is that it is futile to study teacher selves or teacher identities in isolation. What matters is how they fit into a person's moral character and resonate with one's overall life plan. The Aristotelian message, then, can be nothing short of proclaiming that the currently dominant epistemological constructivism obscures the goals of identifying and influencing teachers' professional identities, and that it does disservice to all those engaged in that endeavour.

The Emotional Practice of Teaching

Even for advocates of the claim that the professional teacher must be a moral teacher, the role of emotions in the moral life has not always taken hold. In her otherwise enlightening account of the moral dimension of teaching, for instance, Campbell harps on the idea that teachers' moral knowledge is demonstrated through their *actions* and classroom *behaviour*, and that such knowledge is 'necessarily action-oriented' (Campbell, 2003, 139). In the detailed subject index of her book, there are no entries for 'emotion', 'feeling' or 'affect'. It is no wonder, perhaps, that emotions were virtually absent from the mainstream educational literature before the 1980s, as they were from the mainstream moral philosophy literature. The Aristotle-inspired revival of emotions in recent mainstream moral philosophy, however, has taken some time to find its way into educational discourse. Maybe the tenacity of Kohlberg's Kantian formalism, which influenced whole generations of teacher educators, is to blame. In any case, one is more likely now than before to come across handbooks for teachers making bold claims like: 'People often talk as though emotions should be banned from the teaching relationship. Impossible. Emotions are at the heart of [it]' (Wilson, 2004, 30). Notably, this quotation is taken from a book on 'the emotional business of teaching and learning' (Wilson, 2004, 1).

Zembylas (2003a) writes about three 'waves' in the introduction of emotions into educational discourse. The first wave was that of the teacher burnout literature of the 1980s. Theorists suddenly became alert to the fact that teaching, as well as many other 'people professions', involved hard emotional labour, the burden of which constituted the typical reason given for early exits from these professions. It is not as if this realisation came as a bolt from the blue; but after the invocation of scientific measurements of experienced burnout (see especially Maslach and Jackson, 1981), folk wisdom about the effects of long-term emotional stress was finally incorporated into a theoretical framework. Among the key indicators of burnout in human service institutions, including schools, turned out to be 'emotional exhaustion' (frustration, stress and fatigue) and its resulting 'depersonalisation' (evidenced as self-dehumanising cynicism and callousness). Every teacher has a story to tell: the hurt produced by spending hours preparing stimulating materials, only to have them sabotaged by a handful of disrupters (Wilson, 2004, 31); the feelings generated by an expectation that the distinction between personal emotions and public image in the classroom must be erased (see various examples in Nias, 1989); the price of maintaining the appearance of a cheerful and enthusiastic professional while worrying about a critically ill mother (Day and Leitch, 2001, 411). Such examples can, of course, be multiplied many times over.

The burnout literature focused on personal emotional strain and the adverse effects of emotional labour. The second wave of research on teacher emotion widened the perspective to include the sociological aspects of emotion. I am referring here to the literature sparked by Hargreaves's seminal article on the 'emotional practice of teaching' (Hargreaves, 1998). We must not overemphasise personal factors (private origin, individual responsibility) when gauging teachers' emotions, Hargreaves argued, for such an approach aggravates guilt and increases burnout. Rather, we should understand emotion as an institutional factor: part of the structure of the job. The sources of teachers' specific emotional vulnerabilities are not to be sought inside their heads, but in the policy measures and complex professional relationships that create an impact on their work (see Kelchtermans, 2005). Think here of all the strict curricular requirements that must be met and the fearful 'school inspections'; the policy-makers' constant demands for change; the steady increase in administrative responsibilities and paperwork; the constant lack of time, certainty and emotional space (see Wilson, 2004, 30–33). But we should also remember that emotional labour can be 'pleasurable and rewarding – when people are able to pursue their own purposes through it' (Hargreaves, 2000, 814).

The most notable contribution of the sociological approach was probably its helpful conceptualisation of the emotional landscape. Concepts help to structure thought; and in Hargreaves there is no shortage of new frameworks of thinking. Apart from the notions of (a) 'emotional practice' and (b) 'emotional labour', which he fleshes out in some detail, there is also the notion of (c) 'emotional geographies of schooling' (referring to the specific 'spatial and experiential patterns of closeness and/or distance in human interactions' within schools; Hargreaves, 2000, 815) and that of (d) unique 'emotional understanding'. One of the defining features of Hargreaves's sociological approach emerges in explaining (d). Emotional understanding differs from cognitive understanding, because emotions are essentially non-cognitive (Hargreaves, 1998, 840; Hargreaves, 2000, 815). Cognitive reflection can help us to guide and moderate emotion (Hargreaves, 2000, 812) – control it, if you like – but emotions constitute affects, not beliefs or judgements. When we are captured by strong emotions, it is the emotional mind that swamps the rational mind (Day and Leitch, 2001, 406). Schools should, as much as possible, be structured in such a way that this does not happen.

Non-cognitivism is common in psychological natural-kind approaches to emotion. So is the notion that emotions can be divided according to their 'valence' into positive (read: pleasant) and negative (read: painful). When we feel bad, we are in the grip of negative emotions – and the good life is life with as few of these emotions as possible. It is not clear whether Hargreaves accepts this characterisation, but in subsequent works influenced by the sociological approach, it is rife: 'If teachers cannot feel good about themselves in the classroom,' Wilson remarks, 'there is little chance of them being able to cause pupils to feel good about themselves.' Moreover, 'negative emotions may have a malign effect on teacher–pupil relationships' (Wilson, 2004, 31). Changing the emotional structure of the school is tantamount to diffusing the channels of potentially negative emotions (Wilson, 2004, 151).

Zembylas (2003a) writes about the postmodern movement as the third wave in research on teacher emotion, and is a vocal representative of that movement. He faults the burnout literature for its myopic personal perspective, and the sociological literature for reifying existing school structures and taking them for granted, while overlooking the causes of emotion in reigning political ideologies and oppressive power relations. He does not even hesitate to state that previous approaches have done 'little to improve our knowledge about teacher emotion' (Zembylas, 2003a, 121). What, then, is the postmodern approach to emotion? Zembylas unpacks it into four assumptions (Zembylas, 2003b, 110): First, emotions are not private, universal or passive experiences ('the Aristotelian view'), but rather public, local and active discursive practices. Second, power relations are inherent in 'emotion talk', and shape the expression of emotion. Third, by using emotions, one can create sites of social and political resistance. Fourth, emotions are embodied (corporeal and performative). According to this view, teachers' emotions 'are not internal states, but … are about social life' (Zembylas, 2004, 187). More specifically, they are about social life inside the school as it plays out power structures inherent in society. Emotions may either help or hinder teachers in constructing strategies of resistance and self-formation; the postmodern route would be to try to overcome the hindrances.

Now, what would Aristotle say about those three approaches? I am not sure he would have much to say about the first approach – which is essentially descriptive rather than normative – except to acquiesce to its insights: To be sure, emotional labour can be difficult, and teaching is rarely easy. As to the sociological approach, Aristotle would condemn the restrictive cognitivism underlying the dualism of cognition (or reason) and emotion: of head and heart. The fact that an issue is emotionally loaded, stemming from the 'heart', does not mean that it disrupts the governance of the 'head'; rather, emotions can be properly thoughtful, just as thoughts can be properly felt. Hargreaves relegates emotions to the status of such mere feelings as toothaches or palate pleasures. Aristotle does not deny that emotions incorporate painful and/or pleasant affects, but he notes that they also incorporate cognitions – beliefs or judgements – and rather than different 'feels' setting them apart, they are set apart by different cognitive consorts. A teacher does not become angry with students without warning, but only because he or she believes that they have done something inappropriate. Even more unsettling for Aristotle would be the idea that a teacher's emotional repertoire should be developed so as to maximise pleasant emotions and minimise painful ones. Surely some of our most valuable and morally worthy emotions are painful (compassion with those in need, for instance), and some of our most despicable ones are pleasant (*Schadenfreude*, for example)?

I gather that Aristotle would be baffled by the postmodern approach, as expounded by Zembylas. In any case, it hardly requires an Aristotle to notice that Zembylas's four 'assumptions' about emotions are little more than a collection of misconceptions and platitudes. First, emotions *are* private 'internal states', in the sense that they are psychological processes that happen to individuals. By rejecting this fact and claiming instead that emotions are 'about social life', Zembylas is confusing the location of the emotion with its intentionality ('aboutness'). True, when a teacher feels angry with her students, the anger is *about* the students, but the emotion is still inside her. Moreover, one needs to do no more than pick up an ancient tragedy or a novel written in another country to realise that emotions such as anger, jealousy or pride are universal rather than local. And the view that emotions happen to passive sufferers – which Zembylas ascribes to Aristotle, and rejects – was not Aristotle's view at all. Admittedly, if a teacher has allowed an emotional disposition of excessive anger to grow within, he or she may not be able to control bouts of episodic anger. But Aristotle had a proactive view on the cultivation of emotional dispositions: In the end, it is within the power and the responsibility of each individual to develop the proper dispositions of that kind.

Second, Zembylas's point that power relations shape 'emotion talk' is true, given a typically bloated postmodern conception of power according to which any attempt at control of, or influence on, another person constitutes an exercise of power. But its truth then also becomes trivial. The angry teacher may succumb to the power of disruptive students and try to control them with angry shouting. But has anyone ever denied the claim that all occurrences of emotions are reactions to some outside influence, and are themselves attempts to influence some states of affairs? Zembylas's third assumption is also platitudinous. To be sure, one can create sites of social and political resistance by using emotions; Aristotle's main discussion of emotions was even set within his treatment of political rhetoric. Against whom, then, is this assumption supposed to be directed? The behaviourism inherent in Zembylas's fourth assumption is strangely old-fashioned. It is true that the body is normally used to express emotions. However, well-known experiments with subjects completely paralysed by curare have shown that these subjects can experience intense emotions. More mundanely, every teacher has surely had the experience of being angry in class but succeeding in hiding their emotional state from students. Thus, why can anger not be non-performative?

Just as in the previous section on teacher identity, I do not work out an alternative Aristotelian paradigm of teacher emotion. Suffice to say that Aristotle's focus is on emotions as enduring states of character. As such, emotions constitute virtues or vices that comprise one's selfhood. An emotional virtue is not policed by reason, but infused with reason. And when emotional virtues conflict, the moral agent relies on *phronesis* to adjudicate the conflict (see Kristjánsson, 2007, ch. 2). Applying those general insights to teachers' emotions in particular obviously requires more work than I can undertake in this chapter. In any case, it should already be patently clear to readers why Aristotelians will reject approaches to teacher emotion that consider emotions essentially as non-cognitive thrusts – or worse still, as localised social capital exchanged by anguishing postmodern bodies. Moreover, it should be clear that if the discourse about teachers' identities is really about their selfhoods, as Aristotelians claim, and selfhoods are essentially constituted by emotions, as they also claim, then the two discourses that have been canvassed in this chapter are actually, in the end, one and the same discourse: What is the good life of a person – who in this case happens to be a teacher – and how should it be lived?

Concluding Remarks

To see anything like an Aristotelian approach required for understanding teachers' professional identities and teachers' emotions, one must, of course, have become dissatisfied with other, current, approaches. I hope to have given readers reason to be dissatisfied with some such approaches. Consider finally again the story of Runner Fan. A *constructivist* analysis of his reaction would focus on the putative conflict between his personal and professional identities – with both being seen as 'voices' in a chorus of multiple constructed identities. A narrowly construed *cognitive* approach would see him as having become overpowered by the emotion of fear as a non-cognitive thrust. A *postmodern* approach would consider him to be an unfortunate actor in ubiquitous power relationships.

In contrast, an Aristotelian analysis of the story would focus on the teacher's self rather than his identity (let alone identities) – and on possible emotional dissonances within that single self. It would look for the beliefs and judgements underlying Fan's fear and his lack of emotion with regard to his students. It would subject these emotions to moral scrutiny with the aid of *phronesis* – notably not *phronesis* as mere intuitive artistry, but as an intellectual virtue guided by general moral truths as well as situation-specific observations (Kristjánsson, 2007, ch. 11; see also Carr, 2000, 167). Aristotelians would seek congruence between professional and personal values, and not hesitate to pass judgement on the moral rightness or wrongness of emotional reactions. Rather than understanding teaching as a unique practice with its own independent set of norms and rules, Aristotelians would generally be ready to concur with Campbell's view – provocative as it may seem in our fractured times – that professional morality is nothing but the extension of everyday morality into the nuances of professional practice (Campbell, 2003, 12).

References

Aristotle (1985), *Nicomachean Ethics*, trans. T. Irwin. Indianapolis, IN: Hackett Publishing.

Armstrong, A.E. (2006), 'Towards a strong virtue ethics for nursing practice', *Nursing Philosophy*, 7(3), 110–24.

Banks, S. (2006), *Ethics and Values in Social Work*, Basingstoke: Palgrave Macmillan.

Beijaard, D., Meijer, P.C. and Verloop, N. (2004), 'Reconsidering research on teachers' professional identity', *Teaching and Teacher Education*, 20(2), 107–28.

Burke, J.W. (ed.) (1989), *Competency Based Education and Training*, Lewes: Falmer Press.

Campbell, E. (2003), *The Ethical Teacher*, Maidenhead: Open University Press.

Carr, D. (2000), *Professionalism and Ethics in Teaching*, London: Routledge.

Connelly, F.M. and Clandinin, D.J. (1999), *Shaping a Professional Identity: Stories of Education Practice*, London, ON: Althouse Press.

Datong, L. (2008), 'China: After the quake, the debate', <http://www.opendemocracy.net/article/china-after-the-quake-the-debate> (accessed 25 March 2011).

Day, C. and Leitch, R. (2001), 'Teachers' and teacher educators' lives: The role of emotion', *Teaching and Teacher Education*, 17(4), 403–15.

Fenstermacher, G. (1990), 'Some Moral Considerations on Teaching as a Profession', in J. Goodlad, R. Soder and K. Sirotnik (ed.), *The Moral Dimensions of Teaching*, San Francisco, CA: Jossey-Bass, 130–51.

Flanagan, O. (1996), *Self-expressions: Mind, Morals, and the Meaning of Life*, New York: Oxford University Press.

Hansen, D.T. (2001), 'Teaching as a Moral Activity', in V. Richardson (ed.), *Handbook of Research on Teaching*, Washington, DC: American Educational Research Association, 826–57.

Hargreaves, A. (1998), 'The emotional practice of teaching', *Teaching and Teacher Education*, 14(8), 835–54.

—— (2000), 'Mixed emotions: Teachers' perceptions of their interactions with students', *Teaching and Teacher Education*, 16(8), 811–26.

Hume, D. (1978), *A Treatise of Human Nature*, 2nd edn, ed. L.A. Selby-Bigge and P.H. Nidditch, Oxford: Clarendon Press.

Kelchtermans, G. (2005), 'Teachers' emotions in educational reforms: Self-understanding, vulnerable commitment and micropolitical literacy', *Teaching and Teacher Education*, 21(8), 995–1,006.

Kristjánsson, K. (2007), *Aristotle, Emotions, and Education*, Aldershot: Ashgate.

—— (2010), *The Self and Its Emotions*, Cambridge: Cambridge University Press.

Maslach, C. and Jackson, S.E. (1981), 'The measurement of experienced burnout', *Journal of Occupational Behaviour*, 2(1), 99–113.

Maxwell, B. (2008), *Professional Ethics Education: Studies in Compassionate Empathy*, Dordrecht: Springer.

Nias, J. (1989), *Primary Teachers Talking: A Study of Teaching and Work*, London: Routledge.

Sockett, H. (1993), *The Moral Base for Teacher Professionalism*, New York: Teachers College Press.

Wilson, D.F. (2004), *Supporting Teachers, Supporting Pupils: The Emotions of Teaching and Learning*, London: RoutledgeFalmer.

Zembylas, M. (2003a), 'Caring for teacher emotion: Reflections on teacher self-development', *Studies in Philosophy and Education*, 22(2), 103–25.

—— (2003b), 'Interrogating "teacher identity": Emotion, resistance, and self-formation', *Educational Theory*, 53(1), 107–27.

—— (2004), 'The emotional characteristics of teaching: An ethnographic study of one teacher', *Teaching and Teacher Education*, 20(2), 185–201.

8 On the Gender of Professional Wisdom

Liz Bondi

Introduction

Professions came into being as masculine domains. The traditional professions of the law, the clergy and medicine developed as self-regulating occupations that defined their own domains and controlled admission to their ranks (Berlant, 1975). They secured legal recognition and protection, and developed in tandem with the universities, through which access to the relevant degree programmes was managed. In these ways, both the state and higher education were integral to the constitution of these professions and to their maintenance as male preserves. Studies of women's subsequent entry into the traditional professions have shown how deeply and exclusively traits associated especially with nineteenth-century middle-class masculinity were inscribed within their values, ethos and forms of wisdom, which valorised individualism (especially heroic individual effort), objectivity, impartiality, impersonality, control and mastery (Davies, 1996; Glazer and Slater, 1987). The epitome of the nineteenth-century professional was an autonomous individual unfettered by personal concerns and entanglements, able to act on the basis of wholly detached, rational, dispassionate judgement. Such attributes accorded closely with nineteenth-century ideals of middle-class masculinity, and until the second half of the twentieth century, were deeply antithetical to ideals of middle-class femininity (Hall and Davidoff, 1987). In brief, professions were not merely male-dominated in their origins, but masculinity was deeply inscribed in their character and image.

During the twentieth century, the three classic professions were joined by many more as a range of occupations sought the status and prestige accorded to professions. In each case, this has typically entailed the development of voluntary membership bodies through which an occupational field is explicitly demarcated, standards of training and practice are codified, and discipline maintained. Having organised the field, at least some of these bodies then sought to secure statutory underpinning for authority over their various professional domains. In addition, the term 'profession' has been claimed by numerous occupations as a signal of coherence and quality, in the absence of any legally binding framework (Wilensky, 1964). The expansion and extension of the reach of professions has been accompanied by many other changes, including the erosion of their traditional exclusion of women.

If professions are somehow intrinsically masculine in their origins and character, does the entry of women into professional domains propel such women into the position of 'honorary men', or is that intrinsic masculinity being undone? Whatever the gender characteristics of the traditional professions, are attributes of one or other gender inscribed within newer professions, especially those numerically dominated by women, and if so, how? Is professional wisdom in general or in particular professions intrinsically gendered? This chapter seeks to begin the task of addressing such questions. It does not attempt to provide definitive answers, but rather to illuminate some ways of thinking about the gender of professions and professional wisdom.

Fundamental to my argument is an understanding of gender that differentiates between the categorising of human beings as men or women, and the assignation of the descriptors 'masculine' or 'feminine' to traits and characteristics that are culturally associated with, but not intrinsic to people's status as, men or women. The concept of 'honorary men' illustrates this differentiation: the woman who is described as an 'honorary man' is viewed as capable of performing in ways that might be viewed as 'masculine', but is clearly also still recognised to be a woman. So women and men can acquire or adopt attributes more typically associated with the opposite gender without changing their underlying gender. There may be benefits to doing so where the attributes are highly regarded or bring sought-after rewards, for example greater opportunity, prestige or salary. But there may also be costs, in the form of loss of these rewards, and very importantly, in ways more closely linked to gender identity. For example, the woman who works as a bricklayer may encounter numerous reminders that many view her as 'out of place', and she may find perceptions of her 'femininity' negatively impacted by her employment, while a man who works as a nursery nurse may find his occupational choice perceived as 'unnatural', whether under suspicion of paedophilia or as revealing him as somehow less male than would otherwise be the case. Thus, to distinguish between the designation of people as men or women and the cultural associations of gender is not to suggest that the two are unrelated. To complicate matters further, the dualistic form of the concept of gender, which categorises people or attributes into two discrete, non-overlapping either/or classes, is itself sometimes described as an intrinsically masculine way of thinking. In this chapter, I draw lightly on gender theory, through which such complexities have been explored in great depth, and use these ideas to illuminate some of the ways in which gender influences professional wisdom.

In the context of substantial changes in the range of occupations thought of as professions, I outline what is sometimes called the 'feminisation' of professional occupations, and explore some of its consequences, especially in relation to professional domains that might be construed as 'feminine' or 'feminised'. I begin by clarifying what is meant by, and differentiating between, various elements of the feminisation of professions, showing not only that women have become members of professions, but also that values and practices traditionally associated with women have become recognised components of professional work. One example of the latter form of feminisation is the contentious rise in importance attached explicitly to matters of emotion. Thus, while the idea that entry to professions should be equally available to women and men has become very widely accepted, this is less true of other forms of feminisation, which impact upon the character of professional wisdom. Against this background, I discuss how persistent or habitual aspects of gender influence the value attaching to different forms of professional wisdom. In this discussion, I do not distinguish sharply between professional skills and expertise on the one hand and professional wisdom on the other, preferring instead to view skills and expertise, as much as wisdom, and practices that require practitioners to exercise judgement in ways that are sensitive to specific cases and contexts.

The Feminisation of Professions 1: Demographic Trends

The term 'feminisation' covers several different processes. Demographically, it refers to a trend for an increasing proportion of whatever is subject to feminisation to be composed of women. In relation to professions, this has occurred in two distinct ways. First, women have entered the ranks of professions through the achievement of professional status by female-only or female-dominated occupations. One of the earliest such cases in the UK is that of nursing. As Anne Witz (1990, 1992) has shown, British nurses campaigned long and hard to secure the legal status of a profession, withstanding numerous setbacks before eventually achieving a state-sponsored system of registration governed by nurses themselves in 1919. Those who campaigned for nurse registration were insistent upon the importance of nurses themselves being in control of core aspects of the occupation of nursing, including such matters as the requisite standards and duration of nursing education, the specific domains of nursing practice and the conditions of nursing labour. Securing legally protected autonomy over such matters created a distinctively feminine domain of professional practice, in contrast to the masculinity of medicine and other professional domains. The domains are by no means equivalent, with the position of nurses remaining clearly subordinate to that of doctors, and the degree of autonomy, protection, status and prestige accruing to nursing markedly less than for medicine. For these reasons, nursing is sometimes referred to as a 'semi-profession' (Etzioni, 1969), as are several other female-dominated occupations such as social work and teaching.

The second way in which the masculinity of professions came under pressure demographically was through erosion of limitations on women's entry to the traditional professions and other professionalising occupations. Pioneering women entered the traditional professions in small numbers, sometimes masquerading as men, as in the case of James Barry, who is believed to have been born female but who entered medical training at the University of Edinburgh in 1809 as a man, qualifying in 1812 and practising as a doctor for some 50 years (Brandon, 2004). During the nineteenth century, others challenged the exclusion of women from professions by establishing professional schools or colleges specifically for women, and/ or by successfully securing admission to existing professional degree programmes as women. However, the number of women achieving entry through such means remained very modest. By the inter-war years of the twentieth century, access for women was beginning to increase, although many professions continued either to exclude women altogether or to limit admission to single women, ejecting them as soon as they married. Discrimination on the basis of sex continued to be legitimate until the introduction of sex discrimination legislation in the 1970s. Since then, the gender composition of entrants to at least some professions such as law and medicine has become more balanced.

Equalising the opportunity to enter education programmes required for admission to professions has not necessarily led to gender balance within the professions concerned. For example, while the medical profession overall has moved much closer to gender balance, substantial variations between specialisms remain, while nursing remains a female-dominated domain, albeit less so in the specialism of psychiatric nursing. Several newer professions such as teaching, psychology and social work, are also strongly dominated by women, but again, with variations by sub-field. Thus, probation work attracts a higher proportion of men than other strands of social work (Annison, 2007), and the teaching of young children is very strongly dominated by women compared to secondary school teaching (Drudy, 2008). Conversely, professions such as engineering and accountancy are strongly dominated by men.

The Feminisation of Professions 2:

Feminising Professional Practice

The continued gender imbalances found in the composition of many professions point to familiar and persistent associations between particular occupations and attributes that are culturally linked either to women or to men but which are not intrinsically determined by gender. The rise of nursing as a female profession complementing the maleness of medicine provides an early example of this association: while medical men mastered the book knowledge that enabled them to diagnose and treat using logic and scientific rationality, women adapted and applied their supposedly natural skills to tend and care for their patients. This preserved the contrasting ideals of masculinity and femininity associated with the nineteenth-century middle class. Similarly, the association between women and children readily carried over into primary or elementary school teaching. These associations account for other dimensions of the feminisation of professions, which relate to attributes and practices traditionally associated with femininity, rather than with women *per se*, and which may be undertaken by men. This feminisation is integral to many of the newer professions but also impacts on how the traditional professions are practised, points I will elaborate in turn.

Several of the professions (or semi-professions) that emerged during the twentieth century share with nursing and teaching a focus on working directly with individuals or families in ways that entail the delivery of welfare, care or nurturance of some kind. Examples include social work, occupational therapy, psychotherapy and counselling, and what became pastoral ministry (as distinct from those aspects of ministry that retained greater affinity to professions such as law in their focus on systematic knowledge of texts and doctrine). These occupations have come to be known collectively as 'caring professions', and many of the core skills, aptitudes and attitudes they require continue to be associated with femininity. In this sense, the feminisation of professions is not solely a demographic process, but is simultaneously a process through which the expertise and wisdom associated with professional status has incorporated activities and dispositions traditionally linked to women. The concept of 'caring professions' exemplifies this process. Caring for the young, the old and the sick has traditionally been regarded as women's responsibility, and the professionalisation of practices such as nursing, social work and primary school teaching has entailed securing recognition for such activities as economically valuable work for which practitioners are paid, and as work that requires the acquisition of specialist expertise, which is applied in an arena over which practitioners have a degree of autonomy (Abbott and Wallace, 1990).

The professional status of caring professions remains contested and insecure. Professionals in these arenas cannot conform to the traditional character of the professional as autonomous, detached and impersonal: they need to connect with, relate to and care about those with whom they work in distinctly personal and engaged ways. In addition, practitioners often have significantly less autonomy and control over their work than other professionals: their work is typically subject to considerable bureaucratic control, and in contrast to more prestigious professions (including academia as well as the classic professions of law, medicine and the clergy), they are often accountable to managers or supervisors who are not members of their own professions. Furthermore, one of the paradoxes of the professionalisation of care is that however much specialist expertise may be claimed, caring activity is always also undertaken by lay people (predominantly women) operating outside the realm of employment, let alone professional practices. Indeed, any attempt to define an area of caring work over which a monopoly can be claimed would segment the work so narrowly that its very attributes as 'caring' would be lost. Consequently, this element of the feminisation of professions is a complex process that changes the nature of what it means to be a profession, and that tends to militate against the high status and prestige associated with the traditional and traditionally masculine professions.

The account presented so far suggests that the feminisation of professions has at least in part created a new, less prestigious arena of professional practice in which traits associated with femininity have found a place. Within this arena of professional practice, wisdom and wise judgement are informed by activities, attributes and dispositions traditionally associated with femininity in their focus on attending personally to individuals in the context of their familial relationships. While women are now also able to enter the more traditional professions, just as men are able to enter the newer caring professions, on this account, these women and men are called upon to adopt and conform with norms, attributes and forms of wisdom associated with the opposite gender. This line of argument would help to explain tendencies observed in the distribution of women and men within professions. For example, men in female-dominated professions such as nursing and social work are more likely to be in specialisms that entail more contact with male service-users and that involve the use of 'harder' technical and control skills rather than 'softer' interpersonal skills, including, for example, psychiatric nursing and probation work (Lindsay, 2008; Warner and Gabe, 2008). It would also suggest that what I described at the beginning of this chapter as the profoundly masculine character of the traditional professions has remained largely untouched by the entry of women into their ranks. Certainly, some of the testimony of women in elite professions and in male-dominated environments would endorse this view (for example, Cree, 1997). However, it also underestimates some of the changes evident in high-status professions.

The incorporation of traditionally feminine activities into the domain of professional work through the creation of new kinds of professions (or semi-professions) is not the only change associated with professions to which non-demographic processes of feminisation may apply. The long-standing and high-status professions have themselves been subject to a variety of pressures, which have included extensive criticism of the way in which professionals have tended to conduct themselves in relation to their clients or patients. These professions have been called upon to reconsider their paternalistic assumptions and to develop more open, egalitarian and respectful ways of communicating with the people who consult them. In this context, a variety of 'people skills' have come to be valued more highly in the development of professional wisdom. Examples include the increasing emphasis placed on effective and sensitive communication skills in medicine (Pringle, 1998) and the rising profile of pastoral care within the responsibilities of teachers in higher education. While by no means identical to caring, these skills have also often been construed, or stereotyped, as feminine, at least in part because of the requirement to think about and attend to the felt experience of the other person. This suggests that what are often viewed as feminine attributes and forms of wisdom may be becoming significant labour market assets in prestigious professions (Lovell, 2000). Put another way, alongside the rise of the caring professions, other professions have become increasingly oriented to 'people' dimensions of what they do. Therefore, as well as feminisation occurring through expansion of the category of profession demographically and through the professionalisation of a range of caring occupations, it is also a way of describing trends in professional practice within the traditional core of professions.

Thus, alongside the entry of increasing numbers of women into established professional domains and the rise of new, female-dominated professions, feminisation has occurred through changes in the range of, and importance attaching to, activities and values within the ambit of professional practice. These changes call into question the idea that professional practice and wisdom continue to be intrinsically masculine in the sense of valorising the exercise of an individualistic style of rational judgement that implicitly devalues more collaborative, inter-personal and affective ways of being. They suggest instead that through the professionalisation of traditionally feminine activities associated with caring for and attending to others, together with the integration of people skills within professional practice, professional wisdom has changed in gender-inclusive directions. In due course, I will explore this suggestion further, but first I will consider some of the debates related to one theme in professional practice and wisdom that is itself strongly associated with femininity and feminisation, namely the increasing attention accorded to matters of emotion.

The Emotionalisation of Professional Practice

A range of 'people professions' – that is, professions in which practitioners have a primary focus on working with and for the benefit of individuals or families – attend at least to some degree to the subjective experience of those with whom they work and to subjective qualities of relationship between professional practitioners and their clients or patients. For psychologists, psychotherapists and counsellors, the subjective experience or personal distress of their clients is generally the central focus of the work itself. In other professional domains such as nursing, ministry, occupational therapy and child protection, key aims of the work may lie elsewhere, but attending to subjective experience is nevertheless often understood as integral to the exercise of professional judgement. For example, the wise professional, whether working as a nurse or a teacher, is constantly making judgements that take into account perceptions of the actual or potential feelings of those with whom they work.

The idea of an 'emotional turn' has been widely cited across diverse arenas of human life, and has generated divergent evaluations. For example, Squire (2001) describes public life as 'emotionalised' and offers an equivocal analysis of the consequences of feelings becoming increasingly central to politics and popular culture, while Berlant (2008) advances a more scathing analysis of the public circulation of sentimentality in the United States. In this context, it is not surprising that emotional dimensions of professional practice are attracting critical attention across a variety of professions, both as an expression of and a response to this wider 'emotional turn'. In varying ways, this attention includes consideration of the emotional experience of both those with whom professionals work and the professionals themselves. For example, in her analysis of expertise in nursing, Benner (2001) has argued that the ability of nurses to make emotional contact with patients can impact upon health outcomes. Her analysis draws on Goleman's (1996) concept of emotional intelligence, which has also been picked up in relation to social work practice (Morrison, 2007). While the concept of emotional intelligence focuses on the repertoires and abilities of individuals, other discussions of professional practice have utilised more sociological approaches that focus on the social and organisational cultures through which particular emotions or moods may be encouraged or discouraged. For example, Smith (1992) has drawn on Hochschild's (1983) concept of emotional labour to explore the emotional work undertaken by nurses in a variety of healthcare settings, while Boler (1999) offers a feminist analysis of the politics of emotions in educational contexts.

As with the increasing importance of emotions in public life, the rise in attention accorded to emotions in professional practice has generated a range of responses. For some, it is to be welcomed because it recognises what have always been crucial but too often ignored dimensions of what happens in the work that professionals do, the services that they provide and the experiences of those with whom they work (Carr, Chapter 6 in this volume; Goleman, 1996). In so doing, it enables reflection, analysis and interventions that seek to foster emotional well-being within professional practice (Orbach, Chapter 9 in this volume). However, others have expressed caution or even hostility. At the more hostile end of the spectrum, Furedi (2004) considers the attention paid to emotion to be an integral part of what he calls the cultivation of vulnerability, through which, he argues, people's sense of themselves and their lives is increasingly and very unhelpfully dominated by discourses of weakness, neediness, hurt and damage. According to Furedi's account, the growing emotionalism evident in public life and professional practice is intrinsically anti-rational in that it demotes rational analysis relative to emotional expressivism; individualising in that it emphasises unique individual experience at the expense of shared, collective interests; psychologising in its preoccupation with people's inner states; depoliticising because the emphasis on individual psychological experience detracts attention from social and political action, and infantilising in its encouragement of neediness and vulnerability. Furedi (2004) attributes emotionalisation to the development of what he calls a 'therapy culture', and comparable attacks on therapy as the source of a highly detrimental emotionalisation can be found in specific professional domains as in the case of Ecclestone and Hayes's (2008) argument about 'the dangerous rise of therapeutic education'. These accounts argue against the incorporation into professional wisdom of focused and sustained attention to the emotional experience of those with whom professionals work and to the emotional dynamics of relationships between professionals and those with whom they work.

More equivocal responses seek to chart a middle path, often by challenging ways in which emotion is conceptualised. For example, while emotion is often understood as inherently personal, psychological or neurobiological, arising within the embodied experience of individuals, a variety of sociological and anthropological accounts have elaborated how apparently highly personal feelings are made possible and produced within particular social, cultural, political and historical contexts (for example, Chodorow, 1999; Hochschild, 1983; Lupton, 1998; Rose, 1990). Understanding emotions in this way contextualises the emotional turn in professional practice in relation to wider social, political and cultural trends. These wider trends include the feminisation of professional practice discussed in the preceding sections.

Discussions of the emotionalisation of professional practice that neglect these wider trends effectively ignore links between the increasing attention paid to emotion and the various ways in which professions are subject to processes of feminisation. This neglect prompts questions about whether the critical accounts advanced by writers like Furedi (2004) and Ecclestone and Hayes (2008), in objecting to the expansion of professional wisdom to include attention to emotional experience, might equally be objecting to aspects of feminisation that are about recognising the value and importance of what have been traditionally viewed as feminine activities, such as attending to the subjective or affective experience of those to whom professional practice is oriented. This does not render their criticisms intrinsically anti-women or opposed to all aspects of the feminisation of professions, positions from which they would be likely to distance themselves. However, it does suggest that that the relationship between women, men and the value or prestige accorded to gender-typical attributes requires closer scrutiny.

Valuing Habits of Gender

I have argued that an important component of the feminisation of professions has taken the form of the emergence of female-dominated professions strongly associated with traditionally feminine attributes and activities such as caring and nurturing. I have also pointed to other dimensions of feminisation, including the entry of women into male-dominated professions and the influence of traditionally feminine skills on older as well as newer professions. Twentieth-century trends have therefore gone some considerable way towards undoing the original masculinity of professions, which not only limited access to men, but also imbued the values and wisdom of professions with masculine traits. Today, professions overall are more balanced in terms of gender mix, and there is evidence of the incorporation and positive valuing of feminine traits across the spectrum of professions, such that men as well as women are called upon to cultivate and display supposedly 'feminine skills' like collaborative working, listening to others, attending to feelings and so on. In this sense, femininity is at least partially liberated from its mapping onto women and not men.

It is the case that while the overall gender balance of professions may have become much more balanced, a high degree of gender segregation remains at the level of specific professional fields. But while the demographic composition of many professions is dominated by one gender or the other, there are numerous men in female-dominated professions and women in male-dominated professions. These men and women demonstrate that any penalties incurred by crossing normative gender boundaries associated with particular occupations can be surmounted. These men and women may, moreover, be viewed as pioneers of, or ambassadors for, the de-traditionalisation of gender (Beck et al., 1994), through which the grip of traditional ideas about gender is presumed to be loosening and relaxing. From this perspective, the tendency for women and men to gravitate towards particular 'gender-congruent' professions and specialisms within professions is likely to decline over time.

However, this account is incomplete, and the example of the contention surrounding the incorporation of emotion into professional wisdom and practice calls for a more nuanced interpretation of these trends. Evidence of two kinds draws attention to important and persistent connections between gender, professions and power.

First, studies of men in female-dominated professions show that they do not merely gravitate towards gender-congruent roles, but that they are also markedly more likely than women to progress to positions of leadership (Howe, 1985; Williams, 1995). In nursing, for example, where historically men's opportunities have been tightly restricted and where they remain very much a minority, they nevertheless enjoy significant career advantages in terms of their disproportionate presence in leadership roles (Evans, 2004). Notwithstanding equal opportunities and sex discrimination legislation, maleness appears to be highly valued in the senior ranks of female-dominated professions.

Second, as I have noted above, the female-dominated caring professions remain of markedly lower status than both older and newer male-dominated professions. That there is an intrinsically gendered component to this differential valuation of men's and women's forms of professional activity is reinforced by correlations between gender composition and prestige observed in a number of professions subject to rapid changes in gender mix. According to Philipson (1993, 12), 'when work becomes feminized the chief implications are that it becomes less remunerative and lower status'. Her analysis of how the demographic feminisation of American psychotherapy resulted in loss of status is echoed in studies of the feminisation of teaching (Drudy, 2008). Conversely, the reverse trend of professional occupations in which the gender composition shifts towards men entails enhancement in remuneration and status, as in the case of nurse anaesthesia in the USA (Lindsay, 2007).

These examples suggest that the relationship between gender and professions is not necessarily dissolving, but is instead changing its form. Notwithstanding considerable relaxation in the extent to which men and women are required to limit themselves to traditionally 'masculine' and 'feminine' dispositions and activities, the tendency for caring roles to be taken up by women persists, whether or not these roles are remunerated and/or professionalised. Caring roles and responsibilities are oriented towards others, and especially in familial contexts, entail commitments to relationships. These responsibilities operate alongside women's participation in the workforce, including within professions, where individuals are typically expected to behave as autonomous individuals apparently unencumbered by the needs of others. Feminist scholars have argued that this model of the autonomous individual, associated with nineteenth-century ideals of middle-class masculinity, continues to be more consistently available to men than to women today (Mackenzie and Stoljar, 2000). Thus, while both women and men move between workplaces that engage people as relatively autonomous individuals and home lives within which relationships and connections are paramount, the tendency remains for women to 'carry' responsibilities towards others throughout all aspects of their lives, and for men to inhabit the model of the autonomous individual more readily and more fully (Tronto, 1994). This may be one reason why many roles within the caring professions remain so strongly associated with women and low in status: the direct delivery of care calls upon practitioners to enter into relationships with those to whom care is offered that bear a clear resemblance to familial caring responsibilities, rather than maintaining the image of the detached, autonomous individual. It also helps to explain why men, who often form such a small minority of members of such professions, rise disproportionately to senior leadership positions within them. Not only does this enable them to shift from roles that are not gender-congruent to roles that are, but it also enables them to step back from the conflict between the expectations of putting the needs of others first and normative autonomous professional behaviour.

While it is clearly possible for women and men to cultivate and deploy skills and forms of professional wisdom traditionally associated with opposite gender, the implicit value attaching to activities and attributes strongly associated with one gender or the other remains relatively entrenched. This, I would argue, goes some way towards understanding the intensity of debate around the place of emotion in professional wisdom. In so far as professional wisdom has prioritised autonomous judgement and action over and above commitment to relationships, its expansion to include such requirements as attentiveness to the emotional experience of others presents a challenge. This challenge will be unwelcome to some, and it is not surprising that it should be contested and resisted. Whether or not we call other-oriented and relationship-oriented forms of wisdom 'feminine' is a moot point. Historically, they undoubtedly have been associated with women. The feminisation of professions I have described has drawn men into developing and using such wisdom, too. But if it requires men to 'colonise' and thereby 'de-feminise' what have previously been regarded as feminine domains for their value to increase, then the underlying devaluation of forms of wisdom associated with women remains unchallenged. For professional wisdom to shed its historical association with masculinity, these subtle and increasingly hidden gender-based value systems need to be recognised and challenged.

References

Abbott, P. and Wallace, C. (1990), *The Sociology of the Caring Professions*, Basingstoke: Falmer Press.

Annison, J. (2007), 'A gendered review of change within the probation service', *The Howard Journal*, 46(2), 145–61.

Beck, U., Giddens, A. and Lash, S. (1994), *Reflexive Modernisation: Politics, Tradition and Aesthetics in the Modern Social Order*, Cambridge: Polity Press.

Benner, P. (2001), *From Novice to Expert: Excellence in Clinical Nursing Practice*, Englewood Cliffs, NJ: Prentice Hall.

Berlant, J.L. (1975), *Profession and Monopoly*, Berkeley, CA: University of California Press.

Berlant, L. (2008), *Female Complaint: The Unfinished Business of Sentimentality in American Culture*, Durham, NC: Duke University Press.

Boler, M. (1999), *Feeling Power: Emotions and Education*, London: Routledge.

Brandon, S. (2004), 'Barry, James (c.1799–1865)', *Oxford Dictionary of National Biography*, Oxford: Oxford University Press, <http://www.oxforddnb.com/view/article/1563> (accessed 25 March 2011).

Carr, D. (2011), 'Virtue, Character and Emotion in 'People Professions': Towards a Virtue Ethics of Interpersonal Professional Conduct', in L. Bondi, D. Carr, C. Clark and C. Clegg (ed.), *Towards Professional Wisdom: Practical Deliberation in the 'People Professions'*, Aldershot: Ashgate.

Chodorow, N. (1999), *The Power of Feelings: Personal Meaning in Psychoanalysis, Gender and Culture*, New Haven, CT: Yale University Press.

Cree, V. (1997), 'Surviving on the inside: Reflections on being a woman and a feminist in a male academic institution', *Social Work Education*, 16(3), 37–60.

Davies, C. (1996), 'The sociology of professions and the professions of gender', *Sociology*, 30(4), 661–78.

Drudy, S. (2008), 'Gender balance/gender bias: The teaching profession and the impact of feminisation', *Gender and Education*, 20(4), 309–23.

Ecclestone, K. and Hayes, D. (2008), *The Dangerous Rise of Therapeutic Education*, London: Routledge.

Etzioni, A. (1969), *The Semi-professions and their Organisations*, London: Macmillan.

Evans, J. (2004), 'Men nurses: A historical and feminist perspective', *Journal of Advanced Nursing*, 47(3), 321–8.

Furedi, F. (2004), *Therapy Culture: The Cultivation of Vulnerability in an Uncertain Age*, London: Routledge.

Glazer, P. and Slater, M. (1987), *Unequal Colleagues: The Entrance of Women into the Professions, 1890–1940*, New Brunswick, NJ: Rutgers University Press.

Goleman, D. (1996), *Emotional Intelligence: Why it Can Matter More than IQ*, London: Bloomsbury.

Hall, C. and Davidoff, L. (1987), *Family Fortunes: Men and Women of the English Middle Class 1780–1850*, London: Hutchinson.

Hochschild, A. (1983), *Managed Heart: The Commercialization of Human Feeling*, Berkeley, CA: University of California Press.

Howe, D. (1985), 'The segregation of women and their work in personal social services', *Critical Social Policy*, 5(15), 21–35.

Lindsay, S. (2007), 'Gendering work: The masculinisation of nurse anaesthesia', *Canadian Journal of Sociology*, 32(4), 429–48.

—— (2008), 'The care-tech link: An examination of gender, care and technical work in healthcare labour', *Gender, Work and Organisation*, 15(4), 333–51.

Lovell, T. (2000), 'Thinking feminism with and against Bourdieu', *Feminist Theory*, 1(1), 11–32.

Lupton, D. (1998), *Emotional Self: A Sociocultural Exploration*, London: Sage.

Mackenzie, C. and Stoljar, N. (2000), *Relational Autonomy: Feminist Perspectives on Autonomy, Agency and the Social Self*, Oxford: Oxford University Press.

Morrison, T. (2007), 'Emotional intelligence, emotion and social work: Context, characteristics, complication and contribution', *British Journal of Social Work*, 37(2), 245–63.

Orbach, S. (2011), 'Work is Where We Live: Emotional Literacy and Psychological Dimensions of the Various Relationships There', in L. Bondi, D. Carr, C. Clark and C. Clegg, *Towards Professional Wisdom: Practical Deliberation in the 'People Professions'*, Aldershot: Ashgate.

Philipson, I. (1993), *On the Shoulders of Women: The Feminization of Psychotherapy*, New York: Guilford Press.

Pringle, R. (1998), *Sex and Medicine: Gender, Power and Authority in the Medical Profession*, Cambridge: Cambridge University Press.

Rose, N. (1990), *Governing the Soul: The Shaping of the Private Self*, London: Routledge.

Smith, P. (1992), *Emotional Labour of Nursing*, Basingstoke: Macmillan.

Squire, C. (2001), 'The public life of emotions', *International Journal of Critical Psychology*, 1, 27–8.

Tronto, J. (1994), *Moral Boundaries*, London: Routledge.

Warner, J. and Gabe, J. (2008), 'Risk, mental disorder and social work practice: A gendered landscape', *British Journal of Social Work*, 38(1), 117–34.

Wilensky, H. (1964), 'The professionalization of everyone?', *American Journal of Sociology*, 70, 137–58.

Williams, C. (1995), 'Hidden advantages for men in nursing', *Nursing Administration Quarterly*, 19(2), 63–70.

Witz, A. (1990), 'Patriarchy and professions: The gendered politics of occupational closure', *Sociology*, 24(4), 675–90.

—— (1992), *Professions and Patriarchy*, London: Routledge.

9 Work is Where We Live: Emotional Literacy and the Psychological Dimensions of the Various Relationships There[1]

Susie Orbach

Introducing a Notion of 'Work'

Work is where many of us live for many hours a day, and yet the emotional importance of work in people's lives is often downplayed. This chapter argues for greater emotional literacy at work, focusing on professions for which relationships with others is key. I explore questions of motivations for doing the work we do, the emotional impacts those we work with have on us, and what we can do to make the conditions in which we work as enabling as possible.

If I think over my clinical week, in which people have ostensibly come to see me about relationship problems, I am struck by just how many of the sessions have focused on work and the emotional and power relationships that exist there. This is not including the individuals who have come for 'coaching' or consultancy to do with their work practice. That is a separate group whose focus is particular, as are those who come already accepting the emotional factors at work and the importance of paying attention to them. What strikes me in my ordinary patient load is the way in which work is a critical activity for several people – at least equalling their private lives,

---

1   This chapter was previously published by Elsevier in *Emotion, Space and Society*, 1(1) (2008), 14–17, copyright © Elsevier 2008, and is reproduced here with permission.

and causing as large a range of emotions – and yet there is a general unease or perhaps an irritation with the emotional states that work produces. It is as though, despite work being really important, we shouldn't really get hot and bothered – or pleased and delighted – because work is not quite accepted as a legitimate site for what is considered emotionally important or valuable.

Even where it is, a hesitation arises about raising work issues, and initially in therapy, emotions associated with work are often expressed as though the feelings aroused there – hurt, ambition, control, competition, the need for recognition – are faintly unsavoury, and certainly unwelcome. People who openly embrace work and spend long hours on it are gratuitously insulted by being termed workaholics.

And yet work is where many of us live – certainly, for myself and my friends – for many hours a day. Indeed, for someone like me in a privileged occupation – not privileged materially, but privileged in terms of the amount of interest, learning, curiosity, engagement, emotional involvement, recognition and brain food I get – work is something that is emotionally, intellectually and economically sustaining. It is more than that, it is self-expressive, a critical identity marker, a source of self-worth, and a place in which interesting and challenging dilemmas get posed, and more often than not, addressed in creative and original ways.

I had best stop. I am sounding to myself like some latter-day Samuel Smiles.[2] And I know well that many of the pleasures from work, my own included, are scarred by the endless email and administration that befalls one. There's not, at least for me, satisfaction there, just what feels like insane and yet compulsive activity: reducing the list of things to be done, so that the next slew of emails can be dealt with – many of which one may not have initiated or wished to be part of, but which fur up the arteries of a professional life. Managing being overwhelmed is something we all have to learn, and we have developed a number of strategies to cope, which in my case involve the psychic mechanisms of splitting – the capacity to sever thinking about the thing I don't have time to think about now, but which I have a slot to think about tomorrow, or next Tuesday, or in six months, and which I hope to hell my brain will be turning over, without my being aware of it, when it has some spare capacity.

But the question I want to pose is this: if work is where we live, how can we make it more emotionally literate and sane? What do we need to be aware of? Is it a question of repositioning (or in today's vernacular, rebranding) work so that we own its imperative in our lives? Do we need to stop elevating intimate life and rest and recreation as the only legitimate

---

2   Samuel Smiles (1812–1904) author of *Self-Help* (1859) and numerous other texts declaring the social and moral benefits of hard work and individual self-improvement.

bearers of emotional scrutiny? I think so. If we listen to *Desert Island Discs*,[3] where accomplished and well-known people are invited to talk about themselves, we notice that the balance of their passions runs quite evenly down pathways of work, hobbies and intimate life. What makes *Desert Island Discs* guests interesting to us is the way they conceptualise their whole life, their scientific endeavour, their acting, their writing, their political activity and its relation to the rest of their lives. I am being obvious here, but I feel a need to insist on the importance of work, not in a riposte to the so-called feckless whom politicians like to attack, nor do I want to insist that it is a moral good. I want to say, rather, that for those of us whose work poses interesting challenges without too much of a downside, work is a lot of where we live.

The Emotional Life at Work

So if Freud was right and work and love are the ingredients for a satisfying life, or in his sophisticated understanding, a life that manages ordinary unhappiness, once we acknowledge the centrality of work, what can we do to increase our emotional understanding of what happens to us at work: what we do there, what gets aroused, what perplexes us, what infuriates us and what kinds of muddles do we get into that need attention so that we are not involved in hopeless battles, a diminished sense of authority and feelings of fury and depression?

If work matters, then relationships at work matter, and perhaps most especially if our work is oriented to others and draws us into professional relationships with others, such as what might be called 'people professions', like psychotherapy, counselling, teaching, nursing, social work and ministry, among many others. Work is a bit like a family. We didn't chose our siblings or our parents, and we don't for the most part create the ambience, but we are initiated into it, and we try to exert some personal agency; but the business of relating once there and getting on with others, being part of some kind of a co-operating enterprise while being effective and delivering on the job, can be a challenge. And despite having passions which have driven us into people professions, we may not understand what has compelled us and what we are seeking emotionally as we teach, nurse, counsel, minister and provide professionally for needs which have been carelessly responded to before. I want to divide my remarks that follow in three different directions:

---

3   *Desert Island Discs* is a long-running British radio programme in which guests review their lives in the context of eight pieces of music they would choose to have with them if cast away on a desert island.

- What might we want to know about our own motivations for doing the work?
- What emotional dilemmas do our client's actions, desires and mental states provoke in us?
- What can we do to make the conditions within which we work – the emotional temperature and ambience – be as enabling as possible?

I could start anywhere in this cycle, because they all feed into one another and affect how we practise and how we feel, but I will start with how we might come to know our own motivations for doing the work.

Reflecting Upon Personal Motivations

As an aspiring psychotherapist who believed she wanted to 'help' people, especially women, I was forced to engage the idea that my wanting to help was only a small part of the story. In fact, altruism as motivation was something that I should question. This is quite a devastating idea to a young, eager, committed and politically aware individual. I wanted to do this job because I wanted to make a difference. Theoretically, I believed – against the views of most of my political comrades – that psychoanalysis had value. It could illuminate – at least in gender-conscious hands – how our individual psychology and felt experience were constructed with reference to the requirements of our culture. Women's subordination worked, in part, because our early experience prepared us for an inferiorised psychology of femininity (Eichenbaum and Orbach, 1982). If we could transform the psychic conditions in which women were schooled to provide for the dependency needs of others rather than expect emotional dependency or nurture themselves, that they should be midwives to the activities and development of others without expecting this kind of attention personally, and that they should garner their sense of self through the enactment of these kinds of identity prescriptions – if we could change these things, then we would be doing satisfying and meaningful work. We would be transforming individual women's lives and challenging the psychic structures that sustained patriarchal social relations (Eichenbaum and Orbach, 1983).

At one level, our goals were noble enough. Cast by the passions and political language of the 1970s, we identified ourselves with the struggle for liberation. We would work to transform the understanding of mental health issues while providing for new gender-conscious theory and practice. Noble enough, as I just said – except there was a wrinkle. Such a project, without serious self-examination, might exempt us out of our own theory if we did not investigate our personal motivation further.

Managing Emotional Dilemmas

Psychotherapy training is particular in this regard. It insists that we understand why we want to do what we are aiming to do, and in an often extreme manner it suggests that our desire to do so may contain pathology. That is to say, the very reasons we are drawn to treat others may be out of some distress of our own, and we may be unconsciously hoping to solve, foist or resolve our own issues through a form of narcissistic gratification – giving to others what we long for ourselves.

Of course, in my own case, this would certainly be true. My own unmet needs as a young woman and the schooling I and my generation of women received as well as to take care of and midwife others would certainly be addressed in a proxy form by my providing for the dependency, attachment and emotional needs of others and by paying attention to their struggles to articulate their desires. My patients' personal psychological dilemmas would be a version of my own. My patients' personal victories would delight me. My patients' hesitations would be completely understandable. They would speak to me at a deep level.

I tell you this personal narrative not because I am desperate for public humiliation or support, but to suggest that there is something in the psychoanalytic practice of self-examination that is potentially helpful to those of us in the people professions. One's knowledge of one's own participation and motivation as an analyst does not take away from a capacity to be effective or helpful. It enables us to do so cognisant of whose interests we are promoting. One benefit of knowing why you are doing what you are doing is that it is protective to your clients and protective to yourself. It means that you are cognisant of your capacity to need them. If you are unaware of this tendency, it can lead you to act in ways which may be unhelpful to both parties. Self-knowledge clears a space so that you can make yourself available for your client's, student's or patient's actual needs and development, and that you can enter the working space with curiosity and interest rather than with a compelling personal agenda of your own needs. It means a level of emotional literacy towards oneself, in which something less instrumental, proscriptive and more open and curious can occur for oneself. With personal ambition understood and hopefully worked on and worked through, one can be more emotionally alive to oneself and to the other.

Of course, this helps our patients, students and clients too. Indeed, I believe this kind of emotional self-knowledge is crucial. We need to track two different trajectories in relation to our client groups: firstly, what they want and how they interrupt themselves from achieving those things, and secondly, what emotional dilemmas our clients' actions, desires and mental states provoke in us.

The first issue of what our clients want is transparent, on the face of it. They want to develop. But as we work with them in whatever setting we find ourselves in, we will doubtless come across the idiosyncratic and personal beliefs and behaviours that mean that they can get in the way of themselves. They can be inclined to do the very things that are not in their best interest. This is where our skills, our compassion and our experience come in. The job requires sensitivity to the individual's capacity to interrupt and thwart her- or himself, as well as to the stated goals of the endeavour. That 'interrupting' feature can be most devilish. It can irritate, turn off, dismay and discourage the client, and it can irritate, turn off, dismay and discourage the people professional, the designated helper, too. The negative or destructive feelings that a client experiences are frequently disavowed or unacknowledged, or they may be so over-present that they overwhelm both the client and the people professional. Psychoanalysis has a term for describing the process by which unwanted feelings are transmitted – consciously and unconsciously – between people. In the case of helper to the helped, we term such feelings that devolve on the professional, the *countertransference* (Freud, 1915). By describing this phenomenon as the countertransference, we name a process that is otherwise somewhat baffling. In naming the countertransference, we are in a position to study it and reflect upon it rather than be engulfed within it.

The countertransference allows us to examine what we and our client might be experiencing and to examine how to deal with it. The child who is frightened to learn, the drug user who has no way of dealing with need if not using a substance she thinks she can depend on, the abusing man who is fearful of his capacity to deal with his vulnerability unless he acts it out through denial and violence towards another, the young, rude boy whose fragile identity relies on negatively impacting on others inevitably show us these attributes of self-sabotage as they try to develop. Being swept up into such feelings ourselves when we are with or thinking about our work with an individual or a group is a precious signal about what needs attending to. By recognising and understanding such dismaying feelings in ourselves, we are able to dig ourselves out of our own negativity and to understand the force of the negative self-representation that we need to address in our client so that we can be useful to him, her or them.

That is one kind of thing that we need to do. The other, which again relies on understanding the countertransference for us to be effective, is seeing what the emotional dilemmas of our client's 'real world' actions and desires and mental states provoke in us. This is a slightly different form of the countertransference (Gorkin, 1987). It is not so much about how their unconscious emotional states affect us, but how their actions and what they do and how they relate to us and others work on us. We all have our personal psychological sensitivities and bugaboos. Whatever these are, we need to know them. I am thinking of the teacher who can get competitive with her or his pupil, the university lecturer who doesn't know how to contain her or his disappointment when her or his most favoured student fails to deliver as she or he had imagined, or the human resources manager who can't bear anyone to weep – nothing extraordinary, no gross emotional pathology, just the vagaries of our individual temperaments which interact with others who are looking to us for counsel and growth and to whom we look to confirm our own value in our daily work. Their behaviours can upset us and make us wobble. We are never going to avoid being affected by the people we work with – and I am not sure any of us would like to remain unaffected. Being affected is part of what it means to be human and engage with others. They will influence, delight and disturb us. We want to be disturbed, otherwise we wouldn't be where we situate ourselves. So we need to know how to relate to that disturbance. We need to find a way of being curious about the uncomfortable aspects so that we are not immediately reactive in a negative manner. We need to pause long enough inside of ourselves so that what we find emotionally challenging is not sent back to the other in an undigested form which reinforces their own disappointments and negative self-regard (Orbach, 1999).

This pause for self-reflection does not mean we should reject our own personal reactions – quite the opposite. It means that we should understand them sufficiently. When uncomfortable emotional states arise in us, we can be tempted to shut ourselves off from them or become defensive, but what is required is more nuanced. It involves receiving and privately acknowledging what is being emotionally stimulated in us so that we can reflect on it by observing how it affects us rather than immediately rejecting it. This done, we have the chance to act from a more considered, neutral position. And once in this more neutral position, we can think about the need of the other, what they are telling or showing us, so that we can help them take up a new position while simultaneously assessing our capacity to read them in ways which will neither overburden us nor unduly frustrate them.

Creating Enabling Conditions

This leads me to my third point, which is that this capacity to be self-reflexive needs to feed into a work environment which provides sufficient support so that we can bring our concerns to our work colleagues. In some social work-type agencies, supervision or staff group meetings exist which support staff so that the motivations and the feelings that clients evoke can be engaged with sympathetically so that they have a chance to be understood and addressed. Usually, managers don't like the expense of supervision-type staff groups. They particularly don't like them if the staff use an external consultant. But the cost of such a group is minimal in terms of the benefits.

The value added of such groups is hugely beneficial. It socialises the dilemmas which staff inevitably face, rather than dumping them on the individual. There is a considerable advantage when dealing with tricky and disturbing situations by building capacity in the staff grouping and in the individual. The problems evoked by the work are properly situated as problems evoked by work. Re-situating the dilemmas in this way allows individuals to bring their corporate resources to bear on a problem rather than stranding the individual professional with a sense of inadequacy. Even clearing a time and space for a group meeting underlines its importance as a place for professionals to reflect on their practice.

Reflective staff groups are one part of the solution. The other equally important one is finding ways to make the ordinary conditions within which we work – the emotional temperature and ambience – as enabling as possible. For most of us in the people professions, the demands on us severely outweigh our capacity to provide. There are always more deserving people needing things than we can actually meet. Because we are, as a group, highly responsive to meeting needs, we can be faced with a dilemma. How do we meet the demand when we do not have the capacity? How can we set limits to what we are able to provide so that we can provide it well? How can we deal with the emotional conundrum of being unable to provide and thus refusing to give?

The Challenge and Boundaries of Giving

This conundrum is well known to all of us. We have to find mechanisms to create a boundary which does not feel damaging to our own self-worth. We want to be bountiful, but following through on the desire when we are not able to actually deliver can be self-destructive, as well as harmful to the client, who will experience a jagged response from us as we try to shape ourselves to the demands of a situation which we are in fact unable to meet. So how do we emotionally handle the making of a boundary? How do we cope with saying 'no' inside of ourselves and not become angry or defensive or shut off and uncaring?

Each of us will find our own response. For me, the overall feeling I find myself experiencing when I find I have to say 'no' is regret. It hurts not to be able to do many of the things that I would wish to do. The feelings that saying 'no' engenders are not easy; they also include sadness and feelings of selfishness. But put together, the mix of feelings has a personal authenticity which makes it possible for me to stay connected and related to my desire without feeling overtaxed by the request of the other. It is, in a way, a very ordinary sort of feeling. I'd like to be able to say 'yes', but sadly I can't. The emotional honesty of that stance gives one a ground to stand on and allows one to see that often we are pressurising ourselves as much as we are being pressurised by others. It enables one to pull back from the projection that it is the manager who is pressurising us, and to join with her or him to say, 'Yes, it would be really good if we could meet x demand, but we can't', and to empathise with the dilemma of having to refuse what is clearly required and needed and yet cannot be delivered.

In most late capitalist work environments, people are rewarded for hopping to it, working longer hours and staying ahead of the game. Those jobs bring bonuses and status gratifications. They depend on a set of values that until recently did not have much impact on the people professions. But today, business values have infiltrated all of our thinking and many of our work practices, and of course, we are also being pressurised, we have to justify our time and produce sufficient billable income, even if it is theoretical as in the health service. Paradoxically, as the people professions become more infused with corporatised values, the corporation itself is borrowing heavily from the skills that have been learnt in our sector. Today, coaching, professional development, counselling, group process and communication skills are available in many corporate settings. The corporate sector is recognising that emotions count, so that they are seeing the value of emotional literacy and emotional intelligence as adjuncts to achieving their goals. If one was cynical, one might say that this allows the corporate sector to bully their staff or have high expectations of extraordinary commitment on the one hand; on the other hand it recognises how burdensome this is for the individual, so they 'throw in' a little staff development. Maybe so. One could say that attention to emotional life enables people to work more peaceably and efficiently. One could also argue that people at the top are pulling enormous salaries, and that if their performance gets overloaded by stress, then it is very expensive to buy them out of their contracts, and much cheaper to provide some kind of therapeutic help with the aim of bringing them back to peak condition. And this is indeed what occurs.

There are companies that provide psychoanalysis by proxy. They visit the home town of a chief executive, interview schoolmates, teachers, football coaches, parents and siblings – people of significance to the individual. They then prepare a psychological dossier of their findings and map out what they believe to be the client's weaknesses and strengths and a programme for psychological rehabilitation. It is an expensive exercise whose value is questionable. For most people, it is the process of self-reflection and self-discovery that enables wanted change. In this formulation, the client is told who she or he is in a sort of 'this is your psychological life' and what she or he needs to change and how they can most efficiently go about it. It is funny, and we could ridicule it, but it points to something that business wants to use: the expert understanding of emotional processes and their impact on an individual's performance.

What the process tacitly recognises is that those in leadership positions are crucial to the health of an enterprise. In seeing how stressed those in leadership can be and in attempting to underpin their functioning, they are providing value added to the enterprise. While I don't advocate such externalised practices for those of us in the people professions, I do think we could take back some of what we ourselves already know, which is that supporting our own professional and non-professional staff is critical to the work that we do.

There is one last point that I want to raise, which is the way in which the avowed intentions of even the best kind of endeavour can be undercut because there is a devilish tendency of organisations to manifest the very opposite of their intended ethos. I am sure you know what I mean. Women's Liberation organisations of the 1970s dedicated to inclusivity could get in awful wrangles as they excluded or ranked groups of women based on a hierarchy of oppressions. Therapy organisations dedicated to theoretical openness with a rhetoric of being concerned with the importance of benign relationships to foster development turned into authoritarian structures which could not countenance difference. Churches dedicated to care and spiritual practices harboured sexual transgressions that emphasised materiality over the sacred. Certainly, the Church, psychotherapy and political parties have to cope with damaging splits in their ranks as the disaffected or the outcast from a kind of cult mentality seek to hold on to professed shared values from which they have been expelled or thought to deviate.

The Jungians have a concept that is extremely useful here: *the shadow*. They believe that it is always present, always a potential, and that it is naive to assume that an individual or a group exists without the opposite of what it professes or wants to be. Recognising this process allows it to be addressed. The individual or the organisation has an opportunity to incorporate an understanding of the workings of the shadow, rather than being drenched in shame when its manoeuvres surface. And if we reflect on our personal ethos and ask ourselves about our personal shadow, we may come up with some surprising aspects of self which we unconsciously foist on to others through projection or denial or splitting. If we then think about the organisation we work within, we can ask whether the organisation's statement of values is rendered less effective because of the shadow operating. Doubtless it is. This is not something we can entirely rid ourselves of. Our altruistic impulses, as I tried to say at the beginning of this chapter, are linked to, in some cases, a personal need to be given to and/or recognised. This does not render our efforts meaningless, but it does mean that it is worth understanding the underbelly, and thus the complexity of our own impulses to give.

Conclusion

Work, as I hope I have shown, is a dramatically passionate place for many of us. It is boring and deadening, too. It is not a place we stop in at or feed from materially in order to do our serious living: it is as much where we live as are our other activities – familial, filial, sexual, artistic, horticultural and so on. If we can accept the significance of work, we will have more emotional energy to solve some of the psychological tensions and pleasures that arise there. We won't have a perfect work experience, any more than we can hope to have a perfect private life, but we will be able to approach it more accurately, as a place we live a lot of our lives in.

References

Eichenbaum, L and Orbach, S. (1982), *Outside In, Inside Out*, revised as *Understanding Women* (1984), Harmondsworth: Penguin.

—— (1983), *What Do Women Want? Exploding the Myth of Dependency*, London: Michael Joseph.

Freud, S. (1915), 'Observations on transference love', in *The Standard Edition of the Complete Works of Sigmund Freud*, vol. 12, London: Hogarth Press, 157–71.

Gorkin, M. (1987), *The Uses of Countertransference*, Northvale, NJ: Jason Aronson.

Orbach, S. (1999), *Towards Emotional Literacy*, London: Virago.

10 The Wisdom of L'Arche and the Practices of Care: Disability, Professional Wisdom and Encounter-in-community

John Swinton

My Background – Traversing Three Professions

I approach the issue of professional wisdom from a rather unusual professional background. I am currently professor in Practical Theology at the University of Aberdeen. However, my background is in nursing and hospital chaplaincy. I nursed for 16 years within the areas of mental health, and latterly intellectual disability. Later, I became a community mental health chaplain, working with people who were moving from long-term institutional care back into the community. Along the way, I became an ordained minister in the Church of Scotland before taking up my current post as an academic. So my life traverses three professions: nursing, ministry and divinity. Each of these professions has a slightly different perspective on what it means to be a professional, and each has a different mode of wisdom and encounter.

In this chapter, I want to draw from the wisdom I have gained through my engagement with these professions and offer a perspective on professional wisdom which I hope will throw some fresh light on our understanding and practices of care. As someone who comes from and remains theoretically located within the caring professions, my focus will be on the significance of professional wisdom for the types of practices we choose to engage in as we offer care and support to people in various contexts. My particular interest is in disability, so a good deal of what I will focus on relates to what it means for professionals to 'be with' people who have various forms of disability, particularly intellectual disabilities. However, the perspective I offer is applicable to caring professionals wherever they work.

I will begin by offering a general perspective on what we might mean by 'professional wisdom' before moving on to explore what can be learned from reflecting on the specific context of the L'Arche communities. These communities are a particular mode of intentional community which offers an approach to the process of caring *with* people who have intellectual disabilities. It is subtly different from traditional models of professional care and professional relationships, and as I will argue, it offers new and challenging perspectives on how we might understand professional wisdom. Reflection on these communities will allow us to reclaim some aspects of the traditional understanding of professionalism and to develop new and refreshing complementary perspectives.

What Do We Mean by Professional Wisdom?

Professionalism

It will be helpful to begin by briefly exploring the term 'professional'. Historically, the term 'professional' was reserved for:

> practitioners of medicine, law, divinity, and (eventually) teaching. Professionals did not produce goods for sale or artistic pleasure; instead they were guides and healers to individuals, particularly in times of personal crisis. (Donovan, 2000, 13)

It is this traditional emphasis on professionals as guiders and healers that I want us to hold onto as this chapter moves on. Professionals held together theory and practice in critical tension:

> The traditional professions were characterized by the acquisition of systematic and valuable knowledge (knowing), the practice of application of this knowledge through technical skill and training (doing), and the value placed on putting this knowledge and skill to work in the service of others (helping). (Donovan, 2000, 13)

They retained a high degree of internal control over their members, with particular forms of behaviour being central to what it meant to be a professional. Thus, each profession developed its own code of ethics to govern and place boundaries on its practice. Entry into the profession was guarded, and breaching of rules could lead to expulsion and exclusion. Consequently, professionals have a great deal of autonomy in judgement and authority (Donovan, 2000). The boundaries of a profession are thus seen to be clear, guarded and protected against breach and abuse. A professional is one who professes intent to practise in quite specific ways. In ancient times, this 'profession' was a public declaration; nowadays, it finds itself enshrined within particular ethical codes and assumptions, and embodied in the various skills and practices that fall within the boundaries of any particular profession.

Wisdom

With these provisional thoughts on the nature of a professional in mind, we can move on to explore the nature of wisdom before bringing the two together. Basically, wisdom has to do with the process of accumulating knowledge, experience and intuitive understanding over a lifetime, and developing a capacity to apply such things within a life that one considers to be lived well. Wisdom is more than knowledge. People can know many things, but that does not make them wise. Similarly, people can be wise in certain areas, but they do not need to be particularly knowledgeable. The wise person has a broader understanding of the ways things are, and is not trapped or limited by the apparent limited options of the present. Rather, a wise person has an ability to move backwards and forwards across his or her history and experience in order to be able to make decisions that are not simply reactive or instinctive, but which are the product of the accumulated knowledge of the person's whole life. Such wise knowledge enables the person to make sense of any situation in the light of this whole, and to act in ways which reflect not just the current situation, but the accumulated experience of all of the person's life. Wisdom is therefore not one single thing. It is in fact many things that come together within the unifying context of a single life or the life of a community and work together to enable people to live well. Importantly, *wisdom requires imagination*. I will return to this observation below.

Professional Wisdom

How, then, do these two concepts come together to form our professional wisdom? At a basic level, professional wisdom relates to the accumulated body of authoritative, historical, reflective and practical knowledge that is gained by a profession over time and which guides it in the development of its theoretical and practical activities. It is this knowledge that informs the standards of the profession. Professional wisdom is both personal and public, relating both to the individual and the institution. It is personal in so far as individual practitioners gain their wisdom through their life experiences and the experience of working in a particular professional realm over an extended period of time. Within this realm, personal wisdom is passed on, among other ways, through contact with mentors and exemplars who have been imbued with the wisdom of the profession and who are comfortable in working that out within their professional activities. At the personal level, someone becomes a wise practitioner as they reflect on their practices and learn the multidimensional nature of the professional tasks.

Professional wisdom is public and institutional in so far as it is handed down not simply between individuals, but between and within institutional structures. At the institutional level, the professions have particular assumptions and boundaries that make certain modes of knowledge and practice acceptable and wise, and other perspectives unacceptable and unwise. It therefore functions at the often tense interface between the personal and the political, and is negotiated in the sometimes fraught space between the passing on of personal knowledge and the imposition of practices and ethical norms 'from above'.

Professional wisdom is thus contextual – unique to the individual practitioners and their mentors – and general – relating to the whole profession and supported by codes of ethics, rules, regulations and so forth. Such general rules and regulations are, of course, necessary to protect the professional and the one to whom she or he seeks to offer care, and to place boundaries on the shape and texture of professional practice. However, this boundary-forming aspect has another often overlooked dimension to it. As well as placing boundaries on the profession, it also shapes the professional imagination. In other words, the boundaries imposed by the perceived structure of the profession can also act as a way of inhibiting possibilities for developing and increasing wisdom in new directions. I previously suggested that wisdom requires imagination. Let me develop this point here.

Wisdom and Imagination: Shaping the Professional Imagination

We sometimes equate imagination with fantasy, assuming that its product is a fictional movement away from the normal rules of the world. That is a mistake. Theologian Stanley Hauerwas (1994, 178) describes the imagination as 'a pattern of possibilities fostered within a community by the stories and correlative commitments that make it what it is'. Imagination is not autonomous and free-floating. It is the product of the particular narratives and traditions that our communities develop which determine the nature of what we accept might be real and possible. All of our knowing activities are, in essence, imaginative. We organise our world and our social reality according to dominant images, narratives and assumptions which we assume to be normative and which offer us the possibility of stability and growth. If we had no imagination, we could make no sense of the world. Imagination allows us to anticipate and understand what is going on around us, based on previous experiences and expectations; it allows us to draw on the wisdom of our years and to explore the possibility that there might be other ways of addressing the present situation. Far from being fantasy, it is through our imagination that we make sense of the world and make decisions as to how we should respond to our experiences. Imagination is thus seen to be a powerful practical conduit for the development and practice of wisdom. Importantly, it is the boundaries of our imagination that enable us to ask or prevent us from asking particular questions and responding in ways that might be different to current practice.

It is important to reinforce the point that our imagination is not an independent, free-floating entity, somehow filled with innate ideas and concepts. Rather, imagination is deeply tied in with culture and the assumptions and values of the communities we inhabit. You can only imagine what you have been taught to imagine. So, for example, we could look at the literature within the caring professions not simply as sources of knowledge to help us to practice better, but as providing new visions which fund our imaginations in ways that allow us to see the world differently. Take, for example, the issue of spirituality in medicine and nursing: For many years, it was assumed that spirituality had no place within a highly secularised professional healthcare context. Our imaginations were shaped by the promises of science and technology, leading us to assume that religion and spirituality had become a thing of the past. Then, in the 1980s and 1990s, from within medicine and nursing there began to emerge a series of research reports which indicated that religion and spirituality were good for a person's health (Koenig et al., 2001). People were reminded of the religious wisdom of the past and the importance of such things as meaning, purpose, hope, love and God for the ways in which care is delivered (Swinton, 2001b). Previously, we had imagined that the proper role for the professional was distance and objectivity. Gradually, as we as individuals and as professions absorbed the findings of these research reports, we began to learn that closeness and personal encounter form a vital dimension of the role of the professional and the nature of our practices of care. In this sense, such research has re-funded our imagination (Brueggemann, 1993) and opened up new possibilities for the nature and shape of professional wisdom; it has provided us with new ideas, concepts, narratives and possibilities that have reshaped the professional perspectives of healthcare professionals in significant ways. As people have engaged with such research, gradually their imaginations have been extended to include the spiritual wisdom of the past as a potentially useful resource for the professional wisdom of the present. Today, it is much easier for us to imagine spirituality as part of mental healthcare. When I began my nursing training some thirty years ago, it was almost impossible to imagine such a thing.

Guides and Healers: The Professional Wisdom of L'Arche

With these thoughts in mind, I want to explore what it might look like if we used our imagination to reflect on two of the traditional aspects of professionals, namely their role as *guide* and *healer*. It is not immediately clear that these dimensions loom high in the guidelines of the caring professions. Therefore, my intention is to try to help the caring professions to remember or to reclaim dimensions of the meaning of professionalism that may have been forgotten or overlooked. I am not trying to push the boundaries of professionalism. I am simply trying to draw us back to important issues that it will be helpful to reflect on in the light of our current caring practices. In focusing on these two aspects, we will be enabled to begin to re-imagine the role of professional wisdom in interesting and challenging ways. An important thing to bear in mind at this point is that wisdom is not something that is taught simply through the imparting of objective facts and knowledge. Wisdom, as we have seen, is something that comes through experience and encounter. We become wise as we encounter wise people who act wisely. The learning of wisdom requires exemplars and mentors; people and systems who will provide lived examples of ways of being in the world that will engage and challenge current assumptions and in so doing bring about change. It is with this in mind that I want now to turn to the wisdom that is embodied in the L'Arche communities.

What are the L'Arche Communities?

L'Arche is an international organisation of faith-based communities which create places of support for people who have intellectual disabilities. It has a network of more than 110 communities in 30 countries worldwide, and 9 communities in the UK. It is an established care provider for people with intellectual disabilities. However, its approach differs from many other service providers in significant ways.

L'Arche began in 1964 when Jean Vanier, distressed by the institutionalisation and isolation and loneliness of people with intellectual disabilities, invited two men from an institution to live with him in a small house in Trosly, France. He called the house 'L'Arche', a French word for 'the ark' in the biblical story of Noah and the flood. His intention was to invite them to come and share their life in the spirit of the Gospel and of the Beatitudes that Jesus preached (Kearney, 1984). Vanier's intention was not to start a mini-institution. Rather, his desire was simply to live with these two men not as carer and cared for, but as friends. Vanier's initial patterning for community and relationships set the template for the beginning of the worldwide movement that has come to be known as the International Federation of L'Arche Communities. L'Arche grew quickly and spread around the world, attracting many young people who dedicated their lives to *living with* people who have intellectual disabilities.

At one level, L'Arche communities provide what we might call standard approaches to service provision. They seek to meet diverse needs by offering person-centred support in standard and broadly accepted ways. L'Arche strives to meet the highest standards of individual support in partnership with other professional agencies. But it is its perspective on professional wisdom and the positioning of the professional that is importantly different. L'Arche claims to be unique in that it seeks to combine living together, professionalism and spirituality. By the term 'living together', L'Arche does not simply mean that it provides residential accommodation. 'Living together' has a specifically theological meaning and intent. The L'Arche charter makes this statement:

> In a divided world, L'Arche wants to be a sign of hope. Its communities, founded on covenant relationships between people of differing intellectual capacity, social origin, religion and culture, seek to be a sign of unity, faithfulness and reconciliation. (L'Arche Internationale, 1993, 2)

The 'living together' that L'Arche offers is a specific context in which people with disabilities live alongside people without disabilities not as carers and cared for, but within a covenantal relationship of friendship. It is their understanding and practice of friendship which marks their wisdom out as different from that which underpins other service providers. Certainly, those who work in L'Arche have a responsibility to meet the needs of the people with intellectual disabilities and to adhere to the premises of good professional conduct. In this sense, their professional role is the same as any other caring agency. However, the emphasis on the reciprocity of friendship means that within these communities, people with intellectual disabilities are expected to share in meeting the needs of those without such disabilities. Mutuality of relationship and caring together is the key. The model of professionalism is one of reciprocity. The motif of *covenant* sums it up best. The basis of care in the L'Arche communities relates to a covenant wherein both parties intentionally take responsibility for caring for the other. The mode of professional encounter is one of *covenant, partnership, reciprocity,* and above all, *friendship.*

Christian Friendship

The body of wisdom that underpins the ethos of the L'Arche communities is deeply rooted in the wisdom of Roman Catholic spirituality, and in particular the friendships of Jesus with the outsider, the oppressed, the downtrodden and the poor. This gives the meaning of friendship quite specific content. The communities base their understanding of friendship on the friendships revealed in the life of Jesus. Francis Young puts it thus:

> The fundamental spirituality and pedagogy of L'Arche is as follows: It is not just good teaching, trying to make people as independent as possible – rather, it means entering into a relationship of friendship with each person so that together we can discover the joy and inner liberation that comes through belonging and growing towards greater maturity. The new family or community we are forming is not a family of flesh and blood, but is given by Jesus, calling us to a covenant of love; it does not want to be closed on itself, but open and present to neighbours, to parishes and to society in general. Thus, people with handicaps can reveal their gift to all and be like yeast in the dough, affecting the whole neighbourhood. (Young, 1997, 10)

Understandings of friendship within Western cultures have been deeply influenced by models based on the thinking of Aristotle. For Aristotle, friendship could only occur between *equals* – that is, two good people serving to actualise the virtue of goodness within their friendship relationship. In this understanding, the tendency is to work on a principle of likeness. If you have things in common with me, if you are able to give me the types of social goods that I require, then we can become friends. In this model, as McFague (1988, 161) correctly observes, 'friendship is finally not love of another but of oneself. One needs a friend, says Aristotle, in order to exercise one's virtue; one needs someone to be good to in order to be good'.

This understanding is quite different from the friendships revealed in the life of Jesus. In the incarnation, one finds God willingly entering into friendship with creatures who could never be God's equal. In the life of Jesus, one finds a continuing picture of a man entering into friendships not with social equals, but with those whom society had downgraded and considered unworthy of friendship. In the death of Jesus, one discovers a man committed to these same friends even unto death.

Thus, in contrast to models of friendship that insist that like-attracts-like, the model of friendship one sees in the life of Jesus is based on a principle of love, grace and acceptance of those whom society tends to downgrade and marginalise. Christian friendship therefore calls for attempts at intimacy which reach beyond the barrier of otherness and the need for personal gain and affirmation.

The types of friendship upon which the L'Arche communities are built therefore function on two levels: political and personal. In light of the way that society marginalises and excludes people with intellectual disabilities, voluntarily entering into friendship with people whom society constantly seeks to marginalise makes a profound countercultural statement which serves as a significant sign to the politics of the world. At a personal level, such friendships demand the removal of the idea of carer and cared for, and the development of types of relationships within which care and support are mutually given and received. Thus the L'Arche charter states that:

> Whatever their gifts or limitations, people are all bound together in a common humanity. Everyone is of unique and sacred value, and everyone has the same dignity and human rights. The fundamental rights of each person include the rights to life, to care, to a home, to education and to work. Also, since the deepest need of a human being is to love and to be loved, each person has a right to friendship, to communion and to a spiritual life. ... Home life is at the heart of a L'Arche Community. The different members of a Community are called to be one body. They live, work, pray and celebrate together, sharing their joys and their suffering and forgiving each other, as in a family. They have a simple lifestyle which gives priority to relationships. (L'Arche Internationale, 1993, 2–3)

The Way of the Heart

Jean Vanier (1999) describes this mode of relational wisdom as *the way of the heart*. The way of the heart is a way of putting people first, of moving beyond the boundaries of the label of 'intellectual disability' towards a recognition of the person-as-person. The 'way of the heart' is not simply another way of delivering care. It is a way of encountering people, a way of *being with* and *learning from* people with intellectual disabilities. It is an aspect of professional wisdom that allows all parties to learn deep truths from those with whom they share care:

> Power and cleverness call forth admiration but also a certain separation, a sense of distance; we are reminded of who we are not, of what we cannot do. On the other hand, sharing weaknesses and needs calls us together into 'oneness'. We welcome those who love us into our heart. In this communion, we discover the deepest part of our being: the need to be loved and to have someone who trusts and appreciates us and who cares least of all about our capacity to work or to be clever and interesting. When we discover we are loved in this way, the masks or barriers behind which we hide are dropped; new life flows. We no longer have

to prove our worth; we are free to be ourselves. We find a new wholeness, a new inner unity. (Vanier, 1999, 89–90)

This form of professional wisdom brings about healing, facilitates mutual guidance and re-engages the caring professional with the roles of guiding and healing by emphasising the quality and mutuality of their encounters. Within this approach, the professional becomes guide and guided, healed and healer. Through these quite specifically oriented relationships of friendship, professionals are enabled to take time to notice that which often is unnoticed. They are enabled to take time for the trivial, to notice the gentleness of their actions and the vulnerability of the other and themselves, to come close and notice, rather than to stand at a distance and observe (Hauerwas, 1988).

What we discover here is a way of developing wisdom through encounter with those whom society often considers as deeply 'Other', a way of offering care and support that is '*persons*-centred' and focused on the transformative nature of the relationship of friendship, rather than simply 'person-centred' – that is, focused on the needs of only one party in the relationship. L'Arche therefore expands the professional imagination, but does so in a way which maintains integrity and continuity with the wisdom of the wider caring professions.

Learning from L'Arche: Finding Time to Become Friends

Friendship, as we learn it from L'Arche, is thus seen to be a powerful exemplar of a different but not uncomplementary model of professional wisdom. It is a particular form of relating and relationship which offers the possibility of reclaiming the ideas of guiding and healing which we previously saw were significant dimensions of the historical role of the professional. In this way, the wisdom of L'Arche communities offers a challenge to our imagination which offers new possibilities.

Finding Time to Become Friends

However, the suggestion of incorporating friendship into the professional role does raise certain important issues. First among these issues is the question: do people with intellectual disabilities actually want carers and support workers to be their friends? There is a good deal of empirical evidence to suggest that a desire for friendship is one of the primary marks of the life experiences of many people with intellectual disabilities (Swinton and Powrie, 2004; Swinton, 2001a). Unfortunately, it is also true that such friendships are often hard to find (Nunkoosing and John, 1997). At the level of the importance of expressed need, the L'Arche communities have clearly identified an aspect of the lives of people with intellectual disabilities that is of some significance. In the following section, I will draw on my own work on spirituality and intellectual disability to try to show the significance and texture of friendship as it relates to the lives of people with intellectual disabilities.

Do People Want Friends?

In our work on spirituality and people with intellectual disabilities, the desire for friendship frequently came to the fore. People wanted more quality time with carers, although they were aware that staff were busy and often had limited time for developing meaningful friendships:

> What is important to me? I would say me having friends: people staying with you and … listening to the telly with me, and company …. But I know the staff here are busy all the time. The staff come round at four o'clock, and I like to have a chat with them but they don't seem to have the time. (Swinton and Powrie, 2004, 27)

The issue of staff time is, of course, significant. Irrespective of whether or not one assumes friendship to be an appropriate aspect of professional relationships, the reality is there is often very little time to do anything other than basics. Developing friendships take time. Professional carers and support workers often do not have time, or are not prepared to make time, to develop friendships. The community-oriented structure of the L'Arche community is intentionally structured to be conducive to taking time and developing friendships. Many services are not. Bearing in mind the current emphasis on needs-oriented service provision, this is a rather unusual omission.

Professional and Voluntary Friendships

While people desired friendship, their relationship of choice was voluntary friendship – that is, friendship that is given freely and not simply the product of professional roles. Professional friendships were acceptable and desirable, but not people's first choice. This did not necessarily exclude friendships with paid carers and support workers, but it did suggest a need to be needed which went beyond the normal boundaries of professional responsibility and duty. Table 10.1 will help clarify this point.

Table 10.1   Characteristics of professional and voluntary friendship

Professional Friendship	Voluntary Friendship
People become friends as part of their role as paid professionals.	Both enter into the relationship for reasons that are not simply related to profession or vocation.
People are paid to be friends with people with intellectual disabilities.	Neither receive any form of remuneration for their relationship.
People begin their relationships with people primarily because they have an intellectual disability. If the person did not have an intellectual disability, the relationship would not have come into existence.	The relationship may involve, but is not dependent on, one person having an intellectual disability. They are there for one another.
People become friends with people within the context of a professional relationship that is bounded by the number of hours that a person is paid to be there.	The amount of time that they spend together is determined by themselves according to criteria which both are open to negotiate.
Professional friendships have fixed boundaries and codes of ethics and professional conduct to prevent these boundaries being abused.	Friendship has no official boundaries. They must negotiate the parameters of their relationships between them.

Source: Swinton and Powrie (2004), 27.

Some of the professionals in our research made a concerted effort to develop friendships, and some of the carers and support workers we met gave up their own time in order to develop meaningful friendships with people with intellectual disabilities. Here they made a clear movement out of their normal professional roles and into a role which placed them in a position wherein they were more personally committed to the individual, but at the same time more open to being cared for, supported and influenced by them. The line between professional and voluntary friendships was in many cases quite blurry. In other words, while friendship might not be the norm for the professional, it certainly wasn't impossible.

Of course, such a movement brings with it certain expectations. The question of whether or not such expectations can be met is an important one. All potential befrienders (lay or professional) must ask themselves whether or not these expectations can be met, or whether they are creating a situation where the person with an intellectual disability may end up deeply disappointed. One support worker made this point poignantly:

> I think that in today's services where there's constant change of staff, people are constantly losing their history … it is being lost all the time. It's the most devastating lack of belonging, to be faced with yet another team of people. Everything of your history, maybe in the house you're living in, is wiped out. You can also lose what is a spiritual experience – that of being asked or involved or having a role in your community – because the new people don't know that last year you were responsible for this, or did that, or had that job. (Swinton and Powrie, 2004, 28)

Put slightly differently, when significant individuals – professionals or non-professionals – move out of a person's life, they leave gaps that can be devastating for the person concerned. Unless the staff member is prepared to carry on a friendship over an extended period, as has traditionally been the case within the L'Arche communities, with all the implications that involves, it might be better not to offer the relationship at all. 'Voluntary' friendships that end when the staff member moves on can be highly problematic.

This in turn raises another issue. The type of friendship that people are culturally likely to use is closer to Aristotle than to Jesus. By that, I mean that because of the specific form of wisdom upon which they are founded, the types of friendships made available within the L'Arche communities differ in shape, form and emphasis from many forms of friendship that are available within today's society. The question then is, even if we accept that friendship is an appropriate aspect of professional relationships, might the Christ-centred friendships that have shaped and formed the wisdom and practices of L'Arche actually be transferable to a secular context which has come into being via a different mode of professional wisdom?

Learning from L'Arche

The answer to this question would be both 'yes' and 'no'. It is clear that within a secular and secularising social context such as the UK, implementing models of friendship specifically based on the friendships of Jesus would not be deemed appropriate outwith organisations that are specifically based within the Christian tradition. However, on this point it is interesting to reflect on the ecumenical nature of contemporary L'Arche communities. It is true that they spring from religious roots. However, as one surveys the L'Arche communities worldwide, one soon finds them to be ecumenical and inter-religious, with some of them having no obvious religious commitment. And yet the ethos and wisdom of encounter and the way of the heart remains. Clearly, it is possible to take the wisdom of L'Arche and recontextualise it in ways which retain its radicalism yet remain flexible to a variety of religious and non-religious perspectives. Wisdom, it seems, is not a set of disembodied facts that remain open only to these who adhere to certain belief structures. Wisdom is a way of life within which one learns that the way of the heart is actually a wise way to live one's life. That being so, with L'Arche as an exemplar and its wisdom tradition as a possible path, it may be possible for other service providers to learn and be mentored by the way of life revealed in these communities.

Hospitality and Friendliness

Perhaps one way of working with the 'way of the heart' within a context which is different from L'Arche and which professes different modes of wisdom is by working with two concepts: *hospitality* and *friendliness*. Hospitality provides the relational context for the development of the covenantal relationship of friendship. In order for me to be hospitable to you, I need to accept you as you are, with absolute integrity. Such acceptance means that one has to open one's self fully to the other and be prepared not only to listen to what they have to say, but to allow what they say to affect you. Hospitality is something that is both given and received. If we reflect back on the ministry of Jesus, we see him sometime as host, sometimes as guest, but *always* as himself. This free movement from host to guest without either role swallowing up the other is the basic dynamic of hospitable living. It is precisely this dynamic that the L'Arche communities try to capture and live out. Hospitality through friendship enables the professional to pick up on the cadence of such a dynamic and to realise that to be a guide and a healer requires that as well as offering it, one receives both guidance and healing.

So the initial step in bringing the way of the heart to a context other than L'Arche might be to explore whether or not the relational context within which people with intellectual disabilities are being cared for and supported is truly hospitable. If such hospitality is an 'added extra' to the daily chores of caring, then it may be that even though our professional obligations are being full met, there is a need for a deeper recognition and working out of the roles of guide and healer. Such a focus on hospitality leads to an atmosphere of genuine friendliness. Friendliness is the context out of which friendships that embody the way of the heart have the possibility of emerging.

Conclusion

The development of professional wisdom is an act of the imagination. It is an ongoing process of shaping, re-thinking and practising wherein individuals and communities learn the shape and form of the meanings and practices that make the profession what it actually is. Wisdom is flexible, contextually bound and always open to imaginative expansion as it encounters new forms of wisdom. I have suggested that the wisdom that has been passed down by the L'Arche communities has implications beyond the boundaries of these communities. It may be that genuine person-centred care has a covenantal dynamic wherein it is the person of both carer and cared for that forms the locus for the loving encounter. The question is: do we have an imagination that is broad or deep enough to begin to listen to the wisdom of L'Arche and learn what it means to be wise professionals who see the world just a little bit differently, and who, in seeing things differently, begin to practise differently?

References

Brueggemann, W. (1993), *The Bible and Postmodern Imagination*, New York. Fortress Press.

Donovan, G.K. (2000), 'The Physician–patient Relationship', in D.C. Thomasma and J.L. Kissell (ed.), *The Healthcare Professional as Friend and Healer*, Washington, DC: Georgetown University Press.

Hauerwas, S. (1988), 'Taking Time for Peace: The Ethical Significance of the Trivial', in *Christian Existence Today: Essays on Church, World and Living in Between*, Durham, NC: Labyrinth Press, 253–66.

—— (1994), *Dispatches from the Front: Theological Engagements with the Secular*, Durham, NC: Duke University Press.

Kearney, T. (1984), 'Discovering the Beatitudes at L'Arche', *The Furrow*, 35(7), 460–64.

Koenig, H.G., McCullough, M.E. and Larson, D.B. (2001), *Handbook of Religion and Health*, Oxford: Oxford University Press.

L'Arche Internationale (1993), *Charter of the Communities of L'Arche*, <http://www.larche.org/charter-of-the-communities-of-l-arche.en-gb.43.3.content.htm> (accessed 25 March 2011).

McFague, S. (1988), *Models of God: Theology for an Ecological, Nuclear Age*, London: SCM Press.

Nunkoosing, K. and John, M. (1997), 'Friendships, relationships and the management of rejection and loneliness by people with learning disabilities', *Journal of Intellectual Disabilities*, 1(1), 10–18.

Swinton, J. (2001a), *A Space to Listen: Meeting the Spiritual Needs of People with Learning Disabilities*, London: Mental Health Foundation.

—— (2001b), *Spirituality and Mental Health Care: Rediscovering a 'Forgotten' Dimension*, London: Jessica Kingsley Publishers.

—— and Powrie, E. (2004), *Why Are We Here? Understanding the Spiritual Lives of People with Learning Disabilities*, London: Mental Health Foundation.

Vanier, J. (1999), *Becoming Human*, 2nd edn, New York: Paulist Press.

Young, F.M. (1997), *Encounter with Mystery: Reflection on L'Arche and Living with Disability*, London: Darton, Longman & Todd.

Part III

Legislation, Regulation and
Professional Judgement

11 Fabled Uncertainty in Social Work[1]

Sue White

Introduction

In this chapter, I explore the place of certainty, uncertainty and professionalism in social work practice. I argue that certainty and uncertainty are a good deal more context-dependent than has sometimes been suggested, and professional identities a good deal more malleable. Specifically, in the UK at least, the notion that the day-to-day practice of professional social work can accommodate, let alone embrace, uncertainty is erroneous.

My ideas on this matter developed substantially while I was analysing a corpus of data from a two-year ethnographic study of an integrated child health service (White, 2002; White and Stancombe, 2003). The service comprised paediatric inpatient and outpatient facilities, a child and adolescent mental health service, a child development centre and a social work team. Methods included observation of clinics, ward rounds and staff/team meetings, audio-recording of inter-professional talk in meetings and other less formal settings, such as before and after clinics, the tracking of a number of individual cases through the services, and a documentary analysis of medical notes. The study generated many hours of audio-taped, naturally occurring conversations between various professionals in meetings, over coffee, in corridors and so forth. On analysing these data, I was struck by how many markers of uncertainty

1   The research referred to in this chapter was supported by the ESRC, and in relation to the more recent work, I am indebted to my co-investigators at the Universities of Cardiff, Huddersfield, Lancaster and Nottingham. This chapter draws extensively on my paper 'Fabled uncertainty in social work: A coda to Spafford et al.', previously published by Sage Publications in the *Journal of Social Work*, 9(2) (2009), 222–35.

– 'it might be, but I'm not sure', 'I know the test says this, but you can never tell' – there were in doctors' talk about relatively 'technological' matters like test results. I was equally struck by how relatively few such markers there were in social workers' talk, which often took the form of complex characterisations of people, relationships and so forth. Moreover, when doctors were discussing relationships, their talk also became much more apodictic in flavour, with fewer markers of uncertainty. This was something of a surprise, but it did not prove too difficult to generate what I think are reasonable candidate explanations.

These I shall articulate in due course, but first, some data. The following extract is taken from pre-clinic briefing sessions between a consultant paediatrician (Con.) and a registrar (Reg.).

Extract 1

Con.: He's been in with asthma but that's not why he comes to see us. The main reason is some hydronephrosis[2] – I think I've got the last scan, seems to have a problem attending [reading]. Repeat ultrasound October 99, it's still hydronephrosis, further up urinary tract infection, yeah, for definite.
Reg.: That's back in April.
Con.: Back in April. DMSA [dimercaptosuccinic acid-test to assess scarring and relative function of kidney] clear. Mild right-sided hydronephrosis with prominent renal pelvis mainly extra-renal, no scarring and no … reflux. So, I suppose I thought that the best way was to do repeat the ultrasound if the kidney was blowing up. It's difficult sometimes with these mild hydronephroses. You never know whether it's the beginning of –
Reg.: Or whether it's borderline –
Con.: Or whether it's just the way they're made –
Reg.: Yeah, yeah –

The consultant's account has a number of markers of certainty – 'urinary tract infection, yeah, for definite' – but these are juxtaposed with markers of uncertainty, warranted principally by clinical experience – 'It's difficult sometimes with these mild hydronephroses' – accompanied by references to the limits and fallibility of the technology. The difficulty in adjudicating between the normal and pathological is explicitly stated.

This kind of exchange was more commonly seen when clinicians were discussing what appeared to be the more technological aspects of medicine,

---

2   Hydronephrosis is a condition in which one or both of the kidneys become swollen, due to a build-up of pressure when urine cannot drain from the organ.

with fewer markers of uncertainty when they were discussing psycho-social cases which demanded judgements about matters such as parental competence or love.

Extract 2

Con.: Ben Owen – you've not had the pleasure of this mother. Mother is under our psychiatrists, she is a [2.0] … factitious illness gives the wrong impression. She's got a [neurotic] state really, somatisation –
Reg.: Right, right.
Con.: Somatisation, really severe somatisation disorder –
Reg.: Right, yeah.
Con.: You, you may have met her, as soon as you meet her, she'll go on – he's constipated, severely constipated.
Reg.: I think I probably, what's he got? Yes, it's all, yes –
Con.: She looks ill, and as soon as you meet her she looks ill and she'll come out with all of her complaints. He has severe constipation, actually required a manual when they first brought him in to extract the masses of faeces, but recently he's relapsed and the problem seemed to be that mum had relapsed as well, so everything went down and he had to come in for an enema –
Reg.: That's right, that's right. That's how I know him, I didn't see him.
Con.: No, well, and mum couldn't, it had to be done here because mum can't cope at home, she can't cope. He was much better, but he was on sort of 30 ml of Picolax a day. His bowel is just sort of –
Reg.: – Huge.

This extract is again taken from a discussion at the beginning of a paediatric outpatient clinic. The consultant begins by stating the child's name, but the 'mother' is immediately introduced as a troublesome party with the ironic statement 'you've not had the pleasure' and by assigning her to the deviant category 'psychiatric patient'. With the statement, 'You, you may have met her, as soon as you meet her, she'll go on – he's constipated, severely constipated', the consultant makes an implicit link between the symptom (constipation) and the mother's character. This needs very little elaboration; its relevance is not questioned by the registrar, who appears to hear it as an account of what caused the problem. That is, by describing the mother and her behaviour, the consultant establishes the child's complaint as a psychological response to inappropriate parental management.

In the next extract, a social worker is describing one of her clients. Here, there is no explicit reference to theory, but the popular version of psychological ideas is used to produce a formulation about the case which is clear and unequivocal, and forms the basis for the social worker's work.

Extract 3

> Yes, I mean she's a very angry person, but, so there are a lot of issues probably in the past that she could perhaps do with working through, whether she will or not, I don't know. Her family have all turned against her because she drinks. ….
> In fact, really, if she had a more supportive family, I think her problems would be a lot less, it's just that she's completely on her own with an aggressive nature. I mean, I was quite pleased today because I've had quite a few conversations with her about her aggression and how she deals with people, and in the core group today, I mean, she started off saying she was going to kill the head teacher, she was going to fucking punch her and all this sort of thing, but she was quite assertive, really. She said what she had to say, not in a way that I would … so perhaps a bit of it's sinking in, I don't know.

Here, the social worker makes use of popular psychological knowledge. Her formulation draws implicitly on the ideas about early trauma associated with psychodynamic theory – 'so there are a lot of issues probably in the past that she could perhaps do with working through'. It makes explicit attributions of cause and effect – 'really, if she had a more supportive family, I think her problems would be a lot less' – but also blames the client, or rather her drinking habits, for her not having a 'supportive family' – 'her family have all turned against her because she drinks'. She uses reported speech to support her claims about the client's aggressiveness, but goes on to mark the effect of her own interventions – 'but she was quite assertive, really. She said what she had to say, not in a way that I would … so perhaps a bit of it's sinking in, I don't know.' This relatively popularised knowledge grants an apodictic, undisputed and irrefutable status to the formulations, and enables the social worker to categorise and process the case, and also to account for her actions. Moreover, because it invokes her status as eyewitness, it would be exceedingly difficult to challenge without compelling contradictory evidence.

These tendencies are even more evident in this next extract from Sally Holland's ethnography of child and family social work.

Extract 4

> Mrs. James presents as a passive young woman, expressing little change in her emotions. Engaging with her has been difficult, not only due to her missed appointments, but her personality is such that she does not initiate and maintain conversation. However, once given the attention, she can appear cooperative, she holds no strong views or opinions on matters relating to her life circumstances. Factors of her background, her motivations, the concerns she has, or her plans for the future are not known. (extract from assessment report; Holland, 2000, 156)

The language in this written format has a more technical gloss, and a certain expertise is implied. The social worker is not easily duped: she can see beneath the surface, Mrs James only 'appears' co-operative. However, the claims are similar to those in Extract 3. They require very little in way of argument or persuasion. They appear straightforwardly as simply so.

* * *

The data above illustrate that in technological domains, clinicians often seem to display a degree of scepticism and uncertainty about the technologies themselves and the diagnoses they may suggest, whereas when opinions are proffered about human relationships, these appear to be delivered with much less equivocation (for further detail and other exemplars, see White and Stancombe, 2003). In the domain of human relationships, then, professional talk centres not so much on uncertainty, but on complex characterisations. These formulations may or may not be accompanied by references to specific theories. That is, the popular nature of the ideas invoked apparently exempts practitioners from the imperative to justify their actions using formal knowledge. In the slippery world of relationships and interaction, professionals seem to suspend disbelief, while in more rational-technical activities, they seem to be more likely to display scepticism. So how do we explain this apparent paradox?

In a recent article by Marlee Spafford and her colleagues (Spafford et al., 2007, 155) they report that 'Social Work students viewed the acknowledgement and examination of uncertainty as a touchstone of competent social work'. At least three factors can be identified which may predispose social workers to depart prematurely from a position of 'respectful uncertainty' (Laming, 2003) about their assessments of people and situations.

1. Social work texts often rely substantially on relatively popularised, handbook versions of theory.

2. Social work often operates in the moral domain. We know from work in cognitive neuroscience that moral judgements rely substantially on affect – emotion – and that 'reasoning' appears to be added *ex post facto*. The emotional dog subsequently wags his rational tail (or tale!) (Haidt, 2001). Moreover, rather than destabilise these judgements, group discussion tends to solidify them, since affective judgements generate group norms.

3. Certainly in the UK, a combination of retrenched and over-stretched services, the demands of performance management and the impact of various information and communication technologies mean that decisions are made quickly on the basis of limited information, which means the kinds of discussions that, for example, Spafford et al. (2007) have seen in a pedagogical context are not typical of day-to-day talk in social work agencies.

Let us examine these arguments in turn.

Social Work and 'Take-away Knowledge'

The work of microbiologist and philosopher of science Ludwik Fleck is relevant to my argument. Fleck was concerned with the processes whereby the tentative 'exploratory' science of the laboratory becomes transformed into something more stable. Fleck sought to understand how science changes as it moves from the 'esoteric' domains of the laboratory into more applied settings, and finally into 'popular' or 'exoteric' domains. He investigated this empirically by analysing the structure of scientific literature, which he sub-classified as 'journal' and 'handbook' (vade mecum) science (Fleck, 1979, 111–12). Fleck pointed to the way in which laboratory science becomes gradually transformed and simplified as it becomes popularised. 'Journal science' is tentative and provisional, characterised by forms of expression such as 'it appears possible that ...' which invite the collective (community of scientists or practitioners) to adjudicate on the rightness or wrongness of the claims. In the extracts above, it seems that the scientific language of technological medicine may provide a vocabulary through which uncertainty can be expressed as competence and savvy.

Fleck argues that over time, journal science is moulded into a simplified form via vade mecum (or handbook) science, which results from the migration of ideas through the collective. *Vade mecum* literally translated from the Latin means 'go with me'. In English, however, it has come to mean the kind of 'take-away knowledge' we find in textbooks. As handbook science travels further away from its sites of production via the media into the domain of popular science, its status becomes even more simplified and 'certain'. Popular science is characterised by the omission of detail and of dissenting or controversial opinion. This transforms knowledge into something '[s]implified, lucid, and apodictic' (Fleck, 1979, 112). Thus, where judgements depend extensively on a combination of vade mecum (handbook) science and popular wisdom, we may find professionals are often actually very good at carving certainty from ambiguity, as in relation to medicine (see Atkinson, 1995).

So Fleck's argument is that however specialised our field, a major portion of the knowledge we use is popular wisdom, or knowledge for non-experts. I suggest that this is particularly the case where judgements about people, relationships and personality are a central feature of the work – as is the case in social work (White and Stancombe, 2003; Taylor and White, 2006).

Moreover, social workers are particularly exposed to vade mecum versions of psychological theories of various kinds. There are a number of obvious examples. The versions of attachment theory made available to social workers often lack the equivocations and caveats of the original works (Taylor, 2004). Indeed, the simplifying 'lens' effect is intentional, as Howe et al. argue:

> theories help to organize what we know. Theories also provide an economy of effort. They allow conceptual short-cuts to be taken. If the theory is powerful one, it might only take a few observations to locate a particular phenomenon as an example of a class of objects or behaviours …. Hypotheses help to guide future observations, the results of which aid practitioners in further testing and refining their initial assessments and observations. (Howe et al., 1999, 228)

The knowledge of the vade mecum provides just such powerful theories, but that is not altogether a good thing. Imagine for a moment Arnold Gesell (for example, Gesell and Ilg, 1943) undertaking the seminal experiments that led to his classification of the ages and stages of cognitive and sensori-motor development in infants. In his laboratory work, he observed any number of variously compliant or recalcitrant infants with the aim of charting what *most* infants do at various developmental stages. Of course, for each of the behaviours he eventually mapped, there would be a good few infants who did not display the behaviour in question for any number of reasons, yet these variations are obscured in the line drawings he eventually produced of children doing what *most* children did, which in turn populate various professional textbooks. These texts do not invite scepticism, they invite categorisation. When observing paediatric outpatient clinics, for example, it is striking how many children are referred from primary health screening because their bladders and bowels stubbornly refuse to follow the developmental trajectory at the pace dictated by the charts. Paediatricians have a set of questions which help to identify those children who may have an underlying disorder, but the vast majority are simply defined as 'maturational problems', and the therapy is parental reassurance. A 'diagnosis' of an attachment disorder by a social worker is far harder to falsify, since there are few human behaviours that attachment theory cannot reasonably plausibly account for. In sum, 'technologies' of assessment are the handbook embodiments of theories. As such, they can construct versions of reality and affect what we 'see' when we 'observe', as John (1990) notes:

> just as theories are underdetermined by facts, so facts are overdetermined by theory, which means that situations may be capable of a range of factual interpretations depending on the theory selected. Furthermore, individual psychological theories have been shown to be capable of such a degree of interpretive flexibility as to virtually incorrigible; it has sometimes been difficult to find situations, even when they involve quite contradictory outcomes, which they could not plausibly explain. (John, 1990, 127)

There is a danger that all that is revealed in the application of a theory are its own metaphysics expressed in the diagnostic fables of its votaries (Wastell and White, 2009). When we add supple theory to our innate equipment for making emotional judgements and our tendencies as information processors towards seeking to confirm our initial hypotheses (Kahneman et al., 1982), we have an intoxicating concoction rendering us dizzy and drunk on our own convictions. The cocktail is all the more sweet and heady when supped in the company of like-minded friends.

Social Work, Moral Judgement and Emotion

I have said that there is compelling evidence from cognitive neuroscience to overturn the Cartesian separation of reason from emotion (see, among others, Damasio, 1994). The perspectives, closely allied to each other, carry a number of appellations – for example, the 'sentimental rules hypothesis' (Nichols, 2004) or 'social intuitionism' (Haidt, 2001). Based on sound empirical work, they convincingly demonstrate, in the words of neuroscientist Antonio Damasio, that:

> certain aspects of the process of emotion and feeling are indispensable for rationality. At their best, feelings point us in the proper direction, take us to the appropriate place in a decision-making space, where we may put the instruments of logic to good use. We are faced by uncertainty when we have to make a moral judgement …. Emotion and feeling, along with the covert physiological

machinery underlying them, assist us with the daunting task of predicting an uncertain future and planning our actions accordingly. (Damasio, 1994, xiv–xv)

The social intuitionist approach articulated by psychologist Jonathan Haidt (for example, in Haidt, 2001) is particularly apposite for social work. Based on painstaking empirical work in experimental psychology Haidt shows that *reasoning* follows moral judgement, not the other way round. So, to use Haidt's example, the process goes as follows: 'Abortion feels wrong.' Why? 'Well, life begins at conception' – *not* 'Life begins at conception,' *therefore* 'abortion is wrong'. Emotions are, then, indispensable (but not infallible) guides to decision-making. We had affect before we had language, thus verbal reasoning is often the postscript to judgements made on other grounds (Nussbaum, 2001). If emotion and moral judgement are inevitable and necessary but are constructed as murky contaminants to reason, then we face at least three potential problems:

1. Affective/moral judgements are justified using other warrants, and therefore are concealed and not debated.
2. Positive emotional responses, such as compassion, can be bracketed out by technological vocabularies, procedure, habit, rule and routine.
3. Certain behaviours can become transformed into 'moral violations' by normative understandings of the group; for example, a team's views on mothering may predispose them to certain judgements, as Haidt notes:

Because moral positions always have an affective component to them, it is hypothesised that reasoned persuasion works not by providing logically compelling arguments, but by triggering new, affectively valenced intuitions in the listener … Because people are highly attuned to the emergence of group norms, the model proposes that the mere fact that friends, allies and acquaintances have made a moral judgement exerts a direct influence on others, even if no reasoned persuasion is used. (Haidt, 2001, 819)

I have seen this effect many times when analysing extracts of inter-professional talk. When professionals make moral judgements which are congruent with group norms, very little argument is generated. This brings me to my final points about practice cultures and contexts.

Culture, Organisation and Social Work

I have argued that certain aspects of occupational culture operate in exactly the way Haidt has expounded above. Team talk is often confirmatory, and group norms and understandings are often reinforced by humour and story-telling. The following extract is taken from a transcript of a weekly social work allocation meeting in a children and families team in the late 1990s.

Extract 4

> **Team Leader**: … One that Deborah's been out on today with Bev, and Deborah and Sally are going to finish it off this afternoon was a family called [name] where there's a sort of marital conflict and where father's made allegations about mother's treatment of the children which does appear to be over the top.
> **Others**: Uuuuurgh [laughter].
> **Team Leader**: I know, I know … Deborah is either trying to see Mum this afternoon, or she and I will try to see them together tomorrow, but it just is possible that this is one that will appear again, and I just think that I want people to be aware. There are four children in the family, and there's been a marital dispute, mother left and dad said the children had made allegations which sound a bit over the top, so that's one that may be coming back to us, I suspect, but at the moment we're trying to deal with it very clearly as a one-off and getting them to get legal advice.

The team leader categorises this case as a 'sort of marital conflict', which implies that the father's account may be subject to bias or partisanship. This ironises the father's version and trivialises any risk to the children. By the collective exclamation 'Uuuuurgh' followed by laughter, social workers display their shared knowledge that allegations of abuse made by estranged partners are problematic. This is typical of this kind of case-talk. As Haidt suggests, the team leader's description of the referral draws out 'affectively valenced intuitions in the listener[s]', who respond with shared laughter.

The tendencies to rush to categorisation are exacerbated by organisational impacts of current policy in the UK. With colleagues, I recently completed a two-year ESRC-funded study of the impact of ICTs on professional practice (see, for example, Connolly et al., 2007; Peckover et al., 2008; Hall et al., 2011). We are currently engaged in a further project under the ESRC's public services programme looking at the impact of performance management in children's services. Both these studies show how, in various ways, judgements *have* to be precipitous and *have* to be coded as certain – the technologies demand it, and the timescales imposed by government preclude equivocation about cases, which simply *have* to be categorised as this or that. Table 11.1 shows a set of referrals which greeted the team manager of a referral and assessment team in one of our sites.[3]

Allocation and disposal decisions are made very quickly, often based upon little more information than is shown here. They are thus likely to involve substantial amounts of tacit knowledge, and to require the exercise of moral judgement about normality and deviance. This leads to early categorisation of the case – for example, 'This is a non-familial assault' or 'This is a behaviour support issue' – and these are associated with plans about what is done in these sorts of cases. More importantly, the referral team manager explained that she undertook a risk assessment score 'in her head', and then filled in the form to evidence her decision. This again suggests an *ex post facto* rationalisation for a decision taken on intuitive grounds, bearing out Haidt's thesis above. The risk scoring is undertaken on the computer, and forms part of the e-record that is 'workflowed' through to the assessment team; it is also printed out and signed, symbolically suggestive of scientific risk assessment processes, but in truth it is an expedient re-packaging of an 'intuitive' professional judgement. Institutional categories, then, exist precisely to carve certainty from ambiguity, and they are more than fit for purpose.

Conclusion

While Spafford et al. (2007) argue that uncertainty is a touchstone of professional competence, rather than a personal deficit, in UK children's services, where my empirical work is located, uncertainty is rarely an option for practitioners. The raft of government reforms, and particularly the implementation of various e-enabled assessment instruments, push social workers towards precipitous categorisations and action. Institutional categories are the pistons inside a swift disposal device. Varieties of moral judgement and the limber knowledge disseminated in handbooks provide the lubrication for the machine's efficient execution. It is noteworthy that a similar categorical tendency has been described by Gerhard Riemann in his work with German social workers:

> many practitioners seem to expect from themselves – and assume that the others expect it from them, too – that they can demonstrate quickly that they have reached professional insights .... The speedy determination of 'what's the case' seems to be a prestigious and often competitive activity. (Riemann, 2005, 423)

---

3   These data were collected by Dr Sue Peckover, University of Huddersfield, Senior Research Fellow on the project.

Table 11.1   'Monday morning': Cases referred to 'Erewhon' office

1	Police referral following weekend call-out. Three children witnessed domestic violence. Mother taken to hospital with fractured nose. Father arrested.
2	Sexual abuse, and child assaulted by mother.
3	Information that child is having contact with offender who has convictions for sexual assault.
4	Young child (3) shot himself with airgun while in care of father over weekend. Parents separated. Child in hospital.
5	Extra-familial assault.
6	Referral from police following domestic violence call-out. Children in household.
7	Fight between step-father and young person.
8	Behaviour issues with a teenager. Police called by parents.
9	Out-of-area child placed in 'Erewhon' area. Older half-brother has alleged that he was assaulted by this foster carer when he was living there.
10	Police referral. Called to argument between a mother and her sibling. Baby present. No assaults or damage reported. Baby not involved.
11	Referral from police following call-out to a domestic violence incident. Ex-partner attacked a woman who has young children.
12	Father with alcohol and mental health issues. Police referral.
13	Catering worker at school hit a child in the dinner queue.
14	Child with severe head lice. Non-engagement with services.
15	Referral from probation. Substance misuser in relationship with woman with three young children.
16	Allegation of physical assault by father on 14-year-old son.
17	Notification from police they need to interview a minor who witnessed an extra-familial assault.
18	14-year-old boy with learning difficulties and past history of abuse from his father. Now concerns about his mother's parenting.
19	Children in care of their mother. Father has a Residence Order, but children and mother have moved away. Allegations from father about their care and role of new boyfriend (using alcohol, abusive attitude).
20	Telephone call from mother saying she needed help with the baby as she couldn't cope.

While research-informed approaches appear to offer the possibility of challenge to received wisdom, they are unlikely to change the problematics of 'case formulation', where the imperative is to decide what is wrong, not what works. The bald fact is that many social workers in statutory settings do not to have the time to notice uncertainty in their work. They may repent at leisure after they have acted, or when mistakes become retrospectively obvious, but they go about their business nevertheless, and are forced to so do by the organisational systems that are in place. If we are to have a debate about what might be done, it must start with some clarity about how social workers in their day-to-day work 'think'. In order to consider further the place of uncertainty in social work, a tentative and sceptical vocabulary of the emotional and moral domain is the very least that is required, and we are unlikely to find it in easy-read psychology or e-enabled assessment frameworks. Rhetoric of complexity and reflection should not be confused with uncertainty. We have just to peer through the cracks in the wall at our elderly neighbours the psychoanalysts – ministers without rival of a heady brew of certainty – to see that the two are not the same.

References

Atkinson, P. (1995), *Medical Talk and Medical Work*, London: Sage.

Connolly, M., Hall, C., Peckover, S. and White, S. (2007), 'e-Technology and information sharing in child welfare: Learning from the English experience', *Children Australia*, 32(4), 4–8.

Damasio, A.R. (1994), *Descartes' Error: Emotion, Reason and the Human Brain*, New York: Avon Books.

Fleck, L. (1979), *Genesis and Development of Scientific Fact*, Chicago, IL: University of Chicago Press.

Gesell, A. and Ilg, F.L. (1943), *Infant and Child in the Culture of Today. The Guidance of Development in Home and Nursery School*, New York: Harper and Brothers.

Haidt, J. (2001), 'The emotional dog and its rational tail: A social intuitionist approach to moral judgement', *Psychological Review*, 108(4), 814–34.

Hall, C., Peckover, S. and White, S. (2011), 'e-Solutions to Information Sharing and Assessment', in N. Thrift, A. Tickell and S. Woolgar (ed.), *Globalization in Practice*, Oxford: Oxford University Press (forthcoming).

Holland, S. (2000), 'The assessment relationship: Interactions between social workers and parents in child protection assessments', *British Journal of Social Work*, 30(2), 149–64.

Howe, D., Brandon, M., Hinings, D. and Schofield, G. (1999), *Attachment Theory, Child Maltreatment and Family Support*, Basingstoke: Palgrave Macmillan.

John, I.D. (1990), 'Discursive style and psychological practice', *Australian Psychologist*, 25(2), 115–32.

Kahneman, D., Sloveic, P. and Tversky, A. (1982), *Judgement under Uncertainty: Heuristics and Biases*, New York: Cambridge University Press.

Laming, H. (2003), *The Victoria Climbié Inquiry: Report of an Inquiry presented by the Secretary of State for Health and the Secretary of State for the Home Department by Command of Her Majesty, January 2003*. Cm 5730, Norwich: The Stationery Office.

Nichols, S. (2004), *On the Natural Foundations of Moral Judgment*, Oxford: Oxford University Press.

Nussbaum, M. (2001), *Upheavals of Thought: The Intelligence of Emotions*, Cambridge: Cambridge University Press.

Peckover, S., White, S. and Hall, C. (2008), 'Making and managing electronic children: E-assessment in child welfare', *Information Communication and Society*, 11(3), 375–94.

Riemann, G. (2005), 'Trying to make sense of cases: Features and problems of social workers' case discussions', *Qualitative Social Work*, 4(4), 405–22.

Spafford, M., Schryer, C.F, Campbell, S.L. and Lingard, L. (2007), 'Towards embracing clinical uncertainty: Lessons for social work, optometry and medicine', *Journal of Social Work*, 7(2), 155–78.

Stewart, J. (2006), 'Asking for Senior Intervention: Conceptual Insights into the Judgement of Risk by Junior Doctors', unpublished PhD dissertation, University of Newcastle upon Tyne.

Taylor, C. (2004), 'Underpinning knowledge for child care practice: Reconsidering child development theory', *Child and Family Social Work*, 9(3), 225–35.

—— (2006), 'Narrating significant experience: Reflective accounts and the production of (self) knowledge', *British Journal of Social Work*, 36(2), 189–206.

—— and White, S. (2000), *Practising Reflexivity in Health and Welfare: Making Knowledge*, Buckingham: Open University Press.

Taylor C. and White, S. (2006), 'Knowledge and reasoning in social work: Educating for humane judgement', *British Journal of Social Work*, 35, 1–18.

Wastell, D. and White, S. (2009), 'Unsettling Evidence and Lively Language: Reflexive Practitioner as Trickster', in H. Otto, A. Polutta and H. Ziegler (ed.), *Evidence-based Practice: Modernising the Knowledge Base of Social Work?*, Leverkusen: Verlag Barbara Budrich, 227–244.

White, S. (2002), 'Accomplishing the case in paediatrics and child health: Medicine and morality in interprofessional talk', *Sociology of Health and Illness*, 24(4), 409–35.

—— and Stancombe, J. (2003), *Clinical Judgement in the Health and Welfare Professions: Extending the Evidence Base.* Maidenhead: Open University Press.

12 Crowding Out Wisdom: The Mechanisation of Adult–child Relationships

Kathleen Marshall and Maggie Mellon

Introduction

This chapter is based on the work of one of us (Kathleen Marshall) during her term of office as Scottish Commissioner for Children and Young People (SCCYP). The Commissioner is a statutory appointment, on the nomination of the Scottish Parliament, with a remit to promote and safeguard the rights of children in Scotland.[1] The chapter draws on a number of reports published or commissioned by the Children's Commissioner during her five-year tenure from April 2004 to 2009.

After a wide process of consultation with children directly and with relevant organisations, it was agreed that 'proportionate protection' should be a policy priority for the Commissioner. The children and many organisations consulted complained of the impact of a range of inter-related and sometimes contradictory legislation, guidance and practices on children's welfare and relationships with adults and each other. The impact of contradictory expectations was particularly an issue for children whose care is wholly, or in important aspects, provided and regulated by the state. This includes children in care and those with disabilities who require respite or specialist additional support and services. However, the problem identified was wider than this, and affected most children and families in some way.

An example of policy or regulation that adversely affects all children is what is interpreted by many adults as a 'don't touch' approach to children in the public, and even private, domains. In school, in friends' homes, on the

---

1   For more information about the role of the Commissioner, see <www.sccyp.org.uk>.

street, even in their own family homes, adults are anxious to avoid suspicion and accusation of harmful intentions towards children. Adults, particularly men because of the greater suspicion that attaches to men in relation to child harm, hesitate before approaching and helping a child apparently lost or in need of assistance and unaccompanied by any obviously responsible adult. This 'hands-off' approach causes parents as much anxiety as the possibility of sexual or physical abuse. Therefore, parents complain that teachers will not help even very young children apply suntan lotion, or give them help with toileting, or administer necessary medication. In the research, parents of children with disabilities complained of not being allowed to get on the school bus with them to help with seatbelts as they had not been 'police checked' and therefore might take the opportunity to abuse or molest the other children. Residential workers for children in care told of policies which stipulate a hands-off approach to children in distress: if they attempted to run away, they should not be physically restrained, but instead the police should be called to find them and bring them back. Policies of this kind clearly carry risks of harm to children that are greater and more likely than those that supposedly prompted their development and implementation.

However, what is promoted as child protection can also be understood as organisational and adult self-protection. What apparently originated in the desire to protect children from the risks of harmful attention by adults has led to a pernicious environment which not only puts children at risk, but also acts corrosively to undermine the good protective and nurturing relationships that children need from adults, and which adults need to be fully human and fulfilled. This is what the term 'mechanisation' is intended to convey: the deliberate quashing of our humanity, and its replacement with mechanical procedures. To focus on this issue and to advocate change, the Children's Commissioner undertook a programme of research and consultation with children and young people.

The following three stories, based on real events uncovered in the research and consultation, exemplify the mechanisation of adult–child relationships that is evident today, and the unattractive consequences in terms of child welfare, professional timidity and the banishment of joy. Of course, the 'crazy' picture painted by these stories is not the whole truth. There are shining beacons of good practice by responsible and caring professionals who recognise the nonsense for what it is and act accordingly. The SCCYP reports on which this chapter is based aimed not just to publicise bad and unhelpful practice, but to highlight and disseminate good practice, and to encourage those who were acting out of fear to see that things did not have to be that way.

Story 1: My Crazy Parents

The first story takes the form of a fictional film script written by Kathleen Marshall to illustrate the impact that 'mechanisation' can have on children and young people in care. It is called 'My Crazy Parents'. One should imagine it trailed by the kind of caveat one finds attached to biopics – that while this film is based on real events, names, places and identifying details have been changed in order to protect confidentiality, and some scenes have been merged in the interests of the narrative.

Scene 1

The central character and narrator of the film is a young person aged 15. A seemingly normal family home. The young narrator begins:

> Most teenagers think their parents are crazy, but mine really are! You would not believe the things they do, or make me do, before they will let me have any fun. It is totally embarrassing and sometimes it makes it just not worth it. It's much easier to stay in the virtual world of the games console – much more exciting. This is what happened last week.

Scene 2

> It all started at breakfast. As usual, I got fed up waiting for things to get served. Sometimes I just want something to eat when I want it. But my parents say the kitchen is too dangerous a place. I might get electrocuted, or cut myself on a knife. And then what would people think of them? So here we are again – cold milk and cornflakes at the dining table at 8.30 a.m.

Scene 3

> It was nice last Saturday. I thought I might go out on my bike, but I couldn't be bothered with the rigmarole. This is what happens.

The film shows a parent pulling a risk assessment form out of the drawer and questioning the narrator on where he wants to go. Then the parent writes out where he is allowed to go and gets the narrator to sign it. Then he gets the young person all covered up in helmet, knee and elbow pads and insists on accompanying him, carrying a first aid kit and a puncture repair kit. The narrator says:

> So, as you might understand, I decided not to bother.

Scene 4

But my crazy parents had noticed the nice weather too and suggested a trip to the lake. That sounded fine. But this is what happened next.

The film shows them on a beautiful lakeside with others, who are having fun, looking on in a puzzled and amused way as the parents tie a rope around the young person's waist and then to a nearby tree before he is allowed to jump over a small inlet that other children (much younger) are happily splashing around in.

Scene 5

I wanted to escape! There was a cruise boat on the lake, taking people for one hour trips. That looked cool! Amazingly, my parents seemed OK about going on it. At least, I thought so until we reached the kiosk where you pay for the tickets. There they were – talking seriously to the guy selling them. The guy was looking puzzled. My parents looked deadly serious and increasingly frustrated. The people in the growing queue behind them were getting impatient. I couldn't help listening in, even though I didn't really want to because I was afraid of what I might hear.

The film listens in to the conversation, where a parent is saying, 'If I can't see the boat driver's insurance and qualifications, you are not having my custom. I can't expose the boy to that danger'.

Scene 6

I was feeling a bit depressed when I got home after that. Then I got a text from Harry, a boy at school. He asked if I could go and stay at his house that night. I asked my parents. They looked at each other in an anxious way, and this is what happened next:

The film shows the parents quizzing the narrator about the friend and his family and whether they have any criminal convictions. They explain to him that they can't let him stay overnight until they have thoroughly checked the background of everyone staying at the house and asked the police about them.

Scene 7

The young narrator says:

You will be glad to know that all of this stopped this week – very suddenly. What happened? A sudden revelation? A change of heart? No. On Monday, I turned 16. And this is what happened next.

The film shows a birthday celebration with the narrator blowing out the candles. Then you see the parents putting his belongings into a black bin bag and escorting him to his new accommodation – a bed and breakfast establishment in a rather scary area. The camera pans back from the narrator's face to show the bedroom. The young person says:

It's not all that brilliant, is it? But at least I am free from all the rules. It doesn't matter that I haven't been taught to cook or use a washing machine, because I am not allowed to do that here anyway. I can eat out and go to launderettes. After all, they're giving me £43 a week to live on. That should do me nicely – shouldn't it? And it doesn't matter that the guy in the next room is a convicted murderer. He's not on the Sex Offenders Register, so that's OK, isn't it?

Then comes the dénouement:

By the way, my parents are the local council. This is all about what can happen when you live in a children's home.

END
Words appear on the screen:

Everything depicted here has really happened to young people in and leaving care. Practice varies across the country, and some young people have better experiences than others. Who is this protecting?

The fact that highly risk-averse practices in care give way very suddenly to a complete lack of care and some potentially very dangerous situations feeds the suspicion that child protection, in its truest sense, is not at the heart of the agenda depicted here. The rules that form the basis of the 'corporate parent's' actions in this script often have some basis in truth, but tend to be distortions of it. The script up until the point at which the boy leaves home is based upon research conducted for SCCYP by the Scottish Institute for Residential Child Care (McGuinness et al., 2007). The scenarios about bike-riding, proximity to water, overnight stays, police checks and so on all arose out of that research, and can be sourced and evidenced (for example, SCCYP, 2010). The scenario about leaving home – being pushed out at age 16, belongings in a plastic bin bag, the bed and breakfast establishment with a convicted murderer as a fellow resident – is taken from, and evidenced in, an SCCYP report laid before the Scottish Parliament in 2008 entitled *Sweet 16? The Age of Leaving Care in Scotland* (SCCYP, 2008b).

Building upon suspicions raised by answers given to a previous questionnaire, the researchers visited six residential childcare establishments and spoke to some of the residents and staff about opportunities for outdoor play and activities and the surrounding rules. Most of those interviewed could not supply any written source of the 'rules' that were said to shape their actions; they had learned them by word of mouth. The one institution that did give a written source produced a 1992 document from the former Strathclyde Regional Council that had been based on 1980s guidance for schools and which, read in its proper context, was fine. However, it was being applied to quite a different set of circumstances. The rules followed in relation to the child who wanted to go out on his bike – the risk assessment, the equipment the child had to wear, the member of staff accompanying the child with a first aid kit and a puncture repair kit – had been extracted from a part of the document addressing organised trips in the open country – mountain biking, hill-walking and other outdoor pursuits with adult instructors or supervisors. In that context, they were appropriate, but not for an individual child who just wanted to go out to play on the bike. What it shows is that adults are so frightened of getting the blame if things go wrong that they are looking for rules they can follow to protect themselves. And if there are no rules or guidance designed specifically for the occasion, they will take anything that seems vaguely relevant and likely to protect them from suspicion, accusation, investigation and their terrible personal and professional consequences. For this, adults cannot be entirely blamed. The climate for childcare has been one of suspicion, accusation and investigation – and of presumed guilt rather than innocence or simply a mistake when anything goes wrong.

This conclusion is supported by other research published by SCCYP on *Adult Attitudes to Contact with Children and Young People* (SCCYP, 2007). It showed that the biggest barrier to contact was fear of being accused of harming a child through neglect or abuse, specifically sexual abuse. This latter fear was leading many adults, particularly men, to avoid any contact, or when they did have contact, to dehumanise it, to avoid any touch or speech that might be misinterpreted, and to cling to rules like safety ropes on a stormy deck. Common sense went out the window – crowded out by fear and regulation, whether real or imagined.

Story 2: Helping Children in Difficulty

A second story, also arising out of the research on adult attitudes, concerns a situation in which 'a child aged 9 is left alone after an activity that you have helped to arrange. No-one has come to pick them up. It is dark. Neither of you has a phone. You have a car'.

This was one of a number of scenarios put to a properly sampled survey of 1,093 adults across Scotland in February 2007. They were asked whether they would drive the child home.

- 37% said they were 'very likely' to do so;
- 31% said they were 'quite likely' to do so;
- 20% said they were 'not sure';
- 8% said they would 'probably not';
- 4% said they would 'definitely not'. (SCCYP, 2007, 24)

The survey was followed by a series of focus groups designed to explore the scenarios in greater depth. The responses from these groups indicated that people would be much more cautious about intervening to help than the survey scores would suggest. It seems that people like to think they would act to protect a child even in the face of their own fears, but the fears are a strong, and possibly persuasive, disincentive. With regard to this particular scenario, the researchers observed:

> The scenario provoked significant debate from focus group participants. Many people suggested they would be very reluctant to take the child home in this situation and whether [they did so] might depend on how well they knew the parents and whether there were other adults present. Some people suggested they would be worried about what the parents would think, or accuse them of, if they turned up at their home with their child, rather than being grateful. The privacy of the car seems to be a key issue: people were reluctant to be alone with a child in a private situation and a few suggested they would rather leave the car and walk than be alone with a child in [a] car. The suspicion that was feared was accusation of sexual abuse or of intention to sexually abuse.

> 'It's a difficult situation, what do you do?'

> 'I'd be worried. I would have to stand and wait.' (SCCYP, 2007, 23)

It is good to see people thinking creatively about how they could respond appropriately without putting themselves at risk of accusation or suspicion, but alarming to think that there might be some, possibly a majority, who would feel unable to help the child. It has echoes of the terrible tragedy of two-year-old James Bulger, who in 1993 was dragged, crying, through the streets of Liverpool by two ten-year-old boys who had abducted him from a shopping centre and then killed him. At that point, the media profiled the question: 'Why did none of the adults who saw this intervene to help?'

The SCCYP research shows that, for some adults at least, the risk to themselves of intervening to help a child outweighs care, compassion or responsibility. Fear outweighs, and crowds out, wisdom. Some adults would rather leave a child alone on a dark street than intervene to help if that might raise suspicions about their motivation.

Story 3: Helping Disabled Children

In the first two stories we see rules and practices that have developed supposedly to protect children being taken up as a means of protecting adults from blame. This has unfortunate consequences for children's safety, welfare or development. The third story is about rules that are supposed to keep adult workers safe, and about their impact on children and on the adult workers. It focuses on the approach to moving and handling children and young people with physical disabilities.

Evelyn (aged 14) has a considerable disability and uses a wheelchair. She does have some mobility, and can be helped into a standing position with support for short periods. It is important that she is allowed to do this or she will lose the limited mobility she has. Evelyn has carers who help her out at home, in school and on any outings. The carers have been told by their employer that on no account must they lift or manually handle Evelyn. It is 'against health and safety', and is a rule designed for the workers' protection. So when Evelyn slumps over in her wheelchair, as she often does, they are not allowed to straighten her up. When this happens at school, Evelyn has to contact a parent to come to the school to perform this service for her. When Evelyn needs to go to the toilet, carers are not allowed to help her move towards it. They have to use a hoist and sling, which makes Evelyn feel undignified, 'trussed up like a turkey', manoeuvred 'like cargo'. It also takes time to do. While she is waiting, she sometimes wets herself, which does nothing for her confidence or dignity. Some of her carers realise that this is nonsense and help Evelyn get to the toilet without the hoist. They do it secretly, because they will be disciplined if they are found out. Evelyn worries about the carers hurting themselves, since because they are forbidden from handling her, they have not been taught how to move and handle her safely.

The incidents in this scenario are evidenced in a SCCYP report laid before the Scottish Parliament in 2008, *Handle With Care* (Paton, 2008), and the associated DVD, *Dignity in Practice: Reflections on Moving and Handling* (SCCYP, 2008a). The irony is that by acting out of compassion and breaking the rules, the workers may not only be handling Evelyn in a way that is unsafe for her, but they may be leaving themselves open to disciplinary action, and also putting themselves out of the reach of any employment protection if they get hurt. So these rules, which are supposed to help the workers, do not always even do that. In some cases, where rules breach common sense, wisdom and love, the only entity they end up protecting is the employing institution. Of course, there are some cases in which recourse has to be made to mechanical aids, but blanket 'no lifting' policies are unhelpful to everyone. It would be better for everyone if individual assessments of people with disabilities took full account of their capacities and preferences, and workers were trained to move and handle appropriately and safely without resort to mechanical aids where it was possible to do so.

The Mechanisation of Relationships

The third story portrays the mechanisation of relationships between adults and children in a very concrete form. But even when there is no brute, physical presence of machinery such as hoists and slings, a more subtle mechanisation is evident, manifest in rules and myths, and fuelled by fears of blame or liability on the part of individuals and agencies. Media reports and genuine public concern following death or injury to a child often focus on whether or not 'guidelines' were followed, and can be quick to blame those who were not aware of them or did not follow them. It is natural that we should reflect on tragic events and do our best to ensure that the bad things that happened do not happen again. This often translates into the production of guidelines. However, as these thicken in content and pile up as discrete publications, it can become pure fiction to assume that workers have read and internalised them. And workers can feel fearful and guilty in case they have missed something. All of this can hamper the development and application of professional wisdom which informs a humane response to difficult situations.

When guidelines have not been followed, there are often calls for them to be made statutory – to turn the guidance into law. This is mechanisation in its purest form, where the professional is reduced to a cog in a child protection machine, and where the child is the product swept along the conveyor belt, untouched by human hand. In the child protection factory, no human can be held accountable because no individual is empowered to make decisions – it is all the responsibility and the fault of the system.

It is important that we recognise and acknowledge the reasons why we feel compelled to produce ever more laws and guidelines. Some see it is an aspect of a privileged position children hold in our society – where everything possible is done to protect them from harm. A phrase that has come into vogue in the past few years is 'the cotton wool kids'. This refers to our reluctance to allow children the freedom to engage in stimulating play and activities that might involve risk: the freedom to roam, to climb, to jump, to gather, to have fun with no adults present. The 'cotton wool' analogy does seem appropriate for some contexts, especially some parent–child relationships, but in a professional context, the image of cotton wool is too soft and cosy. The more sinister image of barbed wire may be more appropriate. Cotton wool is designed to protect the child. Barbed wire can perform that function too, but it also – and in some cases, largely – serves to protect adults from the threat that contact with children can pose to their reputations, livelihood and even family life. The cotton wool kid is bathed in an aura of protection – even if it is over-protection. The barbed wire kid is surrounded by notices saying 'Danger', 'Keep Out' or 'Do Not Touch'. Barbed wire is dangerous to adults and children. The barbed wire kid is one that you are not allowed to comfort when they are hurt, to hug when they are celebrating, to put sun cream on for protection during a primary school outing. Some adults even avoid *looking* at or talking to the barbed wire baby or barbed wire kid for fear that their interest will be misunderstood.

It is important not to ignore or overlook the impact that this climate of suspicion must have on children and how they understand the world. If adults are not supposed to be interested in contact with children, and suspicion attaches particularly to men, then children will be suspicious. If relationships between children and men have been tainted by fear of accusation of sexual abuse, then children will pick up on these anxieties and have their own fears and suspicions. This is indiscriminate, and not proportionate to the risk. There is a difference between children understanding that *some* adults may be dangerous, and children apprehending from adult behaviour that *all* adults are dangerous. That some strangers are dangerous does not mean that all strangers are dangerous. If all adults behave as if the child is a sexual object at huge risk from other adults, how can children be expected not to see the world in that way? And how, then, can children be taught about and protected from real risk by adults who are informed and confident in their role?

It is ironic that the 'solution', the mechanisation of relationships with children, in itself helps create and reinforce the climate of suspicion. If we want to solve the problem of the mechanisation of adult–child relationships, and the simultaneous instilling of fear and sexualisation, we need to understand and address what lies beneath the fears of adults and the over-cautiousness of organisations. This could include the relevance and impact of the publicity that can accompany even an unproven allegation; the concern that information about unproven allegations might surface in later years in police checks associated with future employment, and the perspective that the world views a suspected person as 'guilty until proven innocent' so that the 'mud will stick', come what may. Allegation, suspicion and investigation taint every relationship – professional and personal. Once 'out', it can never wholly be forgotten, and the fear must be that one's life must in future be lived under the shadow of suspicion. The provisions of successive legislation on this area now enforce the disclosure of any record of suspicions or allegations, even if these have been thoroughly investigated and disproved. This can drive perfectly innocent people out of their chosen professional careers – or from unpaid voluntary activity.

These negative aspects are things that people have been whispering about but are sometimes disinclined to say too loudly for fear that they will be accused of acting against the child protection agenda – of making children vulnerable or even of wanting them to be vulnerable. The fear of being suspected of ulterior motives for questioning what seems to be hurting rather than protecting children can act as a powerful disincentive to challenge. It is no good just dismissing adult or organisational fears. If we ignore them or dismiss them as unworthy, they will remain entrenched as substantial impediments to the full realisation of the rights of children, not just to be protected, but to develop through involvement in stimulating activities – and simply to have fun, by themselves and with adults. The fears of adults have to be acknowledged and addressed in a way that safeguards and promotes the whole spectrum of children and young people's rights to a safe, active and happy childhood, warmed by satisfying relationships with trusted and responsible people.

In addition to recognising the fear and self-protection of individual staff members, we also need to identify and acknowledge the fears of institutions. Institutions can contribute to the over-'protection' agenda on grounds of financial and not just of reputational risk. Institutions can feel required to impose harmful policies and procedures in the face of insurers' strict conditions, which necessarily entail the kind of mechanistic measures described in Story 1 in relation to children 'in care'.

It is absolutely right that policies should not be so sensitive to adults' fears and feelings that children are silenced and vilified. In addition, it could be argued that this might be over-protection of adults, and lend weight to the claim that there is a population of vicious children eager to make false allegations. Getting this balance right is an endeavour fraught with difficulties. Suggestions of a more considered approach to responding to allegations against adults – one that does not immediately assume guilt and does not allow a person still 'innocent' in law to be 'named and shamed' – can lead to accusations that you are 'on the side of' abusive adults against children.

However, this is a false dichotomy. The human rights of different individuals and groups are generally inter-connected rather than opposed. It is no doubt true that some children sometimes make false claims, or are mistaken in their claims, but it is the adult response to these claims that is the problem, not the children who voice them. It is much more likely that an 'over-the-top' response will silence rather than empower children and adults. It is children who end up suffering the consequences of indiscriminate and disproportionate responses. When we have reached a stage where innocent, well-meaning adults are afraid to interact with children – and are even *afraid of* children – that is clear evidence that we have got something wrong (see Marshall, 2005).

There are therefore two separate but related aspects to the problem. One is about fear of blame if there is an accident, and this links in to 'health and safety' issues and the desire for rules that will keep adults safe. These fears concern individual and organisational liability. For organisations, the risk of criminal prosecution or civil liability, and/or losing insurance cover, can and does drive the kind of restrictive practices described in Story 2. For individuals, the fear of disciplinary action, of investigation, and of criminal or civil action drives them to cling to rules or interpret and make rules that might serve to protect them from this. The other aspect concerns fear of being accused of a sexual interest in children, and the suspicion or allegation of abuse of a child. This is as significant as 'health and safety' liability as a reason for reluctance to engage with children at all. The two concerns have somehow become mixed and confused, and this has led to the development of a mixed and confused public policy towards the safety and welfare of children.

On the health and safety front, we have to decide whether it is better to give people the rules they want, but more appropriate ones, or to try to reduce the fear and move towards a more human and humane response to these situations. Some situations will require one approach, and some another. This chapter is not a plea for *no* regulation, but for policy and guidance informed and driven by a perspective that helps rather than hinders the realisation of the rights of the child.

During the research about adult attitudes, people were asked what they thought would alleviate their concerns about contact with children and young people, and their fear of being blamed if things went wrong and they were accused of harming a child through design or neglect. Depressingly, the most common answer was 'don't know'. However, some proposals came forward and were aired by the Children's Commissioner at that time. We now turn to these for a discussion of their merits and risks.

Towards Reducing Adults' Concerns about Contact with Children and Fear of Blame

Our first pair of proposals is addressed to employers and professional associations, and calls for better guidance and training. The second pair of proposals would require government action.

Better and More Even-handed Practice by Employers

Employers should develop a more considered approach to allegations of misconduct towards children. They should not automatically suspend an employee from work as a precautionary measure when an allegation is made or suspicion is voiced, regardless of the degree of risk posed to children. Whether suspension is necessary or not, investigations should be speedy, carried out by those with a sound training and experience, and focus on children's welfare rather than organisational or professional self-interest or self-protection. The possible hazard with an informed and sensitive case-by-case approach rather than a catch-all but uninformed response is that without rules, uninformed or careless employers might ignore complaints or concerns about child's welfare. However, this could be mitigated by imposing clear policy and duties, with accompanying guidance and training, to support the correct use of judgement.

A Strong Lead from the Professional and Regulatory Organisations

The Care Commission, the Scottish Social Services Council, the Association of Directors of Social Work, together with their counterparts in health and education, are concerned with developing professional wisdom in their members. They are charged with arriving at balanced judgements and recommendations about professional or organisational change in cases that have ended badly. There may well be an apprehension of organisational risk attached to taking a more measured approach in cases of alleged misconduct. Recommending professional judgement rather than tick-box procedure does require courage and confidence in the standards of professional practice. There will be cases where professional judgement fails to protect children, whether through incompetence, error or force of circumstance.

A Public Insurance System

A system of public insurance for childcare organisations is needed to help defuse the fear of litigation. It would relieve organisations from having to meet the requirements of the private insurance sector. Currently, the private sector charges prohibitively for cover against what they see as risks that would require them to pay out, while other risks which are just as real are not covered. These insurance company restrictions might perhaps not be so one-sided if a successful case were to be made on human rights grounds under the European Convention on Human Rights/Human Rights (Scotland) Act on behalf of the children affected, particularly children in care or those with disabilities. A public insurance system would only be effective if it acknowledged the rights of children to enjoy the full human experience, recognising that risk is an occupational hazard of being alive, and insisted on adherence to best childcare practice rather than risk management as the guiding principle.

Anonymity for Those Accused and Higher Standards of Investigation

The case for anonymity for those accused of child abuse has been made by the Children's Commissioner (Marshall, 2004). This would forbid the public identification of persons against whom an allegation had been made, so that the only people who could be publicly identified would be those who had been tried and found guilty. There are possible disadvantages to this approach. One was put forward recently in relation to the proposal for anonymity for those accused of rape until conviction, which was that the publication of an accused's name before trial can prompt other victims to come forward with evidence of previous assaults. However, very few cases actually arrive at the point of criminal prosecution, and these are more likely (though not always) to be those with strong evidence. The damage to reputation is often done in the absence of criminal proceedings and on the basis merely of an investigation taking place. Suspension from work, being required to live apart from one's own children, the inevitability that colleagues will know of, and be involved in, any investigation all mean that the current process can be extremely painful and public. Drawing up national professional guidance and standards for clear, fair, proportionate and informed investigation is a necessary first step to instilling greater confidence in children and adults in what happens when concerns are raised or allegations made.

Conclusion: Innocence to Wisdom

Risk aversion raises serious issues, both in relation to liability for accidents and in relation to protection from allegations of abuse. We need to address both dimensions, but it is the concern with allegations of abuse that informs the following conclusion.

In our view, the challenge faced by this generation is to carve out the path that leads from innocence to wisdom. 'Innocence' represents the state of ignorance about child abuse that characterised society in the recent past. Of course, it was not a universal ignorance, and sometimes it was a wilful 'not knowing' or intentional ignorance in the face of obvious facts such as children suffering venereal disease, sexual injury or pregnancy. This 'innocence' acted to protect the individuals perpetrating abuse. The children suffering it knew what was happening even if, in some instances, they did not know it was wrong because they had never experienced anything else. The 'innocence' of the non-abusing adults and the disbelief that accompanied it acted to silence the children, and even led to their punishment and ostracism until they retracted.

Even today, in the face of proven cases of severe abuse of children by people who are supposed to care for them, it can be hard for some adults to give up that innocence – or ignorance – of the existence and nature of child abuse. This is especially so where sexual abuse is by a parent or respected person in authority (a priest, a doctor, a judge). For some ordinary, decent people, this sort of behaviour is so far removed from their attitude towards their own children – which they assume is innate and universal – that they just cannot contemplate that any parent or respectable person ostensibly 'like us' would do this to a child.

But most people will now, possibly reluctantly, accept that the deliberate sexual and physical abuse of children does happen, and on a scale that most had never before been made to contemplate. The scandals which have shaken residential childcare, the Catholic Church and other previously trusted and respected institutions create consternation and uncertainty. Our reluctance to believe, and the aversion of those who do not yet believe, may be a product of our fear of the consequences of belief – our fear of the very kind of panic and paranoia about abuse that currently characterises our society. It is the worst of fears – a fear of fear itself.

There is panic. Every new scandal shocks us, whether it is in the home, in a nursery, in residential care or within religious organisations. We want to investigate, to root out the culprits, find out why it happened, who allowed it to happen, and how it could have gone undetected for so long. We want assurances that this kind of thing will never happen again. And that is where the paranoia sets in, precisely because we now know that respectable people can do terrible things; every respectable person becomes a potential suspect. When we know and trust, rightly or wrongly, the person or institution under investigation, then inquiry seems to us to be a witch-hunt. And because of that, we feel that nothing will protect *us* if *we* come under suspicion. Nothing is unimaginable any more. No one is safe.

The philosopher Aristotle advised orators who wished to instil fear in their audience to:

> put the audience into the state ... of thinking that they are in a position to suffer by pointing out that others, greater than them, have in fact suffered, and ... show similar men suffering or having suffered ... (Aristotle, 1991, 155)

This is precisely how the current fear of allegations of harming a child has developed into widespread paranoia. No one, we feel, is safe; no one will believe that we are innocent if the finger of suspicion is pointed in our direction.

We have lost our innocence. But we have also lost our ignorance. This loss of ignorance allows us to move beyond our current panic and paranoia to a state of *wisdom*, in which we accept the realities of child abuse, we do our best to prevent it, but we acknowledge that we cannot completely stop it. We must develop the maturity to create a system that gives children the maximum possible protection, while supporting loving and caring relationships and an environment that encourages healthy development. In order to do this, we must take steps to reduce unreasonable and disproportionate fear in innocent adults while at the same time listening to children, and shaping our systems in a way that they can trust to take their concerns seriously and protect them from harm. We should fix our eyes on a future in which we, like the biblical figure of Wisdom, can be:

> at play everywhere on his earth,
> delighting to be with the children of men.
> (Proverbs 8:22–31, *New Jerusalem Bible*, 1994)

References

Aristotle (1991), *The Art of Rhetoric*, trans. H.C. Lawson-Tancred, London: Penguin.

Marshall, K. (2004), *Names Can Never Hurt Me: Does Naming Suspects Help Children?*, The Annual McClintock Lecture for SACRO, Edinburgh, <http://www.sacro.org.uk/lecture2004.pdf> (accessed 25 March 2011).

—— (2005), *The Power to Abuse and the Power to Accuse: Implications of Shifts in the Balance of Fear*, The Annual Research Collections Lecture for Glasgow Caledonian University Library, Glasgow, <http://www.redguitars.co.uk/fbga/doesNamingSuspectsHelpChildren_kathleenMarshall_mcClintockLecture2004.pdf> (accessed 25 March 2011).

McGuinness, L., Stevens, I. and Milligan, I. (2007), *Playing It Safe: A Study of the Regulation of Outdoor Play for Children and Young People in Residential Care*, Glasgow: Scottish Institute for Residential Child Care (SIRRC) for Scotland's Commissioner for Children and Young People (SCCYP), <http://sccyp.net/admin/04policy/files/spo_264931Playing it Safe_SCCYP 200711.pdf> (accessed 25 March 2011).

New Jerusalem Bible (1994), Study Edition, London: Dartman, Longman and Todd.

Paton, L. (2008), *Handle with Care: a Report on the Moving and Handling of Children and Young People with Disabilities*, Edinburgh: SCCYP, <http://www.sccyp.org.uk/publications/adults/policyandresearch> (accessed 25 March 2011).

SCCYP (2007), *Adult Attitudes towards Contact with Children and Young People*, Edinburgh: Rocket Science, <http://www.sccyp.org.uk/publications/adults/policyandresearch> (accessed 25 March 2011).

—— (2008a), *Dignity in Practice: Reflections on Moving and Handling*, DVD, Edinburgh: SCCYP.

—— (2008b), *Sweet 16: The Age of Leaving Care in Scotland*, Edinburgh: SCCYP, <http://lx.iriss.org.uk/sites/default/files/resources/Leaving_Care_Report_for_Web_20080325.pdf> (accessed 25 March 2011).

—— (2010), *Go Outdoors!*, Edinburgh: SCCYP, <http://www.sccyp.org.uk/publications/adults/policyandresearch> (accessed 25 March 2011).

13 Ministry, Homelessness and Professional Deliberation

Alison Elliot

Introduction

Professional deliberation is sensitive to the context in which it takes place, and as that context changes, so will the action of the professional. One of the concerns of this volume is the extent to which wider cultural changes in the UK affect, and perhaps undermine, central features of professional culture and the nature of professionalism itself.

The focus of this chapter is ministry, and in particular one aspect of pastoral ministry seen from the perspective of the Church of Scotland, a Reformed Presbyterian Church which is the national Church in Scotland. Over the centuries, the Church has developed very strong views about what kind of organisational culture and practice are appropriate to its beliefs and self-understanding. As it pursues its long-standing commitment to public welfare, it increasingly finds itself working in partnership with other organisations whose cultures challenge features of the Church's practice. This poses a dilemma for ministers: should they resist practices which their professional judgement would say were wrong (such as accepting money from the National Lottery), should they compromise their principles in the interests of helping more people, or should they attempt to transform the culture and practice of their partners. These questions will be explored in the context of work that is done on homelessness in Edinburgh.

These questions can be addressed in different ways. The approach taken here will stem from a consideration of the nature of professional deliberation in ministry – the question of how the specialist knowledge underpinning ministry relates to practice, and how this interacts with the changing provision for people who are homeless.

Ministry and Professional Knowledge

It is common to assume that the relationship between professional knowledge and professional practice is simple and unidirectional. Specialised, systematic knowledge of a field is applied to a practical situation, and with experience, the process of solving problems in the area becomes easier and faster as the practitioner becomes more familiar with the full range of knowledge that is available and better able to identify the salient features of a particular case. This perspective on professional knowledge and decision-making is called 'technical rationality' by Schön (1991). It sets high value on evidence and transparency, and assumes that the knowledge base is sound and that the application of the knowledge is unproblematic. However, in the latter half of the twentieth century, public confidence in the scientific knowledge base of some areas of professional knowledge was shaken by well-publicised failures. In addition, Schön (1991) traces a greater awareness of the complexities of professional decision-making occasioned by the uncertainty, uniqueness, instability and conflict of values that surround the process. Emphasis moved from the process of problem-solving to the less well understood process of problem-setting. Rather than holding to the model of technical rationality, Schön (1991) promotes the idea of the reflective practitioner, whose knowledge is shaped by action, reflected on in the context of past experience and of current levels of knowing.

As a model of professionalism, reflective practice sits more easily with the practice of ministry than that of technical rationality. There is a strong tradition of scholarship that regards theology itself as based in activity and therefore supports an approach to ministry as reflective practice. Forrester (2000, 21) quotes Martin Luther as saying: 'Divinity consists in use and practice, not speculation and meditation.' More recently, the practice of liberation theology has developed the hermeneutical spiral as a way of addressing questions of theological truth. Rather than taking received biblical interpretation as a blueprint for understanding experience and guiding action, the liberationist position starts with engagement in lived experience and develops a deeper understanding of the Bible and Christian faith in the light of this. For the poor communities of Latin America, where this tradition emerged, this approach to theological understanding had a validity that was grounded in the experience of oppression and poverty that these people shared with many of the individuals and communities that were the concern of the biblical writers. This led to a situation where theology was contested, not through academic dispute, but out of its relevance to contemporary issues and its capacity to throw light on the experience of living communities. For ministers, tasked with the pastoral care of today's people, this offers a helpful model of professional practice.

It creates an interesting illustration of professional deliberation. Rather than professional, scientific knowledge being supplemented and moderated by reflection on experience (as it presumably is in medicine or law), in the case of ministry, the knowledge is located in the reflection itself. In other words, the minister's professional skill is that of reflecting on action through the lens of the body of knowledge that is the core of the minister's training, including biblical study and theology. Moreover, that reflective skill can be put at the disposal of a variety of activities, ranging from individual pastoral care through social commentary to community action. This is important, given the range of activities that constitute ministerial practice.

Contemporary Ministerial Practice

Normally, one speaks of ministry as the professional activity of a minister of word and sacrament. In the Church of Scotland, that person is academically trained, is one of the few people authorised to preside at the sacraments of communion and baptism, and is generally the person in charge of a parish congregation. However, recent reviews of ministry (Avis, 2005; General Assembly, 2010a; Macdonald, 2004) have reconsidered the nature of ministry itself and how it might be facilitated in contemporary circumstances. They reaffirm that Christian mission is, properly, the mission of Jesus Christ. As the body of Christ, the Church as a whole participates in that mission. And ministry is to be understood as the ministry of the whole people of God, not that of selected individuals. Within that ministry, people are called to different roles, some of which require special training and special authorisation, but ministry is more comprehensive than the activities of those specially identified people, and is incomplete if limited to their work and witness.

Alongside ministers of word and sacrament, one also finds people in other roles. There are readers, who are authorised to preach but not to preside at sacraments, and who are ordained to a local ministry. Beyond that, the Church engages chaplains (ministers of word and sacrament who work in specific specialised contexts, such as hospitals or the armed forces) and presbytery and parish workers (such as youth workers), as well as other professionals who work in specialised projects that the Church undertakes. And beyond them, exercising a variety of ministries, come the volunteers – elders or Church members – whose commitment to working *for the Church* makes much of the Church's work and outreach possible.

Along with this range of participants in ministry, it should be noted that there are three principal dimensions to the tasks of ministry. There is the sacramental dimension (the priestly role, which is undertaken only by ministers of word and sacrament), the teaching dimension (carried out by ministers and readers within the Church and by theologians within the academic context) and the dimension of pastoral care. In addition, within the Church of Scotland there is also an important dimension of parish outreach, whereby the Church not only offers to marry and bury members of the local community (whether or not they are members of the Church), but also adopts a stance of caring for the health and well-being of that wider community (see General Assembly, 2010b).

So, in that mix of roles and purposes, the minister of word and sacrament still plays a key role, complemented by the acknowledged significance of other people in the Church. The body of professional knowledge underpinning the ministry outlined here is the theological training given to ministers of word and sacrament, and this provides the basis of the reflection on practice that ministers undertake. Although acquiring this formal academic training is the privilege of only a few, an attenuated form of this reflection pervades the other forms of ministry throughout the Church, and is the basis of the Church's claims that it operates in a way that is distinctive from other organisations.

Ministry to the Homeless

Theological reflection can be exercised in a wide range of situations, from the handling of delicate pastoral problems to a critique of organisational behaviour and the nature of social institutions; its nature and operation will be different accordingly. The rest of this chapter will focus on one particular aspect of the ministry of the Church – its care of people who are vulnerable to homelessness. This is a present-day manifestation of a persistent feature of the Church throughout its history – its work with the poor and marginalised. At times, this work has been carried out by specialised groups, such as religious orders, or by faith-based agencies such as Scottish Churches Housing Action, but it has always been well supported by people throughout the Church. Although it is not one of the more exotic aspects of Christian ministry, therefore, it is an important one.

As with many forms of voluntary action today, Christian work on homelessness quickly moves away from informal sharing of resources between neighbours in a local community to the work of large-scale charities, which are caught up in today's culture of regulation, evidence-based policy development and focus on outcomes. Specialists in mental health, in addiction, in counselling, in social care, as well as specialist fundraisers and full-time administrators, play their part in delivering the services that are run by Churches and Church-based organisations. The question of how theological reflection keeps up with these changes in the culture in which their work is done will be explored by looking at some Christian organisations in Edinburgh that work with people vulnerable to homelessness.

For this chapter, I conducted interviews with Rev. Dr Russell Barr, the chair of a project (Fresh Start) that is run through and by the churches in Edinburgh, and Iain Gordon, Chief Executive of Bethany Christian Trust, a national homelessness charity that has an acknowledged Christian basis and ethos. Quotations from the interviews have been verified by the interviewees as expressing their views. Material is also taken from recorded conversations with a reflection group on homelessness that was part of the research project 'Theology in the Public Square' in Edinburgh University's Centre for Theology and Public Issues, of which I was a co-supervisor.

Fresh Start, Gateway and Bethany

The millennium was approaching, and the Kirk Session of Edinburgh's Cramond Kirk was considering how to mark it. They were unimpressed by the proposal emanating from the UK government that it should be marked by the construction of a dome in London. For them, what was being celebrated was the anniversary of the birth of Jesus, in a stable, because there was no room for his parents in the inn. Consideration moved on to the possibility of focusing on doing something for their homeless neighbours – 'Not a Dome but a home', as one member proposed. Support for the initiative was secured from churches across the ecumenical spectrum in Edinburgh, and initial funding from the Bank of Scotland. Consultation with people who were homeless indicated a gap in provision, namely support to enable people to maintain a tenancy. The rate of turnover in such properties in that part of Edinburgh at the time was six weeks. The charity Fresh Start was established to address this problem.

The charity operates three main kinds of activity. They put together Starter Packs, so that a new tenant has sufficient crockery, bedding, cleaning materials and other basic equipment to turn a house into a home. They get together Hit Squads, volunteers who decorate the property along with the tenant, and are offering training in useful skills at the same time as friendship and encouragement. And they have developed a Befriending Service, since two thirds of people facing homelessness do so as a result of a breakdown in relationships. A survey of 36 Fresh Start tenants showed that at the end of one year, 34 were still in their tenancy.[1]

---

1   Interview with Russell Barr, 19 May 2010.

Fresh Start is supported by over a hundred congregations in Edinburgh, who donate materials for Starter Packs or offer time to the Hit Squads or Befriending Service. The charity has a contract with City of Edinburgh Council to provide 7,500 Starter Packs, 100 Hit Squads a year and 25 hours' Befriending Support a week.

Recently, Fresh Start has teamed up with Bethany Christian Trust as well as three other charities to deliver the Gateway Project on behalf of the council. This is a large three-year project to provide visiting housing support to people at risk of becoming homeless or who are homeless or have recently experienced homelessness in order to enable them to avoid a housing crisis, or to obtain and/or maintain a home. The project identifies four key outcomes with regard to the lives of the homeless people involved, specified in detail in consultation with the charities, as well as 21 additional outcomes. These outcomes focus on sustaining a tenancy, but also cover improving physical and mental health, reducing substance abuse, developing the skills needed to manage a home, feeling part of the local community, and improving personal motivation and self-confidence. This list shows how ambitious, but also realistic, work with homeless people has become, from the period when handing someone the key to a flat was considered a solution to the problem. The churches can claim credit for getting to grips with the underlying aspects of homelessness. Bethany was instrumental in including in Edinburgh's Homelessness Strategy a clause that defined resettlement as helping people to 'change their lives so that they are ... working to achieve dreams and aspirations'.[2]

Bethany Christian Trust was started in 1983 by Alan Berry, a Baptist minister. It is now a significant homelessness charity, with a turnover of around £6 million, raising half of its income from local authorities, a quarter from individuals and trusts, and the final quarter from social enterprises. It provides a range of services, arranged in seven steps, from street work, through emergency accommodation, specialist units, supported housing and home furniture provision to community education and community integration, where former service users are introduced to supportive networks often provided through the churches. It has an impressive track record. Their success rate for integration into the community is 98%, compared with a Scottish average of 60–65%, and their addiction work indicates that, over a four-year period, 86% of their clients whom they were still in contact with were maintaining their tenancy and living an abstinent lifestyle, compared with a national average of 3%.

So charities initiated by Churches play a significant role in addressing the problems of homelessness. The Christians involved in these charities see this work as part of the Church's ministry. The charities are in a position

---

2   Interview with Iain Gordon, 26 May 2010.

to undertake public contracts, whose aims and outcomes are neutral with respect to Christian values, on the same terms as those organisations which are not Church-based and for whom theological reflection has no place in their practice.

This raises the question of what is distinctive about the work of the charities, and what place theological reflection has in this work. This will be explored along two dimensions: the personal motivation and theological reflection of an individual minister involved in the work, and the impact of theological critique on the organisation's practice.

Motivation and Reflection

Firstly, there is the initial motivation to engage with this work. Russell Barr, minister of Cramond and Chair of Fresh Start, sees this work as an aspect of his role as a parish minister in promoting the health and well-being of the community. He recognises that it is not necessary to explain to people that those without a home are in need and that being a good neighbour entails helping them. The biblical narrative (of the Christmas story or the parable of the Good Samaritan) gives shape and purpose to opportunities that present themselves to help in this way. He speaks of how 'doors opened, things happened, and this seemed to me to be an opportunity – it wasn't one I sought but it's one that happened and that I felt led towards'.[3]

Once engaged in the work, its theological underpinning is enhanced. The more one understands about homelessness, the more important human relationships and their breakdown are seen to be in that process, and that releases further reflection on the Christian message, which focuses so frequently on relationships:

> If homelessness isn't to do with property but with relationships, then clearly there's a lot of Christian theology around that. It would seem to me that much of the New Testament is an invitation to come home – to come home in terms of our relationships with God through Christ – and spills out – cascades out, as it were – into our relationships with one another. It seems to me that at its heart, the Christian faith is about bringing people home.[4]

Deeper understanding of the process of becoming homeless also emphasises how little it takes for someone to start down that path, and that has an impact on one's assessment of other people:

---

3   Interview with Russell Barr, 19 May 2010.
4   Ibid.

I'm far, far less judgmental about the human condition. We do need each other, not for the great things in life but for the absolute basics of life. When that network of dependency is taken away, when you become isolated … my goodness! Are you disabled as a human being then! I try to feed that back into my preaching and prayers and leading worship.[5]

Thus, theological understanding is involved in shaping the practice, which in turn gives further depth to the theological understanding – a simple illustration of reflective practice.

Critiquing the Organisation

Among the various contemporary developments that are challenging the nature of professionalism are changes in organisational culture. For some in the Christian community, there are features in these changes that weaken, or are even incompatible with, important aspects of the Christian tradition. For example, Bretherton (2010) discusses the difficulties faced by Church bodies that apply for public funding from the state. Competitive tendering pits one organisation against another, which can accentuate divisions between the Churches (Bretherton, 2010, 42). Moreover, the process of institutional isomorphism can lead to Church bodies copying features of the dominant political culture, such as 'government regulations, bureaucratic structure and professional norms' (Wuthnow, quoted in Bretherton, 2010, 44), and losing their distinctive contribution as free, non-instrumental space. Bretherton concludes that churches should be wary about partnerships with the state, and even argues that:

> In accepting the current terms and conditions of cooperation as structured by the state, the church distorts its ministry and mission and remoulds its witness around the instrumental requirements of the state. (Bretherton, 2010, 45)

In a forthright publication, Pattison (2007) also identifies features of the partnerships between Churches and other organisations which can cause difficulties, though he does not argue that these partnerships should be abandoned because of this. He details the potential dissonance between a Christian understanding of human nature and the various features of organisations whose practice and structure are driven by the requirement to identify and deliver rigid aims and objectives, which is a common feature of organisations in today's outcome-dominated culture. He portrays a

---

5   Ibid.

Christian anthropology that sees people as essentially complex beings, with diverse interests and purposes, capable of imagination and flexibility of skills, and made for a life full of rich experiences. Their horizons are set, not by the limitations of a controlling organisation that demands loyalty, but by the hope, love and grace that people of faith recognise as characteristics of the divine. From that perspective, life is a mystery, and the future is open to surprise and unknown outcomes. In the Christian tradition, wisdom, truth and insight in its most authentic forms do not come from above, but from the margins of society and from the experiences of those who are not powerful. On the face of it, the practice of driving activity towards pre-set outcomes is likely to be at odds with Pattison's (2007) account of the Christian tradition.

Therefore, if Christian organisations extend their pastoral ministry into community development, and enter into partnership with secular bodies in order to pursue this, they are likely to encounter tensions between the expectations of their partners and features of their Christian tradition. Theological reflection can be undertaken not only with regard to features of homelessness itself, but also to a critique of the culture of the partner organisations. Such a critique can reveal why such a partnership is likely to be uncomfortable, and in some cases, may result in the Church body rejecting partnership altogether.

Churches and their agencies are not alone in being wary of the risks to their distinctiveness of getting too close to other bodies or of the danger that their independence is compromised by accepting public funding. Voluntary organisations also grapple with the dilemma of how to hold on to their distinctive vision of how social problems should be addressed while trying to access funding from sources which are pursuing a different, often more minimalist, agenda. They can also find themselves in an uncomfortable position when pressures external to their own enterprise threaten that vision. How they react to this situation can be explored by considering the operation of the psychological contract (Thompson and Bunderson, 2003).

Alongside stated agreements between employee and employer about terms and conditions, there are often assumptions about 'unwritten promises and obligations implicit in [the employee's] relationship with the employing organisation' (Thompson and Bunderson, 2003, 571). These additional dimensions of the agreement between employee and employer, generally unstated, are referred to as the *psychological contract* into which they enter. Much of the value of this approach to organisational behaviour is that unrest in an organisation can often be traced, not to breaches of the stated contract, but to a breach of this psychological contract. Therefore, articulating what motivates people to undertake a piece of work, beyond the stated terms and conditions of the job, and identifying how they respond to breaches of this wider contract become important dimensions of understanding how the organisation can operate smoothly.

The contributions and rewards that are exchanged in this contract have been characterised as economic or socio-emotional. Thompson and Bunderson (2003) argue that they can also be ideological, relating to a wider purpose or mission that the organisation and its employees espouse. The significance and complexity of this contract is often high within the Church as well as within the wider voluntary sector, where people take on a job not just to pay their mortgage, but because they believe in the work the organisation is undertaking and they are prepared to go the extra mile to contribute to it. As long as things are running smoothly, this is a win–win situation for both employee and employer. However, in times of financial stringency or in periods of increased regulation, this contract can be put under considerable strain as organisations negotiate arrangements with funding partners that risk diverting them from their main purpose, or as increased form-filling alters the balance in the components of a particular job.

People respond to breaches of a psychological contract in various ways. For example, it is found that breaches of the economic conditions of the contract are likely to result in the employee leaving, while breaches of a socio-emotional nature often lead to reduced commitment and an emphasis on the detailed transactional terms of the contract. When there is an ideological component to the contract, breach of the contract can sometimes lead to organisational dissent, whereby the employees try to restore the original terms of the contract. For example, in a study of three voluntary organisations that provide social care to disadvantaged groups, Cunningham (2010) looked at how they responded to changes resulting from financial pressures. He found considerable resilience among the workforce in maintaining their commitment to their work and in respecting the psychological contract. On occasions when this led to a reduction in the amount of personal contact between clients and staff, he found that staff would find ways of maintaining that contact in order to provide the kind of service that they believed their clients needed.

This demonstrates that tensions can arise in ideologically based organisations when the mission of the organisation risks being compromised by the conditions under which funding or partnership working is offered. Various responses to this dilemma can be identified, from refusing to participate in the partnership to finding ways to resolve the tensions in order to maintain the ideological integrity of the organisation.

Cultural Negotiation

Let us return to Bethany and the Gateway project, a substantial contract undertaken by these charities and the City of Edinburgh Council on terms that are faith-neutral and outcome-dominated. There is the potential here for tension between the culture of the charity and the terms of the contract. How have Bethany and the wider consortium approached this question?

Initially, the outcomes in the tender request were inadequate for what the consortium wanted to achieve. As was indicated earlier, Bethany had identified the stages that people needed to go through to move from being homeless to sustaining a tenancy and becoming a full member of the community. They were clear about what support they needed to put in place to enable this to happen:

> If we'd stuck strictly to what was requested in the tender document, we wouldn't be able to do that. We looked at other capabilities we might need to have, other outcomes that we might need to be able to deliver to give us the best chance of taking someone from the initial chaotic starting point through what will essentially be a six month programme, to be in a place where they can sustain their own tenancy and have a life for themselves in the community.[6]

Given that they were in a competitive situation, the consortium saw the extra dimensions that they needed to include as adding value to their application, so they were clear and open about what they were offering in the package:

> We'll see your offer and we'll raise you … family networking support, to try and make our offer more competitive and more attractive to them while at the same time do it in a way that wasn't looking purely to undercut the competition but to be of maximum benefit to the people we're here to serve.[7]

The value of this extended package was evident to many of the people evaluating the tenders, who were themselves practitioners. The consortium was able to keep much of the cost down because of the wider volunteer base to which they had access. They were therefore able to respond to the tender request with an application that was attractive in its content and in its cost to the council, that was explicit about the work that was to be undertaken, and that was wholly consistent with the ethos and purpose of the organisations making the application. In this case, any tension between the public outcomes demanded and the principled practice of the organisation were resolved by negotiating outcomes that could be compatible with the consortium's vision.

---

6   Iain Gordon, Bethany's Chief Executive, 26 May 2010.

7   Ibid.

Ministry, Professional Knowledge and Homelessness Charities: A Summary

This chapter has explored the question of how specialised knowledge relates to practice in the case of ministry and the pastoral care of people vulnerable to homelessness.

First, it was argued that the academic tools that theological training provides constitute not a body of technical knowledge that can be applied to specific cases, but training in reflection, which allows the minister to construct a Christian critique of and perspective on a variety of situations. It was further observed that the current view of ministry is that it is a feature of the whole Church, not only of the academically trained ministers of word and sacrament. This allows a range of activities, carried out by bodies which have a Christian base, to be considered as the practice of ministry in a specific context.

The potential tensions surrounding this ministerial practice arising from contemporary pressures were then explored in the case of some organisations which address the needs of people vulnerable to homelessness in Edinburgh. It was noted that these organisations employ people with a range of specific professional skills, as one would expect in the case of a profession whose special skill is that of reflection rather than technical knowledge. An example was given of how the experience of working with homeless people enhanced the depth of theological reflection by a minister of word and sacrament and informed his subsequent preaching. The gap between the perspective on the needs of homeless people specified in a publicly funded project and the perspective of a Christian practitioner were then discussed, and the reconciliation between the two perspectives was outlined.

This illustration has shown that ministerial practice can be remarkably robust in navigating the challenges of voluntary action in the present culture, and that standards of care based on a Christian perspective can be maintained in the face of faith-neutral project goals. It should be noted that these are reasonably well-resourced and mature projects, and there will be many Church-based community projects which, like other small voluntary organisations, are finding it difficult to survive financially or are risking compromising their best vision in order to maintain a service to their clients.

As an example of professional deliberation in ministry, this is of necessity limited, considering only one area of community and parish engagement. Ministry covers a wide canvas, and will face a variety of challenges in today's fast-moving social landscape.

References

Avis, P. (2005), *A Ministry Shaped by Mission*, London: T. & T. Clark.

Bretherton, L. (2010), *Christianity and Contemporary Politics*, Chichester: Wiley-Blackwell.

Cunningham, I. (2010), 'Drawing from a bottomless well? Exploring the resilience of value-based psychological contracts in voluntary organisations', *International Journal of Human Resource Management*, 21(5), 699–719.

Forrester, D.B. (2000), *Truthful Action: Explorations in Practical Theology*, Edinburgh: T. & T. Clark.

General Assembly (2010a), *Ministries Council*, Report 2010:3, Edinburgh: The Church of Scotland Assembly Arrangements Committee.

—— (2010b), *Special Commission Anent the Third Article Declaratory of the Constitution of the Church of Scotland in Matters Spiritual*, Report 2010:25, Edinburgh: The Church of Scotland Assembly Arrangements Committee.

Macdonald, F.A.J. (2004), *Confidence in a Changing Church*, Edinburgh: St Andrew Press.

Pattison, S. (2007), *The Challenge of Practical Theology: Selected Essays*, London and Philadelphia, PA: Jessica Kingsley.

Schön, D.A. (1991), *The Reflective Practitioner: How Professionals Think in Action*, Aldershot: Ashgate.

Thompson, J.A. and Bunderson, J.S. (2003), Violations of principle: Ideological Currency In The Psychological Contract', *Academy of Management Review*, 28(4), 571–86.

14 Pastoral Supervision: Ministry, Spirit and Regulation

Cecelia Clegg

Introduction

Ministry is accepted as one of the original 'professions', along with law and medicine. Today in the UK, it encompasses a wide variety of religions. Ministers, priests, rabbis, imams and gurus have usually been people of learning, whose personal qualities and religious preparation were thought to fit them to be among the wise elders of a community. Given the multi-faith nature of ministry, it is not possible for me to do justice to all faith groups in this consideration of professional wisdom. My focus, therefore, will be on Christian ministry, because that is the world that I inhabit and because it is the largest faith group in the UK, but much of what I discuss will be relevant to leaders in other faith groups. Christian ministry itself is a wide subject because of the number of denominations who have varied practices in terms of ministerial formation and pastoral ministry. My remarks will be based on the practices of some of the larger denominations: Roman Catholic, Church of Scotland and Anglican.

Despite the professionalisation and regulation of medicine and law, ministry has, until the last decade, avoided taking that path. The notion of professionalisation, with its competency and performance indicators, protocols and guidelines, seemed at odds with a profession where preaching the gospel and administering sacraments are cited as key activities in ordination rites (Gibson, 2002, 4). It appears to have been tacitly assumed that clergy had no need of such processes, either because they were educated people who possessed both the wisdom and the prudence for the task or because training and the event of ordination had somehow bestowed the requisite 'gifts'. Professional deliberation and wisdom, if they were considered at all in preparing people for ministry, tended to be treated as a given, and were not directly addressed in some ministerial training programmes until the early 2000s, for example in the Church of England report on formation (Hind Report, 2003). Up to that time, the cultivation of professional wisdom was thought to happen mostly in the course of initial training and probationary practice. But things were slowly beginning to change in theological education, as evidenced by the appearance in 2005 of Frankie Ward's important text on lifelong learning (Ward, 2005). Beyond the initial training stages, however, until 2008 there were virtually no formal structures to support this type of professional development. The change at this point, although driven primarily by the need to meet new regulatory standards for chaplains in the healthcare field, connected with recent developments in theological education and with a need in other areas, such as parish ministry, for tools to support wise practice. This slowness in embracing professionalisation in ministry has many roots. Among these, the most important are the complexities brought by trying to relate the theological element of pastoral ministry to professional wisdom.

In ministry, as in counselling and psychotherapy, the practitioner is the main 'tool', and professional supervision, as distinct from line management, personal therapy or spiritual accompaniment, would seem to offer one suitable way to foster professional wisdom (Brown, 1984; Hawkins and Shohet, 1989). But there is no culture of professional supervision among ministers, and until very recently there was no system of accrediting supervisors for this role. Moreover, the religious world view of the minister and the theological understanding of ministry add a further and complex dimension to the discussion. Supervision in ministry is not just professional, it is 'pastoral', in the sense that the work under discussion has a theological content. Michael Carroll (2001, 80), citing the philosopher Sam Keen, argues that there is a distinction between 'religious' and 'spiritual' supervision: Religious supervision, Keen contends, is about answers, obedience and repetition, whereas spiritual supervision is about questions, openness, waiting and creativity (see Keen, 1994). Apart from being a gross caricature of religion, the too rigid boundaries of this distinction do not take into account the area of pastoral ministry, which draws from both realms in an attempt to be truly present to those for whom the minister cares. A pastoral minister must attend to both formal religious or theological issues like the understanding of forgiveness, sin or death, and also to wider spiritual issues like well-being, loneliness and coping with suffering.

This chapter unfolds in three sections. First, I will look at the context of pastoral ministry, including some changes in the perception and role of clergy in the UK from the turn of the twentieth century to the present, changes in occupational requirements for some clergy, and special features of religious ministry as professional practice. I move on to consider the development of professional ministerial practice through the lens of 'pastoral supervision', in particular by examining the formation of the Association of Pastoral Supervisors and Educators (APSE). Lastly, I reflect on aspects of how the process of pastoral supervision can promote professionally wise practice.

My contention is twofold. My first point is that an articulation of professional standards in ministry enforced through active line management and a requirement to engage in regular pastoral supervision will not only help to safeguard both the public and ministers, but will also advance the development of professional wisdom. My second point is that the religious and theological aspects which are integral to Christian ministry pose very particular issues for professional judgement.

The Context of Pastoral Ministry

Pastoral ministry, in the sense of a role in which a person on behalf of a Church or religious community, provides religious services (such as sacraments, rituals, music ministry) or support (such as listening to, advising, or praying with) directly to a member of the public has been part of the work of the Churches in the UK for centuries. This description distinguishes a theological sense of 'pastoral' work from the type of pastoral or person-centred support which might be offered by, for example, care workers to their clients in a secular setting. Pastoral ministry is conducted out of a religious commitment and world view. It has theological implications, in that it aims not only to benefit the person receiving the ministry, but also to further the transformation of society into the loving community which is envisaged at the heart of the Christian gospel. This work is most commonly associated with ordained ministers, though in the last few decades lay people have been formally appointed by Churches to such work, and even prior to this lay people conducted pastoral ministry, especially in missionary areas outside the UK. For the moment, I want to concentrate on the largest group of pastoral ministers: ordained ministers.

Changes in Perceptions of the Role and Place of Clergy in Society

There has been a sea change in how ministers are regarded in British society over the last hundred years, and the reasons for this are manifold. In this chapter, I point to just a few pivotal moments while acknowledging that other factors, which I do not have the space to examine here, like the effect of the atom bomb in 1945 and the anti-establishment student protests of 1968, drove the movement both deeper and wider. I have opted to choose three moments from the beginning and end of the last century, and one moment from the first decade of this century.

Until the 1900s, people routinely sought help on a wide range of issues, personal and communal, from those in religious leadership. The Churches stood at the heart of their communities, arbiters of truth and of both right thinking and right living. Professional wisdom in ministry was cultivated through theological education, prayer and aspiring to live a holy life. Young ministers were mentored in their early parish duties by older clergy. Ministers also tended to be separated by class from the people in the pews. They were therefore treated with deference and accorded respect. Alongside this, the esoteric nature of religious belief, the authority of ordination, and the confidential nature of pastoral encounters meant that ministers were rarely challenged about how they chose to spend their time or how they acted – provided that they adhered more or less to doctrine, fulfilled basic duties and caused no scandal. This long history of the practice of ministry led ministers to see themselves as 'independent' agents accountable largely to God alone. Line management in the form of bishops, presbyteries and superintendents could extend only so far.

Two seemingly disparate events early in the twentieth century were to prove significant in beginning to alter this situation: the performance of chaplains, particularly Church of England chaplains, in the First World War, and the development of psychoanalysis.

Chaplains who volunteered to minister 'at the front' in the First World War were totally unprepared for the experience. Many stayed in camps behind the lines, conducting worship services in which they incited the men to fight, and ministering to the wounded. Interviews with survivors showed how inappropriate much of this ministry, especially the worship, was seen to be by the troops. The situation of war revealed many chaplains as out of touch with ordinary people and out of their depth in terms of the pastoral task. Rev. Geoffrey Studdert Kennedy ('Woodbine Willy'), who was to change the face of chaplaincy at the front, quickly realised that if he was to be of any use to the men, he had to be at the front with them, to be, if nothing else, a presence. He also taught incoming chaplains how best to serve in the atrocious and despairing situation. His reflections are captured movingly in his poetry written amid the horror of trench warfare (Studdert Kennedy, 2006; Studdert Kennedy and Walters, 2008).

The outcome of the First World War in terms of ministry was twofold. There was a generation of scarred men and families who struggled to believe in God and for whom faith in ministers was irrevocably shaken. There was also a sobering realisation among ministers who had been 'at the front' that the Churches needed to get closer to the people whom they claimed to serve. This gave impetus to a process of developing a more sensitive grassroots pastoral ministry; however, this was much easier to propose than to carry forward, and it would be many decades and several major wars before such an approach to ministry would become a widespread reality.

The second pivotal moment was the development of psychological understanding from the work of Sigmund Freud, which blossomed in the provision of psychoanalysis in the UK from the 1920s and 1930s. Later, other types of psychotherapy, for example person-centred (Thorne, 2010) and gestalt (Parlett and Denham, 2007) became established. This development of therapeutic services led, according to critics like sociologist Philip Rieff, to a relativisation of truth and a focus on the well-being of the individual in such a way as to undermine both virtue and faith commitments (Rieff, 1966). Whatever the validity of Rieff's claims, the psychotherapist offered an alternative to the minister of religion, an alternative that was based in self-fulfilment and individual valuing, in contrast to the perceived strictures and prohibitions of religion. The role of general adviser and wisdom figure traditionally occupied by the clergy began to narrow to those areas associated with religious matters, unless the minister was also trained in some other field.

In the face of these pressures, clergy were forced to learn a new way of being which required new skills, but on the whole, ministerial training programmes were slow to make the changes, preferring to continue to focus on doctrinal education and personal holiness. Only in the last 25 years have mainstream training colleges included people skills, basic psychology and sociological analysis in a sustained way. One of the responses among clergy was to turn inwards, 'mystifying' their role and emphasising the processes of the spirit which are not amenable to ordinary explanation. This allowed ministers, as a group and as individuals, to resist scrutiny, but inadvertently led to their further marginalisation.

Already by the early 1990s, the climate in British society was quite critical of and hostile towards ministers. This made the third pivotal point, the uncovering of sexual abuse by clergy, predominantly in the Catholic Church, even more damaging. The assumption that ministers could at least be trusted to behave decently was proved to be untrue, and the state as well as the public began to realise that regulation geared to protect people from those delivering public services needed to be extended to Church ministry.

By the early 2000s, the state was also beginning to regard the provision of 'spiritual care', particularly in health settings, as something that should be formally provided and regulated. Hospital chaplaincy had been built into the NHS at its foundation in 1948, and both full- and part-time chaplains were funded by the NHS, but their appointments were handled entirely by the Church or religious bodies. Regulation of their work consisted of annual reports to the appointing Church body, and from 1971 onwards, an annual meeting with the Hospital Secretary. From 2002, it moved from being something offered by the Churches and faith communities to being the responsibility of a generic chaplain employed by a hospital trust and working with a multi-faith team (Scottish Executive Health Department, 2002). This change in employment status brought with it a requirement for ministers working in healthcare to adopt a professional framework of standards and competences in order to be taken seriously in multi-disciplinary staff teams (NHS Education for Scotland, 2008).

Regulation in ministry had arrived, and with it a requirement for line management and supervision. This was one major driver for the conversation across ministry groups in the UK which led to the formation of APSE in 2008.

Special Features of Pastoral Ministry as Professional Practice

When religious beliefs are involved in the interaction of a professional person offering pastoral care and a person needing care, there can be particular and complex issues in terms of professional deliberation and wisdom because the professional is balancing not only knowledge, regulation and relationship, but also beliefs, convictions and movements of the Spirit. Of course, religious professionals are not the only people whose beliefs and convictions shape their work: for example, counselling and psychotherapy is not a value-neutral activity. But much depends on the manner in which the professional holds his or her beliefs and convictions. For the most part, ministers try to be open and sensitive in their dealings with people, not allowing their personal enthusiasms or institutional teachings to influence their conduct in inappropriate or unhelpful ways. But there are two circumstances in which religious factors can be brought to bear in ways that are at least questionable, if not simply misguided in terms of wise practice.

The first is when ministers claim that God or the Spirit is telling them to speak or act in a certain way which proves to be unhelpful or even damaging for the person being helped. For example, a minister in a healing service told a young woman suffering from dwarfism that God wanted her to know that if she only had more faith, God would make her grow. As part of a team who tried to support her through the fall-out of this encounter, I witnessed how literally devastating it was for her.

The second is when ministers allow the truth claims of the Church or organisation to influence their actions and decisions to the detriment of the person being helped. For example, a Catholic priest told a woman who was being abused by her husband that she was bound by her marriage vows and should go home and try to be a better wife so that her husband would have no reason to be angry. There is more than just personal values at stake here; this is a misapplication of Church law and its underlying truth claims. While the Catholic Church would hold the marriage bond indissoluble except by death, it would not require anyone to remain in an abusive relationship.

I have chosen extreme but true examples to highlight some issues of wise practice and the potential for the abuse of power, whether unwitting or not, in the exercise of pastoral ministry. In the first case, there was a claim to be discerning the will of God. In the literature on spiritual discernment, it is clear that true spiritual discernment is usually submitted to the community, or at least to another experienced person, for confirmation before it is acted upon (Ivens, 1998). Certainly, there is not always time to undertake this type of confirmation in the midst of pastoral conversations, but the cultivation of a way of discernment through regular supervision and spiritual accompaniment might obviate the worst excesses. In the second case, there was the assertion of a truth claim above any duty of care that the minister should have recognised towards the woman. In both these cases, if the minister or priest concerned had been obliged to submit their pastoral work to a supervisor, there would have been an opportunity to explore, challenge and hopefully change their assumptions and actions.

That said, the issues of discerning how to communicate the promptings of the Spirit in pastoral situations and of how to balance Church law or truth claims with other pastoral considerations can be very complex. For these reasons alone, I would contend that ministers should consider seeking regular supervision of their work.

The Development of Pastoral Supervision

The flip side of the independence of the minister has been the fact that ministry can be an isolating and isolated way of life (Leach and Paterson, 2010, 7). Those ministers who have wanted to find contexts in which to reflect deeply on ministry, and perhaps more importantly to be accountable for their work, have until recently found very few people who were both trained and willing to facilitate such reflection. The inclusion of reflective practice in initial ministerial formation for the last two decades together with increasing numbers of experienced ministers seeking reflective space made the moment long overdue, in 2008, for the formation of a national body (APSE) which could not only encourage reflective practice, but could accredit pastoral supervisors to provide such spaces.

Pastoral Supervision can be described basically as:

> that activity in and by which a pastoral worker brings all the issues, pastoral and personal, that arise in and from his/her pastoral work to an understanding, supportive yet challenging person (or group) who will seek to assist that worker

in becoming more aware of and responsive to those issues and so become more authentic, realistic and mature in the work he/she does in and for the church. (Kofler and Cosgrave, 1994, 2)

It is recognisable as a form of professional supervision for pastoral ministers. Contained within this definition, however, is a question of whether or not 'pastoral' refers to the work which the supervisee brings to the session or to the approach of the supervisor. Kofler and Cosgrave (1994) largely refer to the former; the APSE Web site refers to the latter so that it can allow for 'NHS contexts in which chaplains might, for example, supervise nurses whose practice is not necessarily pastoral in a theological sense' (APSE, 2009c). Pastoral supervision, then, may be undertaken without the supervisor using religious language if the supervisee has no overt religious commitment. In this instance, the supervision might be couched in language more akin to humanistic values, but it would still, from the supervisor's perspective, be rooted in his or her theological understanding. The content of the supervision would remain the pastoral work of the nurse, and would not stray into areas more properly aligned to either personal therapy or line management. In this chapter, I will adopt the APSE usage.

Pastoral supervision is a varied practice which comprises different types, for example clinical pastoral supervision (developed originally in psychiatric hospitals in the USA), and different methods, such as narrative or creative supervision (Leach and Paterson, 2010). In all these forms, the emphasis is on openness on the part of the supervisor. There is an expectation that supervisors will not impose their beliefs or truth claims on supervisees, but that they will 'bear witness' (Leach and Paterson, 2010, 112) to what they know and trust. They will also risk their own meaning, just as the supervisee does in the process of trying to hear what God is saying. Leach and Paterson emphasise being 'deeply hospitable' (Leach and Paterson, 2010, 112) to the supervisee as a factor which is transformational for both the supervisor and supervisee. Pastoral supervision, therefore, is a deeply relational process that demands honesty and openness of all parties.

The Association of Pastoral Supervisors and Educators (APSE)

As noted earlier, a major factor in initiating the conversation which led to the formation of APSE was the looming requirement of regulation in healthcare chaplaincy. However, APSE brought together not only the areas of healthcare and Clinical Pastoral Education, but also parish ministry, theological education and professional bodies and journals in the area of practical and pastoral theology. The pressure towards accreditation was also partially a desire on the part of ministers to set this profession on a footing similar to that of counselling.

The conversations which led to its formation were interesting. There was a struggle to hold on to a Christian language and framework while leaving space for the inclusion of people from other faiths; again, this was driven especially by the needs of healthcare chaplaincy. The founding group also had to work out the requirements for accreditation. The resultant processes mirror very closely accreditation requirements in other people professions, such as counselling (APSE, 2009a).

The intent of APSE is to create as inclusive a body as possible to promote pastoral supervision and to accredit educators who teach reflective pastoral methodologies. Their definition of pastoral supervision is:

- *a regular, planned intentional and boundaried space* in which a practitioner skilled in supervision (the supervisor) meets with one or more other practitioners (the supervisees) to look together at the supervisees' practice,
- *a relationship* characterised by trust, confidentiality, support and openness that gives the supervisee freedom and safety to explore the issues arising in their work,
- *theologically rich* – works within a framework of spiritual/theological understanding in dialogue with the supervisee's world view and work,
- *psychologically informed* – draws on relevant psychological theory and insight to illuminate intra-personal and inter-personal dynamics,
- *contextually sensitive* – pays attention to the particularities of setting, culture and world view,
- *praxis based* – focuses on a report of work and /or issues that arise in and from the supervisee's pastoral practice,
- *a way of growing* in vocational identity, pastoral competence, self awareness, spiritual/theological reflection, pastoral interpretation, quality of presence, accountability, response to challenge, mutual learning,
- *attentive* to issues of fitness to practice, skill development, management of boundaries, professional identity and the impact of the work upon all concerned parties.

Pastoral supervision is not: Spiritual accompaniment – for the sole or primary purpose of exploring the spiritual life and development of the supervisee(s); Counselling – for the purpose of helping the supervisee(s) gain insight into their personal dynamics, or helping the supervisee(s) to resolve or live more positively with their psycho-social limitations; or Line management – for the purpose of addressing professional practice and development issues in relationship to the supervisee(s)'s performance and accountability (whether paid or voluntary) to her/his employer. (APSE, 2009b)

It is clear in this definition that there is a strong emphasis on elements which foster reflective practice and the cultivation of professional wisdom, but there are two distinctive features. First, *theologically rich* not only maintains space for all faiths, but also ensures that the spiritual and theological realms are to the forefront of this type of supervision. Second, *a way of growing* points to the fact that there is 'a wider agenda of human well-being and community at stake than the language of professional accountability alone suggests' (APSE, 2009c). As with all good supervision, accountability is at the heart of the process, but this definition nuances the accountability by setting it in a wider context of the development of a healthy and functioning community. While pastoral supervision is aimed at developing reflective practitioners, it does so in the understanding of contributing to the building up of a loving community – in Christian theological language, the body of Christ. This gives pastoral supervision a particular tone.

It is also linked to two other sub-clauses in the paragraph cited above: vocational identity and spiritual/theological reflection. These aspects come together well in Deborah Ford's description of the aim of pastoral supervision:

> To help the supervisee to recognise and acknowledge his or her own part (motives, gifts and wounds) in order to be able to be there primarily in/for the service and healing of the 'other' and to ask 'Who is God and what are God's purposes here?' (Ford, 2009, 344).

It is important to recall that in my understanding of pastoral supervision, 'pastoral' refers to the supervisor's commitment, and not necessarily to the supervisee's world view. Therefore, the questions about God and God's purposes may never be voiced by the supervisor – especially where the supervisee is not a theist – but are a framework of understanding that she or he uses in supervision. This framework, whether or not it is shared by the supervisee, can have, as I have shown, some serious implications for professional wisdom, for example around discerning the movement of the Spirit and the application of the truth claims of a Church.

There is little doubt that the formation of APSE is a significant step on the way to the professionalisation of pastoral ministry. It has opened up the possibility of structured accountability which has hitherto been lacking and the impact of which has yet to be seen. Certainly, it is a nascent initiative, and the numbers of accredited members are still small, but growing.

APSE also represents a significant breakthrough in the resistance of ministers towards embracing regulation and professionalisation. It is still too early in the British context for there to be studies of the impact of regulation on pastoral ministers in healthcare. However, a small-scale study of standardisation (regulation) in healthcare chaplaincy in the Netherlands has shown, contrary to expectations, some surprisingly positive effects. For example, chaplains report feeling better able to articulate their work, gaining confidence in their role and being better organised in their activities (Mackor, 2009). It will be interesting to see how the first British studies compare to these findings.

Promoting Wise Practice

The model of pastoral supervision which APSE has adopted has some strengths in terms of the cultivation of wise practice. Pastoral supervision is a boundaried space which allows practitioners to bring together insights from psychology/therapy and spiritual life in relation to their professional work and reflect on their ways of being and acting in order to offer to those with whom they work a deeper level of relationship. In particular, it encourages the development of reflective practice (Schön, 1991), accountability and discernment in order that ministers can be truly present to those that they serve. For example, Ford recounts a group supervision session in which she re-enacted her encounter with a patient who had damaged her hands through setting fire to herself as a child (Ford, 2009). The point of the supervision was for Deborah to be in touch with her own responses and to get close to the experience of her patient while being supported, so that she could, as she did, offer the woman a new level of engagement (Ford, 2009).

The assumption of APSE, however, is that pastoral ministers and supervisors will hold their religious beliefs and truth claims humbly, neither claiming a type of special inspiration from God nor imposing their views on others. This approach is more conducive to liberal theological views than to more conservative ones, in which holding to a particular truth claim may take precedence over other pastoral considerations. The challenge facing supervisors in terms of wise practice in this case is how to develop methods and strategies that on the one hand oblige the supervisee to reflect deeply on the relational implications of their stance in the light of the love of neighbour preached by Jesus, and on the other hand to offer ways to mitigate the effects of truth claims that cannot be set aside. For example, one strategy of mitigation for the Catholic priest who wanted the abused woman to honour her marriage vows would have been for him to refer her to Marriage Care (the Catholic marriage and relationship service), where at least she could have received professional counselling help.

If wise practice entails discerned action that engages expert knowledge, practical know-how, imagination and critical judgement, its cultivation in ministry through the structure of pastoral supervision requires attention to the particular issues associated with the prompting of the Spirit and religious truth claims. There is a long tradition of discernment of the Spirit in the Christian tradition, not least in Ignatian spirituality (Puhl, 2003), with ample resources to aid supervisors and supervisees. The tricky element in dealing with issues of discerning the Spirit, however, is how to maintain a focus on supervision without straying into the area of spiritual accompaniment.

Conclusion

As a profession, ministry has turned late in the day to addressing the demands of regulation and professionalisation, and this is still a contentious area. My focus in this chapter has been on the issues surrounding pastoral supervision as a means of cultivating accountability and wise practice and some of the particular issues that a theological world view can entail. I am conscious, however, that this is only one thread of a double cord, the other part of which is institutional management. Given that line management has not been a tradition in Churches and that many ministers do not have contracts of employment, there is some considerable way to go before this may become a reality. It will require a fundamental shift in mentality on the part of Church institutions – one which, if they are wise, might yet be prompted by the continuing fall-out from the clergy sexual abuse scandals.

References

APSE (2009a), *Accreditation*, <http://www.pastoralsupervision.org.uk/html/accreditation.html> (accessed 25 March 2011).
—— (2009b), *Pastoral Supervision*, <http://www.pastoralsupervision.org.uk/html/pastoral_ supervision.html> (accessed 25 March 2011).
—— (2009c), *The APSE Story*, <http://www.pastoralsupervision.org.uk/html/the_apse_story.html> (accessed 25 March 2011).
Brown, A. (1984), *Consultation: An Aid to Successful Social Work*, London: Heinemann.
Carroll, M. (2001), 'The Spirituality of Supervision', in M. Carroll and M. Tholstrup (ed.), *Integrative Approaches to Supervision*, London: JKP, 76–89.
Ford, D. (2009), '"Are you able to drink the cup that I drink?" A reflection on the significance of pastoral supervision in healthcare chaplaincy', *Practical Theology*, 2(3), 343–54.
Gibson, P. (2002), *To Equip the Saints: Findings of the Sixth Anglican Liturgical Consultation*, Berkeley, CA: Grove Books.

Hawkins, P. and Shohet, R. (1989), *Supervision in the Helping Professions. An Individual, Group and Organizational Approach*, Milton Keynes: Open University Press.

Hind Report (2003), *Formation for Ministry within a Learning Church: The Hind Report*, London: Church House Publishing.

Ivens, M. (1998), *Understanding the Spiritual Exercises*, Leominister: Gracewing.

Keen, S. (1994), *Hymns to an Unknown God*, London: Piatkus.

Kofler, L. and Cosgrave, B. (1994), 'Pastoral supervision: A valuable instrument for today's Church growth', *Newsletter of the Institute of St Anselm*, 9(1).

Leach, J. and Paterson, M. (2010), *Pastoral Supervision: A Handbook*, London: SCM Press.

Mackor, A.R. (2009), 'Standardization of spiritual care in healthcare facilities in the Netherlands: Blessing or curse?', *Ethics and Social Welfare*, 3(2), 215–28.

NHS Education for Scotland (2008), *Spiritual and Religious Capabilities and Competences for Healthcare Chaplains*, Edinburgh: NHS Education for Scotland.

Parlett, M. and Denham, J. (2007), 'Gestalt Therapy', in W. Dryden (ed.), *Dryden's Handbook of Individual Therapy*, London: Sage, 227–55.

Puhl, L.J. (2003), *The Spiritual Exercises of St Ignatius*, Chicago, IL: Loyola University Press.

Rieff, P. (1966), *The Triumph of the Therapeutic: Uses of Faith after Freud*, New York: Harper and Row; London: Chatto and Windus.

Schön, D. (1991), *The Reflective Practitioner: How Professionals Think in Action*, new edn, Farnham: Ashgate.

Scottish Executive Health Department (2002), *Spiritual Care in NHS Scotland*, HDL (2002) 76, Edinburgh: Health Department.

Studdert Kennedy, G. (2006), *The Unutterable Beauty: The Collected Poems of G A Studdert-Kennedy*, Liskeard: Diggory Press.

—— and Walters, K. (2008), *After War is Faith Possible? An Anthology*, Cambridge: Lutterworth Press.

Thorne, B. (2010), *Person Centred Therapy*, <http://www.elementsuk.com/libraryofarticles/personcentred.pdf> (accessed 25 March 2011).

Ward, F. (2005), *Lifelong Learning: Theological Education and Supervision*, London: SCM Press.

15 Not a Tame Lion: Psychotherapy in a Safety-obsessed Culture

Nick Totton

'Is he – quite safe? I shall feel rather nervous about meeting a lion.' 'That you will, dearie, and make no mistake,' said Mrs. Beaver; 'if there's anyone who can appear before Aslan without their knees knocking, they're either braver than most or else just silly.' 'Then he isn't safe?' said Lucy. 'Safe?' said Mr. Beaver; 'don't you hear what Mrs. Beaver tells you? Who said anything about safe? 'Course he isn't safe. But he's good.'

(C.S. Lewis, *The Lion, the Witch and the Wardrobe*)

Unlike Aslan in the passage quoted above, therapy is definitely not God; but there are some parallels. The thesis of this chapter will be that if therapy is going to be good, it can't also be safe.

By 'good', I mean tending to increase the range of clients' relaxation, freedom, expression and self-acceptance; by 'safe', I mean free from pain, anxiety and risk of failure. But there are some very different understandings of 'good' and 'safe' currently circulating in the therapy world, and this is part of what I want to write about. Some schools of thought understand 'good' to mean capable of swiftly alleviating presenting symptoms, and 'safe' to mean defensive practice which ticks appropriate precautionary boxes. I think that the main line of development of psychotherapy and counselling cannot be fitted into this second model, and that attempts to do so are deeply problematic.

One of the messages of psychotherapy and counselling – hereinafter referred to as 'therapy' – has always been: 'Relax, nothing is under control (and that's OK).' Therapy has stood against the dominant cultural message, 'Be in control of yourself and your environment': it has tried to help people tolerate the anxiety of not being in control – of our feelings, our thoughts, our body and our future. Some classic texts on this are Freud (1926), Reich (1973

[1942], 1975 [1946]), Fromm (1960 [1942]), Winnicott (1992 [1949]), Rogers (1978), Berne (1968) and Perls et al. (1973 [1951]); there are many others.

There has always been a tussle over this issue. However, new methods constantly arise – such as Redecision Therapy, Neurolinguistic Programming, Cognitive Behavioural Therapy, Eye Movement Desensitisation and Reprocessing – which make the comforting claim: 'You *can* be in control, after all: you can choose your emotions and live according to your conscious will.' Such a claim is far more acceptable to the dominant social structure, which now also says that therapy itself must be controlled, brought within the field of regulation: partly because of because of the strong opposition of many practitioners, psychotherapists and counsellors in the UK will now not be forcibly accredited and monitored; but the overall pressure for therapy regulation remains intense. This is one aspect of a general trend towards ever-widening regulation: as the world becomes increasingly frightening, it becomes increasingly necessary to claim that security *can* be achieved, through monitoring, surveillance and censorship. This is the path our society is taking; but equally, it is an *internal*, psychological process, embracing exactly the anxieties which therapy arose to address.

From a psychological point of view, this path of control is, in effect, a project to eliminate the unconscious. Aslan actually represents in this chapter not God and not therapy, but what I believe to be therapy's true subject: the unconscious, that aspect of our bodymind which is beyond all control. And the social project of regulation and surveillance is closely parallel to that of the White Witch and her secret police chief Maugrim, who forbid all acknowledgement of Aslan's existence. But when the repressed returns to Narnia, the snow melts, flowers spring up, and everyone who has been turned to stone is restored to life. Not a safe process – but a 'good' one.

If Aslan is not a tame lion, then he is a wild lion. Therapy can often be terribly tame; but in my view, it is essentially wild, a focus of resistance to compulsory human domestication. This is the context for what follows, where I shall explore various aspects of the wild/tame dichotomy, including knowledge, expertise, normality and the ubiquitous therapeutic concept of 'boundaries'.

Not Knowing

> Acceptance of not-knowing produces tremendous relief.
> (Winnicott, 1992 [1949], 250)

What perhaps makes psychotherapy truly valuable, beyond all the interpretations and adjustments, is that it can offer a space free of goals and intentions. Goals, however benign, tend to carry with them a demand for their achievement, and demands are what we suffer from – a suffering which brings us into therapy in the first place, and from which therapy can potentially free us. This is paradoxical, since freeing us from demands is itself a goal, and therefore carries a demand from which the therapeutic space must in turn be freed – which becomes a further demand, and so on. But a tolerance of – even an insistence on – paradox is perhaps one of the features which make therapy, like other techniques of liberation, not a tame lion.

Therapeutic practice, from one point of view, is an ongoing struggle by the therapist to live up to the aspirations of therapy – to become aware of and release the biases and fantasies which lead us to demand, implicitly, that the client and reality be a certain way. This ongoing practice of awareness and release is why and how being a therapist, as well as hopefully being good for clients, is good for *us*. But another paradox of therapy is that it can only be good for anybody when it confronts and gives up its *intention* to be good for them. This is a corollary of the paradoxical theory of change (Beisser, 1972): not only does change happen when the client stops trying to change, it happens when the therapist stops trying to change the client.

Therapists' demands on the client express what Layton (2004) calls the 'normative unconscious' – our internalisation of social norms. As Perls et al. (1973 [1951], 108) (along with many others) point out: 'Our society frequently demands the impossible of us. ... Since such demands are so insistently and universally pressed upon us, we feel that they *must* make sense.' These impossible demands are internalised, becoming sticks with which we constantly beat ourselves; out of these demands, and out of our resistance to them, we construct our identity.

According to Althusser (1971), identity is created through a process of 'interpellation', which can roughly be translated as 'hailing' – 'Hey, you!' If we are addressed repeatedly in certain ways, than we take on the identity which is ascribed to us, together with the requirements that attach to it. Maintaining this interpellated self becomes the source of tremendous anxiety and tension. As a body psychotherapist, I perceive this tension to be anchored in the voluntary musculature, as we habitually tighten our bodies to represent, and to resist, the 'self' which has been imposed on us, to resist, and to represent, the spontaneous impulses of the bodymind.

Clearly, therapists have every opportunity to reinforce interpellation, to 'hail' the client in ways that they are accustomed to, telling them that they are who they have always been told they are. We also have the opportunity to tell them that they are in fact someone else, someone new – someone who conforms better to *our own* picture of what people should be like. But we also have a wonderful opportunity *not* to tell them who they are: neither to feed back the familiar picture, nor to create a new one, but rather to allow the familiar self gently to deconstruct and to loosen its grip on the bodymind.

This involves a subtle and continuous exploration of transference and countertransference – the client's ways of 'recognising' us as the familiar interpellator/ critic, and our ways of responding to this recognition.

At this moment in the history of therapy, we are suffering from an increasingly dominant approach which thinks that 'effectiveness' is about the relief of symptoms. If I go to see a therapist because I am suffering from anxiety or obsession or insomnia, then it obviously makes crude sense to judge the effectiveness of the work in terms of how much this suffering has been alleviated by the time therapy ends. However, like most therapists, I often find that someone says when ending therapy: 'I still have my original symptom, but therapy has been a wonderful, life-changing process.' The person's *relationship* with their symptom has changed: it no longer stops them having a fulfilling life. This is what people often refer to as 'feeling better', which is why that rather unscientific term is a crucial measurement of therapy's usefulness. It transpires that all forms of therapy are pretty 'useful' to most people, especially long-term and relational approaches (Cooper, 2008; Seligman, 1995).

Expertise

Slowly but surely psychoanalysis was cleansed of all Freud's achievements. Bringing psychoanalysis into line with the world, which shortly before had threatened to annihilate it, took place inconspicuously at first. ... Form eclipsed content; the organisation became more important than its task. (Reich, 1973 [1942], 125)

I have felt for some years now like a man who is in danger because he has become imprisoned in the profession of therapy. (Thorne, 1995, 141)

I have quoted elsewhere (Totton, 1999) a fascinating complaint made in the early 1950s by the then President of the American Psychoanalytic Association. He stated that the increase in number of trainees and the more structured training of institutes at his time had changed the sort of people coming for training. In the glory days of the 1920s and early 1930s:

many gifted individuals with definite neuroses or character disorders were trained. ... In contrast, perhaps the majority of students of the past decade or so have been 'normal' characters, or perhaps one should say had 'normal character disorders'. They are not introspective, are inclined to read only the literature that is assigned in institute courses, and wish to get through with the training requirements as rapidly as possible. ... Their motivation for being analysed is more to get through this requirement of training rather than to ... explore introspectively and with curiosity their own inner selves. (Knight, 1953, 218)

The result of this was a decade or more in which analysis in the USA became primarily a mechanism of social normalisation – until the human potential movement arose to oppose this. Something similar is happening now, again correlated with a huge expansion in practitioner numbers, leading to what Knight (1953, 218) describes as 'the partial capitulation of some institutes arising from numbers of students, from their ambitious haste, and from their tendency to be satisfied with a more superficial grasp of theory'. We are again in the age of the 'normal' practitioner.

This dovetails with the re-medicalisation of therapy. It took decades to establish that those wanting therapy are not *sick*, since unhappiness, difficulties in living or a desire to change are not illnesses. However, the enormous expansion of training demands a huge increase in clients: and the only way to get enough therapy and counselling paid for is to get the state and other institutions to pay for it. For this, psychotherapy and counselling must present themselves as somehow *medical*, a technical process of fixing something broken. And 'normal' trainees of course lap this up, because it means that someone will tell them what to do, what procedures to follow, what manual to use. The same trainees will fight hard against having to be in therapy themselves – after all, they are not the ones with 'problems'.

The rise of the 'normal practitioner' and the pressure for medicalisation entwine with a third factor: hunger for status. For some years, many have aimed to establish therapy as a fully acknowledged profession, alongside medicine, law, architecture and accountancy. Professions have two defining features: the possession of 'expert knowledge' (Giddens, 1991; Stehr, 1994) and the establishment of an elite group which controls its boundaries through political strategies, including 'social closure' (Parkin, 1974), 'occupational imperialism' (Larkin, 1983), state support and market control (Larson, 1977). The medical profession can serve as a template of such processes (Griggs, 1982; Stacey, 1992).

Powerful groups within therapy are seeking to repeat the success of medicine, responding to the need for a body of 'expert knowledge' by generating one – radically lengthening training, 'technicalising' every aspect of the work, and inserting new levels and meta-levels of expertise and qualification – all this in a field where research shows repeatedly that *technique and outcome cannot be shown to be connected*, that 'There are ... hundreds of different versions of psychotherapy, and many of them seem to work equally well' (Mair, 1992, 146; see also Cooper's measured research summary: 'When bona fide therapies are compared with each other, they are usually found to be about equivalent in efficacy'; Cooper, 2008, 59).

But a profession must have its expertise – articulating with the hegemonic expertise of its society. This expertise:

> would have key characteristics: it would be taught in an organized way, most usually in a university (or at least in an institution that collects, transmits and eventually reproduces knowledge); and it would be standardized and accredited and often have scientific anchorage. … Expert knowledge gives some the privilege to speak, to act as arbiters. (Cant and Sharma, 1996, 6)

The push for this has come from some influential and ambitious people in the therapy world; the pull has come from the 'normal trainees' wanting to be *told what to do*, and from a society which increasingly demands expertise before it will take anyone seriously. Only the vociferous opposition of large numbers of 'rank-and-file' practitioners has held forcible statutory regulation at bay for so long in the UK.

Local Knowledge and Thick Description

Expertise occupies the opposite pole to *local knowledge* (Geertz, 1983), a term developed in anthropology and knowledge studies to describe what James C. Scott calls 'the indispensable role of practical knowledge, informal processes, and improvisation in the face of unpredictability' (Scott, 1998, 6). Van der Ploeg's illuminating essay 'Potatoes and Knowledge' (Van der Ploeg, 1993) studies the difficult relationship between agrarian science and local farmers in the Andes, describing how, from the scientists' point of view, it is 'only logical' to model the needs and procedures of agriculture in a standardised way, with so much nitrogen required equalling such-and-such a dose of chemical fertiliser, and so on. The practical reality of farming, for someone who knows the intricacies of their environment and works by what Van der Ploeg calls *art de la localité*, growing perhaps a dozen varieties of potato each in their appropriate micro-climate, is very different. But because such an approach's procedures and outcomes cannot be precisely specified, they simply do not register for the expert approach: 'Local knowledge … is, under these conditions, rapidly becoming not just a marginal, but more than anything, a superfluous or even a counter-productive element' (Van der Ploeg, 1993, 219–20).

Wynne (1995) characterises local knowledges – which are always, in reality, plural – as:

> interwoven with *practices* … highly dynamic systems of knowledge involving continuous negotiation between 'mental' and 'manual' labour, and continual

interpretation of production experiences. ... However because it is so multidimensional and adaptive, experience is rarely expressed in a univocal, clear form. This is frequently mistaken for lack of theoretical content ... [But] there is indeed systematic theory, even though this is in a syntax linked to the local labour process and does not presuppose a universal and impersonal world. (Wynne, 1995, 67; my emphasis)

Is this not an excellent description of the 'knowledge system' of psychotherapy and counselling – 'multidimensional and adaptive', 'interwoven with practices'? Experienced practitioners generally find that they pay less and less attention to theory and technical rules.

The expert systems/local knowledges dichotomy is explicitly linked with themes of colonialism and imperialism. 'Therapy plc' has used a specious version of expert knowledge to colonise and weld into an empire many diverse local craft knowledges, hence distorting them. It has managed to ignore how 'scientific research' itself – the system's own expertise – repeatedly shows that although therapy seems generally beneficial, *neither technique nor training significantly affect the benefits reported*. What *does* make therapy effective is precisely 'local knowledge' – the 'therapeutic bond' and all the imponderables on which it depends.

Geertz (1973), who coined the term 'local knowledge', also speaks of 'thick description', an expression borrowed from Gilbert Ryle to indicate the need for *contextuality* in any adequate account of human behaviour. Since context is in principle infinite, Geertz asserts the impossibility of ever *getting to the bottom of things,* quoting the well-known story about a Westerner who, told by a native informant that the world rests on a platform which rests on the back of an elephant which rests in turn on the back of a turtle, asks what the turtle rests on. Another turtle. And that turtle? Well, after that it's turtles all the way down.

Domesticated culture, as expressed in phenomena like the state, is constantly trying to shorten the informational food chain to get to the final turtle. This attempt is distilled in the concept and practice of *expertise*, which is:

formulated on a global level, that is, within the abstract 'synthetic nature' constructed by science. And the terms it is built on are to be highly standardized, quantifiable and not subject to subjective interpretations. It is through such a model, its language and its terms that the necessary control, manipulation and supervision ... is established. (Van der Ploeg, 1993, 219)

Facilitating clients' grounding in their own dense and embodied experience as a condition of creative change, therapy is a powerful example of both thick description and local knowledge.

Maugrim

> The inability to tolerate empty space limits the amount of space available. (Bion, 1992, 304)

Therapy is experiencing a ferocious clash between the 'expert systems' approach and the 'local knowledge' approach – a clash in which expertise always has the debating advantage, because it can speak simply and with one voice, simplification and univocality being two of its essential characteristics. The struggle is not a new one for therapy, which has always held a tension between local knowledge and expertise, thickness and thinness, art and science, wildness and domestication. This tension plays a key role in clinical practice, where training focused on domestication installs a self-censorship or 'therapy police' in practitioners – largely through an unexamined notion of *boundaries*.

This amplifies the self-censorship which already tends to be present. Many supervisors have noticed how their supervisees inhibit their own responses, and in fact their own best judgement, in response to an internal modelling of what they believe is expected of them by their profession. This is natural and to a certain extent appropriate for trainees or newly qualified practitioners, though even here it can be unhelpfully exaggerated; but for experienced therapists, it acts as a block to authentic relationships with their clients.

Joseph Sandler, an elder of psychoanalysis, wrote that 'the conviction of many analysts [is] that they do not do "proper" analysis ... that what is actually done in the analytic consulting room is not "kosher," that colleagues would criticize it if they knew about it' (Sandler, 1983, 38). He goes on:

> Any analyst worth his [*sic*] salt will adapt to specific patients ... He will modify his approach so that he can get as good as possible a working analytic situation developing. I believe that the many adjustments one makes in one's analytic work, including the so-called parameters that one introduces, often lead to or reflect a better fit of the analyst's developing intrinsic private preconscious theory with the material of the patient than the official public theories to which the analyst may consciously subscribe. (Sandler, 1983, 38)

Sandler's 'intrinsic private preconscious theory' is what I have been calling local knowledge. Sanford Shapiro describes how the new practitioner's spontaneity can be systematically inhibited:

> My first lesson in being 'proper' was in 1959. ... I began my first psychotherapy case, a young woman with depression and marital problems. ... I had detailed process notes for our first supervisory meeting, and I described how the patient

came in to a session and said: 'Hello, how are you?' 'I'm fine,' I answered, 'And how are you?' Parcells [the supervisor] interrupted me: 'Why did you say that?' he asked. 'Well,' I said, 'It seemed the natural thing to do.' Parcells gently explained that it would be natural in a social situation, but this was therapy, not a social situation. Thus I learned my first rule of proper technique. Each rule that I subsequently learned acted as a restraint and led to an increasing rigidity in my style of working. (Shapiro, 1995, 4)

Many trace this rigidity in psychoanalysis and psychotherapy back to Freud. But Lohser and Newton (1996), who assemble accounts of their analyses by Freud's patients, show that Freud's practice was very different from his recommendations to young analysts. As well as feeding patients who were hungry and raising money for them if necessary, Freud at times revealed himself to patients. After just over a week of daily sessions with the poet HD (Hilda Doolittle):

I veer round, uncanonically seated stark upright with my feet on the floor. The Professor himself is uncanonical enough; he is beating with his hand, with his fist, on the headpiece of the old-fashioned horsehair sofa .... The Professor said, 'The trouble is – I am an old man – you do not think it worth your while to love me.' (HD, 1985, 15–16)

Later in the analysis, when HD revealed her maternal transference onto him, he responded, according to her report:

'But – to be perfectly frank with YOU – I do not like it – I feel so very, very, very MASCULINE.' He says he always feels hurt when his analysands have a maternal transference. I asked if it happened often, he said sadly, 'O, very often.'[1]

Although filtered through HD's preoccupations and projections, this indicates a much more spontaneous and relational way of working than Freud recommended to others. And this is a common pattern in the therapy world. More than once, when speaking at a conference about my use of touch in therapy, I have been told privately by some elderly and experienced figure: 'Well, I'm happy for *you* to work in this way, I can see you know what you're doing – but I would never publicly condone it.'

Touch is one of several issues that create anxieties about 'wild' and out-of-control feelings and behaviour. These anxieties – both within the therapy profession and in wider society – have intensified over recent decades and become condensed into the quintessentially domesticated concept of

---

1   Quoted from a letter in Lohser and Newton (1996), 49, with original emphases; the version in HD (1985), 146–7, is considerably watered down.

'appropriate therapeutic boundaries'. More recently qualified practitioners are so familiar with the notion of boundaries that they may be surprised to discover that they are a very recent introduction. A literature search shows that before the 1990s, therapists did not speak of 'boundaries' in this specific sense: 'lines of behaviour which must not be crossed, by the therapist, by the client, or both'. Of course, issues of acceptable behaviour were always discussed, but under a variety of different headings; and there is something very significant in how all these themes were gathered together under a single rubric borrowed originally from the discourse of sexual abuse.

I make no criticism whatever of the theory of boundaries developed around work with survivors of sexual abuse. It is enormously helpful and clarifying – *within that context*. But its appropriation as a way of thinking about issues like fees, telephone contact or session times has helped to install a subliminal notion of what both advocates and opponents have called the 'slippery slope' theory: that any flexibility or inventiveness around the usual ways of doing therapy – a single toke on the spliff of adaptability, so to speak – leads to the hard stuff, to sexual abuse of clients. It has been claimed in all seriousness by proponents of the 'slippery slope' theory (Gutheil and Gabbard, 1993; see also Simon, 1989) that the use of first names between practitioner and client is a predictor of sexual abuse further down the line!

Freud gets blamed for rigid boundaries because of the technical papers on psychoanalysis which he wrote for new practitioners. Whatever one feels about his recommendations (which is explicitly what they were), it is interesting that Freud very often explains them not as a protection for the *analysand*, but as for the benefit or convenience of the *practitioner* – for example, analysts should not work for free because they will not be able to afford it (Freud, 1913). Freud is mainly thinking practically, flexibly and locally; he might have been quite surprised to find Robert Langs (for example, in Langs, 1998) arguing that these local arrangements match the unconscious needs of *every single patient* – Langs's follower David L. Smith lists a set of 21 'fundamental ground rules', including such matters as a set time, a set fee, and no gifts being accepted, which he claims all psychotherapy clients 'unconsciously want their therapists to follow irrespective of their conscious preferences. They appear to be universal rules' (Smith, 1999, 139). In a note he continues, ludicrously but quite logically: 'this implies that patients' unconscious secured-frame criteria are the product of hominid evolution' (Smith, 1999, 140).

The idea that our species has evolved to require a set time and fee in therapy is not widely held; but it *is* now widely held that all clients at all times should be 'held' by the same set of boundaries. For perhaps 20 years now, the idea that boundaries are a key element in therapy has become more and more dominant, to the extent that for many practitioners it is part of their conceptual wallpaper, an axiom which they have perhaps never questioned. The emphasis on boundaries has been read back into earlier therapeutic formulations, and is now understood as universally present. But is this really the case?

The developing concept of appropriate boundaries, and its codification in legal and quasi-legal structures, increasingly forces all therapists into defensive practice – that is, working in ways based not on giving the client the best therapeutic environment for them, but on avoiding vulnerability to malpractice hearings. Gutheil and Gabbard (1993) develop a distinction between 'boundary violations', which are always harmful, and 'boundary crossings', which may be neutral or beneficial. However, they also argue that even boundary crossings which are justified and consistent with good care should be avoided for fear of being taken to court: 'the risk-management value of avoiding *even the appearance* of boundary violations should be self-evident' (Gutheil and Gabbard, 1993, 188; my emphasis).

Therapy is as much about questioning boundaries as about asserting them; as much about supporting clients to break out of the rules as about teaching them to observe the rules. For some clients, often those who have been abused in childhood, it is crucial to know that the therapist will act within a defined frame. For others – or even for the same client at a different point in therapy – it is equally crucial that the therapist dances outside the frame, and that a trust can be established which is based on authenticity rather than on predictability.

What every therapeutic relationship needs is to be a *relationship*: a place where two subjectivities meet each other, with all of the difficulty and painfulness this implies, but also with a developing willingness and capacity to tolerate the other person's otherness. For a therapist to hold careful boundaries because they believe they *must*, or because they are afraid of the uncontrollability of closeness, cripples the potential for relatedness; but for a therapist to hold such boundaries as an honouring of the client's woundedness is itself relational. The only valid generalisation about relationships is that they are each unique, quintessentially local and 'thick'; and therapists are artisans of relationship, co-creating one-off works with their clients.

Conclusion

The more complex our society is, the less controllable everything is, so that the striving for control becomes less and less sane, more and more about simplifying not *reality*, but *appearance*. The rise of the 'neo-liberal state' heightens this situation: through an ideological conviction that the free market will magically solve all problems, the state resigns many of its traditional functions, leaving a frightening vacuum (Cooper, 2001). Cooper highlights the irreality which results from neo-liberal ideology, and the ways in which this relates to deeper psychosocial issues – issues which psychotherapy has traditionally tasked itself with exposing:

> However capable we may be of improving on past performance, in the domain of health, welfare and mental health practice there always will be mistakes, there will be failures and deaths, there will be guilt, anxiety and the wish to blame. These things will not and cannot go away. (Cooper, 2001, 361)

This is not a tame universe, in other words; and therapy has historically tasked itself with saying so, and also saying that this state of affairs is endurable. But human beings have always found it difficult; and the trend of society at the moment is in the opposite direction, towards the illusion that given enough rules, enough monitoring, enough surveillance, enough punishment, suffering can be prevented. Both individual therapists and therapy as a profession will have to choose whether to appease this fantasy, or to stand against it, or to go underground. Lion? What lion?

References

Althusser, L. (1971), 'Ideology and Ideological State Apparatuses', in *Lenin and Philosophy and Other Essays*, London: New Left Books, 127–87, <http://www.marx2mao.com/Other/LPOE70NB.html> (accessed 25 March 2011).

Beisser, A. (1972), 'The Paradoxical Theory of Change', in J. Fagan and I.L. Shepard (ed.), *Gestalt Therapy Now*, New York: Harper, <http://www.gestalt.org/arnie.htm> (accessed 25 March 2011).

Berne, E. (1968), *Games People Play*, Harmondsworth: Penguin.

Bion, W.R. (1992), *Cogitations*, London: Karnac.

Cant, S. and Sharma, U. (1996), *Complementary and Alternative Medicines: Knowledge in Practice*, London: Free Association Books.

Cooper, A. (2001), 'The state of mind we're in: Social anxiety, governance and the audit society', *Psychoanalytic Studies*, 3(3–4), 349–62.

Cooper, M. (2008), *Essential Research Findings in Counselling and Psychotherapy: The Facts Are Friendly*, London: Sage.

Freud, S. (1913), 'On Beginning the Treatment (Further Recommendations on the Technique of Psycho-analysis I)', in *The Standard Edition of the Complete Works of Sigmund Freud*, vol. 12, London: Hogarth Press, 121–44.

—— (1926), 'Inhibitions, Symptoms and Anxiety', in *The Standard Edition of the Complete Works of Sigmund Freud*, vol. 20, London: Hogarth Press, 75–175.

Fromm, E. (1960 [1942]), *The Fear of Freedom*, London: Routledge and Kegan Paul.

Geertz, C. (1973), 'Thick Description: Towards an Interpretive Theory of Culture', in *The Interpretation of Cultures: Selected Essays*, New York: Basic Books, 3–30.

—— (1983), *Local Knowledge: Further Essays in Interpretive Anthropology*, New York: Basic Books.

Giddens, A. (1991), *Modernity and Self Identity*, Oxford: Polity Press.

Griggs, B. (1982), *Green Pharmacy: A History of Herbal Medicine*, London: Jill Norman and Hobhouse.

Gutheil, T.G. and Gabbard, G.O. (1993), 'The concept of boundaries in clinical practice: Theoretical and risk-management dimensions', *American Journal of Psychiatry*, 150, 188–96.

HD (Hilda Doolittle) (1985), *Tribute to Freud*, Manchester: Carcanet.

Knight, R. (1953), 'The present status of organized psychoanalysis in the United States', *Journal of the American Psychoanalytic Association*, 1(2), 197–221.

Langs, R. (1998), *Ground Rules in Psychotherapy and Counseling*, London: Karnac.

Larkin, G. (1983), *Occupational Monopoly and Modern Medicine*, London: Tavistock.

Larson, M. (1977), *The Rise of Professionalism*, Berkeley, CA: University of California Press.

Layton, L. (2004), 'A fork in the royal road: On defining the unconscious and its stakes for social theory', *Psychoanalysis, Culture and Society*, 9(1), 33–51.

Lohser, B. and Newton, P.M. (1996), *Unorthodox Freud: The View from the Couch*, New York: Guilford Press.

Mair, K. (1992), 'The Myth of Therapist Expertise', in W. Dryden and C. Feltham (ed.), *Psychotherapy and Its Discontents*, Buckingham: Open University Press, 135–68.

Parkin, F. (1974), 'Strategies of Social Closure in Class Formation', in F. Parkin, *The Social Analysis of Class Structure*, London: Tavistock, 1–18.

Perls, F., Hefferline, R.F. and Goodman, P. (1973 [1951]), *Gestalt Therapy: Excitement and Growth in the Human Personality*, Harmondsworth: Penguin.

Reich, W. (1973 [1942]), *The Function of the Orgasm*, London: Souvenir Press.

—— (1975 [1946]), *The Mass Psychology of Fascism*, Harmondsworth: Penguin.

Rogers, C. (1978), *Carl Rogers on Personal Power: Inner Strength and Its Revolutionary Impact*, London: Constable.

Sandler, J. (1983), 'Reflections on some relations: Between psychoanalytic concepts and psychoanalytic practice', *International Journal of Psycho-Analysis*, 64, 35–45.

Scott, J.C. (1998), *Seeing Like a State: How Certain Schemes to Improve the Human Condition Have Failed*, London: Yale University Press.

Seligman, M.E.P. (1995), 'The effectiveness of psychotherapy: The *Consumer Reports* study', *American Psychologist*, 50(12), 965–74.

Shapiro, S. (1995), *Talking with Patients: A Self Psychological View of Creative Intuition and Analytic Discipline*, Northvale, NJ: Jason Aronson, <http://www.selfpsychology.com/twotheories.htm> (accessed 25 March 2011).

Simon R.I. (1989), 'Sexual exploitation of patients: How it begins before it happens', *Psychiatric Annals*, 19, 104–22.

Smith, D.L. (1999), 'Maintaining Boundaries in Psychotherapy: A View from Evolutionary Psychoanalysis', in C. Feltham (ed.), *Controversies in Psychotherapy and Counselling*, London: Sage, 132–41.

Stacey, M. (1992), *Regulating Medicine: The General Medical Council*, London: Wiley.

Stehr, N. (1994), *Knowledge Societies*, London: Sage.

Thorne, B. (1995), 'The Accountable Therapist: Standards, Experts and Poisoning the Well', in R. House and N. Totton (ed.), *Implausible Professions: Arguments for Pluralism and Autonomy in Psychotherapy and Counselling*, Manchester: PCCS, 141–50.

Totton, N. (1999), 'The baby and the bathwater: 'Professionalisation' in psychotherapy and counselling', *British Journal of Guidance and Counselling*, 27(3), 313–24.

Van Der Ploeg, J.D. (1993), 'Potatoes and Knowledge', in M. Hobart (ed.), *An Anthropological Critique of Development: The Growth of Ignorance*, London: Routledge, 209–27.

Winnicott, D.W. (1992 [1949]), 'Mind and Its Relation to the Psyche-soma', in *Through Paediatrics to Psychoanalysis: Collected Papers*, London: Karnac, 243–54.

Wynne, B. (1995), 'May the Sheep Safely Graze? A Reflexive View of the Expert–lay Knowledge Divide', in S. Lash, B. Szerzynski and B. Wynne (ed.), *Risk, Environment and Modernity: Towards a New Ecology*, London: Sage, 44–83.

Index